D1085126

Shifting Lines in the Sand

Shifting Lines in the Sand

Kuwait's Elusive Frontier with Iraq

DAVID H. FINNIE

HARVARD UNIVERSITY PRESS
Cambridge, Massachusetts
1992

This book is printed on acid-free paper, and its binding materials have been chosen for strength and durability.

Library of Congress Cataloging-in-Publication Data

Finnie, David H.
    Shifting lines in the sand: Kuwait's elusive frontier with Iraq /
David H. Finnie.
        p.   cm.
    Includes index.
    ISBN 0-674-80639-5
    1. Iraq–Boundaries–Kuwait.   2. Kuwait–Boundaries–Iraq.
I. Title.
DS70.96.K9F56   1992
341.4'2'026656705367–dc20   92-8938
                                      CIP

FOR SARAH AND CHARLES
with love, thanks, admiration, and joy

Preface

A month after Iraq's invasion of Kuwait in August 1990, I accepted the friendly challenge of a lawyer friend to get to the bottom of Iraq's "historical" claims to Kuwait. Both of us were aware from the news media that Saddam Hussein was seeking to justify his aggression before the world on the basis that Kuwait had at one time been a part of Iraq, and that there had never been a settled boundary between the two countries. I soon found out that in 1963 Iraq's claims had been abandoned and repudiated, and that since that time they could be advanced upon only the most tenuous of grounds. Kuwait, for its part, understandably putting the best light on its own assertions that it had been "independent" since its founding in the eighteenth century, had been tempted into a rather selective reading of its own history. Then there was the discovery that in the first part of this century Great Britain (which for many years held a controlling hand in both countries) had cut corners with Kuwait, with Iraq, with the international diplomatic community, and with the truth. Trying to make sense of this welter of contradiction was to become a challenge indeed.

Crown copyright material in the India Office Records, London; in the Public Record Office, London; and in *British Documents on Foreign Affairs*, Part II, Series B (Frederick, Md.: University Publications of America, 1986) is reproduced by permission of the Controller of Her Britannic Majesty's Stationery Office. Material in the Edmonds Papers and Dickson Papers is reproduced by permission of the Fellow in Charge, Private Papers Collection, Middle East Centre, St. Antony's College, Oxford.

My thanks are due to two former colleagues, H. Francis Shattuck, Jr., and Victor H. King; to my original challenger, Charles J. Johnson; and to Janet Finnie. I am especially grateful to Dr. Roger Owen of St. Antony's College, Oxford, and to Professor

J. C. Hurewitz of Columbia for their constant encouragement and
assistance. My wife has been, as always, an unfailing source of
devoted support and counsel.

March 1992

Contents

Illustrations

"Although Kuwait is fortunate in knowing roughly where her boundaries lie, they have never been demarcated on the ground and the definitions leave much room for dispute. The western and northern boundaries with Iraq are defined as follows: 'The frontier runs from the intersection of the Wadi al Auju with the Batin to a point just south of the latitude of Safwan, then eastwards passing south of Safwan wells, Jabal Sanam and Umm Qasr; leaving them with Iraq; and so on to the junction of the Khor Zubair and the Khor Abdullah.' The vagueness of this definition, which accords with that of the Anglo-Turkish Convention [of 1913], is obvious. 'South of Safwan wells' was at one time interpreted as one mile south of the most southerly palm at Safwan, which was not much more satisfactory as palms can easily be cut down and new ones planted . . . It is not yet known when demarcation will be undertaken, but the task is likely to prove a formidable one for any commission appointed to carry it out."

—*Sir Rupert Hay, 1954*

1. Kuwait: The Beginnings

Although it can be said to have come of age in 1961, Kuwait has no particular birthday. The sandy patch at the head of the Persian Gulf now known as Kuwait had apparently lain undisturbed at least since ancient times—a flat, barren, hot, unpopulated desert; *res nullius* in the lexicon of classical international law: a land belonging to no one, a place without a history or a settled populace, a territory over which human dominion had never been asserted from time immemorial.[1] Then at some moment known only to legend, but evidently in the early eighteenth century of the Christian era, nomadic Arabs from the desert, part of the tribe of the Beni Utub, which in turn belonged to the great Aniza federation, pitched their black goatskin tents near a point (Ras Ajuza: "Cape of the Old Woman") on the southern shore of Kuwait Bay, and they stayed. "Kuwait" means "little fort," but there seems to be no trace of any fort, little or otherwise, at the site.[2] Early European travelers called the area "Grain," thought to be a corruption of the Arabic "Qurain," which means "little horn," and that makes a bit more sense, because the Cape of the Old Woman looks rather like a horn as it juts out into the shallow waters of Kuwait Bay.[3]

The tribal newcomers, having formed a new community, in due course arrived at a consensus about their leadership. Just how this was accomplished can be ascertained only by recourse to tradition, for there are no historical records. But modern Kuwaiti historians suppose that usual customs were followed: the settlers vested their governance in a senior male of their number who had demonstrated or was deemed to possess desirable qualities such as stature, courage, wisdom, and perhaps that indefinable attribute called *hadh*, or luck. In the case of Kuwait the mantle of shaikh fell upon a certain Sabah. The year was about 1752.[4]

1

The House of Sabah (Al Sabah) has been first among equals in Kuwait ever since, in a succession of thirteen rulers, far surpassing any other regime in the Middle East and ranking high in longevity among the dynasties of the world. But from the very beginning Al Sabah did not manage everything alone. A kind of merchant oligarchy evolved: Al Khalifa took prime responsibility for trading and commerce; Al Jahalma was in charge of maritime affairs (including the important pearling and shipbuilding industries); and Al Sabah had general superintendence of civil government. For the protection and leadership provided to the community, Al Sabah received financial contributions from the others.[5] This sense of shared community responsibilities (and privileges) among a few close-knit families has been an abiding and distinctive feature of Kuwait's polity throughout most of its history.

The new community on Kuwait Bay seems to have prospered from the start, taking advantage of a site fairly defensible from the hinterland (the first town wall was built about 1760), an ample and sheltered harbor that came to be acknowledged as the best in the Gulf, and ready access to the caravan routes that snaked across the Arabian interior. It was a notably commercial environment. (One Saudi official observed after Iraq's 1990 invasion of the shaikhdom that Kuwait had been a business long before it ever was a state.) The success of a business community depends above all upon expectations of internal political order and security from outside threats; these, along with favorable geography and good sound business management (perhaps laced with *hadh?*), fostered steady growth and prosperity in Kuwait. The Sabah made it a point of policy to show good will and hospitality toward all their neighbors, including other Arabs, Persians, and the Ottomans. Kuwait became known in particular as a haven for political dissidents from elsewhere in Arabia: Wahhabis from the interior, exiled shaikhs of Bahrain, and a whole miscellany of tribal chiefs temporarily visited by misfortune.[6]

At the turn of this century the population of the shaikhdom was estimated at about 50,000, with some 35,000 in the town itself and the rest in outlying areas. Most of the inhabitants were Arabic-speaking Sunni Muslims, although there were also a Persian community of about 1,000; between 100 and 200 Jews; and some 4,000 black Africans, of whom about one-third were emancipated and the remainder slaves. The most important occupations were fishing, pearling, shipbuilding, and seafaring. A survey of the town in 1904 listed others: 36 dealers in piece goods, 21 gold-smiths, 11 blacksmiths, 132 dealers in "bedouin requisites" (such as carpets, cloaks, nails, horseshoes, ammunition), 32 date merchants, 16 druggists, 12 tea shops, 250 warehouses for the storage of grain, and so on. The chief imports were arms and ammunition, piece goods, tobacco, and other agricultural staples. Exports were few: pearls and ghee (clarified butter); merchants also re-exported tobacco, wheat, and dates.[7]

Until the development of Kuwait's oil resources began after World War II, Kuwait changed very little. A Kuwaiti historian writing in 1926 presented a picture of the pearl-fishing trade at that time that was almost identical with a description dating from the eighteenth century. One factor promoting this stability was the close alliance of Al Sabah with other Kuwaiti families, a phenomenon that had no parallel elsewhere among the principalities of the Gulf.[8]

For almost two and a half centuries the Al Sabah have kept intact their family, their traditions, their political system, their status, their territories, and their people, largely through shrewd diplomacy, political and personal intrigue, manipulation of their neighbors and protectors, and—in recent years—the prudent expenditure of oil revenues to buy off predators. It has not always been easy.

The Ottoman Presence

Long before the establishment of modern Iraq after World War I, the major power to contend with in the Middle East was the Ottoman Empire, founded by Turks from central Asia who overcame the moribund Byzantines and captured Constantinople (modern Istanbul) in 1453. The domains of the Ottomans, centered in Turkey, stretched at times far into the Balkans and central Europe, along the eastern and southern coasts of the Mediterranean Sea, and over much of the Arabian Peninsula.

To the east, the forces of Sultan Suleiman the Magnificent captured Baghdad from the Mongols in 1534 and reached the head of the Persian Gulf with the taking of Basra in 1546. And there the eastward expansion stalled, for the Ottoman Turks found themselves confronted on land by Safavid Persia and at sea by the first generations of explorer-soldiers from Europe: the Portuguese, to be followed soon by the Dutch and then the English.[9]

The Persian Gulf, shown on early maps as *Sinus Persicus,* was bounded on the north and east by the country from which it took its name, and on the south and west by the Arabian Peninsula. Since Roman times and before, it had been a thoroughfare for trade and commerce between Europe and Asia, a grand shortcut in an age when water held undisputed advantages over land for long-distance travel. Although the Ottoman Turks themselves were not particularly noted for their seafaring, Arabs of the Gulf had been involved in maritime commerce since antiquity.

Between Kuwait and the Turkish capital at Constantinople stretched hundreds of miles of deserts and rugged highlands: daunting terrain relieved only by the healing flow of the two ancient and mighty Mesopotamian rivers, the Euphrates and the Tigris. Over the centuries the Turks managed, more or less, to control Mesopotamia, with its fabled cities of Baghdad, Basra, and Mosul, each of which was to give its name to a province, the three together embracing the area we now know as Iraq. Basra, the most southerly of the three, stretched north from the head of the Gulf in the form of a wedge with its point at Fao, where the Shatt al-Arab enters the Gulf; the eastern flank ran along the Shatt (with Persia on the far side), and its western flank wandered vaguely through uncharted salt marshes and tidal flats toward the barren desert wastes of northern central Arabia, where no humans were to be found except nomadic herders of sheep, goats, and camels.

Among the national states that emerged after the Middle Ages in Europe, boundaries were commonly staked out following conquest or treaty, and were carefully delineated on maps published for all to see. Sovereignty based on the division of territory was a specifically European notion; moreover, early exponents of international law "invited European states to take possession of territory inhabited only by mere wandering tribes."[10] In the Middle East, by contrast, even major international frontiers like the one between the Ottoman and Persian empires partook of "the very blurred outlines of tribal space."[11] In the vast expanses of the Arabian desert and its surroundings, there were no boundaries at all except in the minds of the tribal leaders whose flocks and herds wandered here and there in search of forage. Tribal jurisdiction depended first of all on traditional grazing rights and customs, which were subject to adjustment only by agreement (or conflict) among the tribesmen themselves. And as tribal leaders grew or diminished in influence, loyalties and allegiances ebbed and flowed accordingly. Capt. William Shakespear, who as British political agent in Kuwait (1909–1915) was involved in the first efforts to define Kuwait's territorial boundaries, referred to an "unwritten desert law": "All Arab shaikhs base the territorial extent of their power upon their ability to enforce some order over the adjacent tribes, their power to enforce the payment of 'zikat' [alms] by Beduin, and their capacity to prevent and to avenge outrages and raids within the territorial limits claimed."[12] European, especially British, efforts to lay down specific territorial frontiers between newly established national states after World War I were to run afoul of this gap between widely differing cultures, thought, and legal concepts. The cultures were in many respects talking past each other, and in some sense perhaps they still are.[13]

The Ottomans appointed governors in Baghdad and Basra from the earliest days of their conquest right up to the final collapse of their empire in World War I. Mesopotamia was less well-organized than other Arab areas under Ottoman rule; as for effective control of the region, "the problem seems hardly to have been faced."[14] The Ottomans were preoccupied with more pressing matters: fending off incursions by Persia and trying to subdue rebellious tribes in Iraq itself. "In the second half of the eighteenth century," writes Kuwaiti historian Ahmad Mustafa Abu Hakima, "there was no Ottoman ruler in Eastern Arabia. In fact, Ottoman rule was not even nominally acknowledged."[15] Kuwait several times served as a refuge from Ottoman officials. In 1787, for example, the *mutasallim* (governor) of Basra himself fled to Kuwait to elude disciplinary measures at the hands of the pasha of Baghdad; Shaikh Abdullah of Kuwait granted him asylum.[16] On the other hand, Kuwaiti shaikhs ordinarily took pains to keep their fences mended with Ottoman authorities. In 1827 Shaikh Jabir (ruled 1814–1859) put Kuwait's maritime fleet at the service of the governor of Basra; in 1836 he assisted Turkish forces in putting down a tribal uprising in Zubair (a desert way-station between Kuwait and Basra); in 1837 Kuwaiti forces joined in an Ottoman assault on Muhammarah (on the Persian side of the Shatt); and eight years later they helped once more in the defense of Basra.[17] Kuwaiti vessels often flew the Turkish flag. As a reward for his help against Muhammarah in 1837, Shaikh Jabir was given private deeds to some date plantations on the Fao peninsula,[18] the beginning of a long and tortuous relationship between Al Sabah and Basra that continued to cloud relations between Kuwait, Iraq, and the British as recently as the 1950s.

Lt. Col. Lewis Pelly, Britain's ranking representative in the Gulf at midcentury, reported in 1863 that Kuwait was "practically independent despite recognizing Turkish suzerainty"; he attributed use by Kuwaiti ship captains of the Ottoman flag to commercial pragmatism: customs duties at Bombay were lower for vessels thought to be Turkish.[19] Three years later another British officer, Col. A. B. Kemball, pointed out that it was customary for shaikhs of the great bedouin tribes to receive regular subsidies from the Ottomans in return for not raiding settlements on the borders of the desert, and that there was no tribute flowing the other way as far as Kuwait was concerned. As for the shaikh of Kuwait, Kemball wrote that "his feudal obligation, if I may use the term, is to protect the shores of the Shatt al-Arab from foreign attack by sea."[20] The relationship was contractual rather than one of subservience or subordination.

In 1831, when the last of the Mamluks were ousted from power in Constantinople, the central Ottoman government assumed firm control in Baghdad for the first time. Serious attention was given to breaking down tribal power in Iraq and imposing Ottoman authority throughout the country.[21] But there was little real progress until the arrival in 1869 of a new governor, the capable and illustrious Midhat Pasha. Midhat's vigorous tenure (1869–1872) was marked by the introduction into Iraq of a version of the sweeping *tanzimat* reforms, originally adopted by the central government in Constantinople in the 1830s and thereafter applied in various parts of the empire. The *tanzimat* reforms, derived from European models, embraced a wide array of legal and administrative matters, including land registration, a civil code, and municipal government. Some of Midhat's reforms survived his time in Baghdad, becoming the basis for the first steps toward modern government in Mesopotamia. The reforms were most effective in towns and settled agricultural areas, although even here success was problematical and sometimes fleeting. Among the migrating tribes the *tanzimat* reforms were almost impossible to apply.[22] If, as some Iraqi propagandists have recently maintained, Kuwait was at that time effectively a part of the province of Basra, one would expect to find traces of *tanzimat* there; yet not even the most ardent Iraqi partisan has come forward with any such evidence.

Another event of Midhat Pasha's rule in Baghdad had an immediate and lasting impact on Kuwait and the Sabah. In 1871, with the encouragement of the central government, Midhat launched a maritime expedition down the Arabian coast of the Gulf to restore Ottoman authority in various decaying outposts of the empire. (Among the garrisons he established was one in al-Hasa, an extensive area of comparative fertility in what later became the eastern province of Saudi Arabia; the Turkish garrison at al-Hasa remained until 1913, when it was forced to withdraw under fierce attack by Wahhabi tribesmen loyal to Abdul Aziz Ibn Saud.)[23] Shaikh Abdullah II of Kuwait (ruled 1866–1892) lent his full support to Midhat's expedition, supplying 300 seagoing vessels for transport of troops. In recognition of his help the Porte bestowed on Shaikh Abdullah the Ottoman title of *qaimmaqam*, or subgovernor, which carried with it the implication that as an officer of the sultan his shaikhdom fell under Ottoman jurisdiction.[24] In 1875 a new administrative structure for southern Iraq was put in place. Kuwait was grouped with Basra, Nasiriya, Qurna, and Amara into an autonomous "Vilayet of Basra." After 1884, the ambit of the Basra vilayet was expanded down the littoral of the Gulf to incorporate Najd and al-Hasa, including Hofuf, Qatar, and Qatif. This administrative structure provides the specific basis for Iraq's modern claims that Kuwait belongs to Iraq because it was once part of the Basra vilayet.[25]

On the other hand, it is perfectly plain that neither Midhat Pasha nor any other Turkish authority before or after him introduced Ottoman administration in Kuwait. There was never a Turkish garrison in the town. Kuwaiti subjects paid no Turkish taxes; Kuwaiti men were not conscripted into the Ottoman army.

If there was ever an opportune time to bring Kuwait administratively into the Ottoman Empire, it was at this moment, when a forceful, reforming, strong-minded official like Midhat had the sympathetic ear of Shaikh Abdullah II of Kuwait. Yet little was done except to endow the shaikh with the middle-level title of *qaimmaqam* and to hand over to him some more date gardens on the banks of the Shatt al-Arab.[26]

Beginning in 1871, then, Kuwait's status as an independent entity became qualified by the fact that its ruling shaikh had been appointed an official of the Ottoman Empire. The appointment, however, appears to have made no practical difference in the affairs of Kuwait itself, where life proceeded very much as it had before. Shaikh Abdullah seems to have accepted his new title with aplomb, and the expansion of his property holdings in southern Iraq undoubtedly enhanced his material welfare, but he took no orders from any Turk. Only after 1899, when Kuwait began to emerge as a quasi-protectorate of Great Britain, did the Ottomans try to add meat to the bones of their nominal hegemony, as a counter to British encroachment. For the time being, the British themselves made no effort to challenge or contest Ottoman pretensions in Kuwait. In fact, in 1888 and again in 1893 the Ottoman foreign minister was formally advised that Great Britain recognized Ottoman sovereignty and jurisdiction along the Gulf coast from Basra as far south as Qatif.[27]

Britain in the Gulf

Kuwait's reputation as a comparatively hospitable commercial environment was tested early on by the hardheaded managers of Britain's East India Company. Chartered by Queen Elizabeth I in 1600 with a monopoly on trade between England and the East, the Company had maintained a "factory," or trading station, at Basra since 1645.[28] In 1775 Basra was invested by Persian troops, resulting in an evacuation of European traders and a general diversion of trade from Basra to Kuwait which lasted for several years. In 1793 the Company again moved the Basra factory to Kuwait for two years, this time to avoid the vexations of certain unsympathetic Ottoman officials in Basra. A cruiser of the British Indian navy was kept anchored in Kuwait Bay to guard the outpost.[29] This well-documented episode has often been cited to refute Iraq's claim to Kuwait on the basis that the shaikhdom had always been ruled by the Ottomans.

"India," which in the days of the British raj included much of modern Pakistan, came close to the eastern reaches of the Ottoman Empire, the Persian Gulf, and the Arabian Peninsula. Until 1858 the governance of India was in the hands of the East India Company. Commerce, indeed, was the main factor in the evolution of Britain's paramount position in the Gulf in the nineteenth century. Just after the Napoleonic wars, the government of British India began to develop a network of treaties with the chiefs of the Arab communities in the Gulf, with a view to maintaining order, improving navigation, and eliminating the rampant piracy that was a constant threat to commercial shipping.[30]

Later in the century these pragmatic concerns were supplemented by a more general strategic consideration. India was seen by Victorian England as a prize and a responsibility. The "jewel in the crown" required protection from outside powers and dependable lines of communication with the home government. The government of India, even after it was transferred from the East India Company to Her Majesty's Government in 1858, was largely autonomous in most local matters. Its ruler, the viceroy, was appointed by the British government and reported directly to the cabinet through the India Office, presided over by the Secretary of State for India, just around the corner from Downing Street and the prime minister. In the early days, communications with the Indian government were largely around the Cape of Good Hope, although telegraph communication was established through Turkey in the mid-nineteenth century. As early as the 1830s there were dreams and projects for developing British-controlled land routes across Turkey or northern Arabia (including the idea of navigating the Euphrates by river steamer). Interest in those possibilities waned with the success of the Suez Canal after it opened in 1869, only to be revived toward the end of the century with projects for European railways across Anatolia to the Gulf. The Persian Gulf came to be seen by the British, and most acutely by the British in India, as a vital arena of defense and avenue of communication, one whose control could not be sacrificed to a potentially hostile power in the great game of control of the paths of empire. As the weakness of the Ottoman Empire grew increasingly apparent toward the end of the nineteenth century, first Russia and later Germany were seen as the major threats. It became a cardinal point of British policy not to let another power gain a foothold in the Gulf. Lord Lansdowne, the foreign secretary, made the policy explicit in a memorable statement to the House of Lords on May 5, 1903: "We should regard the establishment of a naval base, or of a fortified port, in the Persian Gulf by any other Power as a very grave menace to British interests, and we should certainly resist it with all the means at our disposal."[31] As long as concern for the maintenance of British hegemony in the Persian Gulf guided its foreign policy—and it faded only with the dissolution of British rule in the Indian subcontinent after World War II—the world was on notice that Britain would keep a watchful eye on the Gulf.

The government of India willingly shouldered the responsibility for creating and maintaining this Pax Britannica. The Persian Gulf, often referred to as a "British lake," was in fact more of an "Indian" lake. Authority over the Gulf issued from a "residency" at Bushire, on the Persian coast, presided over by a British Indian officer whose full title was "Her Britannic Majesty's Political Resident in the Persian Gulf and Consul-General for Fars and Khuzistan." The P.R., as he was known to his colleagues, reported to the Foreign Department of the government of India. Only the ablest officers of the Indian Political Service could aspire to such eminence. When Lord Curzon was viceroy he once confided to a friend that the political resident "is really the uncrowned King of the Gulf."[32]

As the British in India expanded their treaty network and their control over the Gulf, they risked stepping on the toes of the Ottomans. Although it was true that Constantinople was far away, and that the exercise of Turkish control was inconsistent and often ineffective, it had to be accepted in Delhi as well as in London that there was no clear way to establish and maintain British hegemony without the risk of offending the Turks. Understandably, these risks were often assessed differently by England and British India. London's concern to support the fading Ottoman Empire against incursions or encroachments by other major powers translated into a general reluctance to become involved in the affairs of the interior of the Arabian Peninsula, including the hinterland of Kuwait.[33] Partly because of its equivocal relationship with the Ottomans, Kuwait came late into the British treaty system.[34] But by the end of the century a pattern of Anglo-Indian administration, gunboat diplomacy, and imperial certitude prevailed throughout the Gulf, establishing ample precedent for Britain's involvement in Kuwait.

2. Britain, Kuwait, and the Turks, 1899–1914

The prosperous little Bedawin town bids fair to be the
scene of a notable conflict (or compromise) between
western rivals in the east, and to matter more to Europe than any other spot in Arabia . . .
—*David George Hogarth, 1904*

By the 1890s Kuwait had become a relatively prosperous community of some 50,000, with a reputation for shipbuilding, pearling, seafaring, and an astute commercial sense that played upon
the town's natural advantages as the best harbor in the Persian
Gulf. The Sabah were well established as the leaders of the community, although they took care to maintain good relations with
two or three other merchant families as a political base. Shaikh
Abdullah and his family were well-to-do, owning among other
things some very extensive and productive agricultural estates
(generally referred to as "date gardens," a name that hardly suggests their extent and value) along the fertile alluvium on the
banks of the Shatt al-Arab, well within the recognized territory of
the vilayet of Basra. And there were other links to the vilayet of
Basra and to the Turkish authorities there. In Kuwait itself almost
the only water was an undependable supply from brackish wells
at the oasis village of Jahra, some twenty miles from Kuwait town
near the western end of Kuwait Bay. So animal skins full of fresh
water were regularly shipped from the Shatt in the characteristic
wooden sailing vessels known as "booms" or "dhows," along with
vegetables and other produce from Kuwaiti-owned estates there.
Shaikh Abdullah II, invested in 1871 with the title of *qaimmaqam,*
had good reason to cooperate with Ottoman officials if only out
of concern for his precious gardens near Basra. The shaikh cus-
tomarily flew the Turkish flag in the town and upon his vessels.

12

On the other hand, no Turkish personnel, civil or military, were stationed in Kuwait. Travelers, visitors, and British officials were in general agreement that although Abdullah had accepted for his shaikhdom a kind of nominal "suzerainty" (the word most often used), the Turks exercised no actual control or influence. Turkish and British vessels chugged past each other to and from Kuwait's port in apparent harmony. Although the British dominated the Gulf region in practice, they were not in a strong legal or diplomatic position to challenge Ottoman territorial ambitions there.[1]

Abdullah was succeeded in 1892 by Muhammad I, who was equally comfortable with the Ottoman connection. He ruled in close cooperation with his brother Jarrah. A third brother, Mubarak, a boisterous and adventurous sort, appeared to thrive upon the role allocated to him as head of the shaikhdom's military forces, until it occurred to him that Muhammad and Jarrah were deliberately sending him off to the desert in order to keep him remote from the center of power. Rumors spread among Kuwaiti merchants that Jarrah was under the sinister influence of one Yusuf al-Ibrahim, a powerful figure behind the scenes at the court, who was thought to be secretly plotting to oust Muhammad and seize power for himself or for his protégé, Jarrah. Many in Kuwait considered Yusuf al-Ibrahim to be committed to allowing Kuwait to come much more directly under Turkish influence. Whatever the truth of all these intrigues and rumors, they were enough to stir Mubarak to action. The story is told by Alan Rush, a modern chronicler of the Sabah:

> One May morning in 1896 after Muhammad I's son, Sabah, had gone out for the dawn prayer leaving open the door of the Sief Palace, Mubarak, his sons Jabir and Salim, and some retainers slipped inside. While Salim kept watch at the main entrance, Mubarak made his way to the roof where Muhammad I was sleeping and shot him dead. This was the pre-arranged signal for Jabir, who later gave this account of his part in the affair: "My father ordered me to despatch Jarrah and himself went in search of Muhammad. I went up to the roof, heading for Jarrah's quarters. I noticed a small door. It was shut. I pushed it open, and there was Jarrah sitting on the bed, and his wife standing nearby. I raised my gun and aimed. I pulled the trigger.

It did not go off, so I stepped back, ordering my servants to finish the job. As Jarrah fell, he cried, 'Fear Allah for the murder of your uncle.'"[2]

Two of Mubarak's nephews, the sons of the brothers whom he had slain, fled Kuwait and settled in Basra with Yusuf al-Ibrahim, a relative on their mother's side.[3] They were to become a serious vexation to Mubarak.

Rumors circulated that somehow the British were behind Mubarak's successful bid for power, based apparently on the fact that Mubarak had paid a visit to the political resident in the Persian Gulf, Colonel F. A. Wilson, at Bushire shortly before the coup.[4] No such conspiracy has ever been documented, however, and on balance it seems unlikely. Be that as it may, Mubarak's accession suited British policy well. He was regarded from the outset as a ruler who might be willing to play by Anglo-Indian rather than Ottoman rules. Threatened as he was by the possibility of vengeance at the hands of his exiled nephews and their shadowy mentor, and perhaps sensing a plot to overthrow him, Mubarak appealed to the British for protection. He was turned down.

"Protection" had by then proved to be a fairly effective governmental instrument for the Anglo-Indians, particularly on the Indian subcontinent itself. Shaikh Isa of Bahrain had acceded to a quasi-protectorate status in 1880 and was seen to thrive from it; Mubarak told a British naval officer in 1897 that his friend Isa had strongly recommended to him that he do likewise.[5] That same year, following an attempted raid by Yusuf from the sea, Mubarak tried again and was refused once more. The first loyalties of the British in the Indian civil service, from the viceroy down through the political resident and the subordinate political agents in Bahrain, Muscat, and elsewhere, lay with the Indian Political Department in Delhi. Their attitudes are graphically illustrated by a letter received by Sir Arthur Nicolson from his friend Lord Hardinge, viceroy from 1909 to 1916, written after he had been in India for two years: "Strongly as I felt when in London on the question of the Persian Gulf, I feel infinitely more strongly out here . . . The Shaikh of Koweit should be protected at any cost."[6] But although the viceroy and the officials reporting to him had a great deal of delegated responsibility, it was not within their authority to create

new political responsibilities for Her Majesty's Government. Mubarak's proposal for a protectorate had to be referred to Whitehall. And in London there was hesitation and caution. Officials
there were tempted by the idea and mulled over various possible
justifications for declaring a protectorate: Russian "designs"? Piracy? Nothing seemed quite appropriate.[7] Britain was deeply en-
meshed in imperial diplomacy, and staying on the right side of
the Ottoman Porte and its sprawling dominions was important for
a number of reasons that had nothing to do with the Persian Gulf.
After all, it was a busy time for colonialism: in 1897 Kitchener
was advancing in the Sudan, the Germans were occupying Tsing-
tao, Crete was in revolt, and Turkey itself was involved in a war
with Greece.[8] Perhaps to the surprise of some Anglo-Indians,
knowing little of European *realpolitik* and caring less, London said
"no." Keep a watchful and friendly eye on Mubarak, was the
message, but we cannot authorize any initiative in the Persian Gulf
that might complicate Britain's delicate relations with the Turks
elsewhere.

Britain Makes Its Move

In seeking protection from the British, Shaikh Mubarak was as
persistent as he was ambitious. Late in 1898 he tried once again,
and this time the response was more favorable. Circumstances
had changed. A Russian promoter named Count Kapnist had
been discussing with the Turks the construction of a railway to
the Gulf. It seemed likely that the plans would include a terminal
at Kuwait, regarded for some time as the most promising location
for that purpose.[9] Instructions went out to Lt. Col. Malcolm John
Meade, the political resident in the Gulf (who had replaced Wilson
in 1897), to call upon Mubarak and obtain an agreement with him
that would foil the Kapnist project. But there was need for
caution. "Any formal declaration," wrote British Ambassador
O'Conor from Constantinople, "would be considered little short
of a hostile act by Turkey, and in any case it would be sure to
produce very serious diplomatic complications not only with this
[Turkish] government, but probably also with Russia."[10]

   Meade was told to move quietly to avoid arousing the Turks.
In January 1899, under cover of a game-shooting expedition to

the salt marshes of southern Iraq, Meade visited Mubarak and, on January 23, 1899, exchanged notes with him that were to affect profoundly the history of Kuwait.

The first document, which came to be known as "the bond," contained promises by Mubarak that he and his successors would neither receive the agent of any power nor give up any part of his territory without the prior consent of the British government. The second was a letter from Colonel Meade in which he assured the shaikh of the "good offices" of the British government as long as the bond was observed, promised to send him 15,000 rupees, and conditioned the entire arrangement upon the shaikh's preserving its secrecy. In reporting on the successful completion of his mission, Colonel Meade predicted proudly that the agreement would "stand in the way of attempts by other Powers, or their subjects, to obtain a foothold in this important place."[11]

Several features of these fateful documents are noteworthy:

First, the British, leery of a reaction by the Turks, deliberately did not establish a formal protectorate in Kuwait.

Second, Mubarak's promise "not to receive the agent or representative of any Power or Government" was meant to apply specifically to officials of the Ottoman Empire. Shaikh Mubarak kept that promise; he was appalled in 1913 when he found out that his British mentors had reached an agreement with the Ottomans allowing them to station an agent in Kuwait.

Third, the British government pledged its "good offices," a usefully imprecise expression falling short of definite legal or political commitment; later generations of Foreign Office civil servants and their legal advisers were to puzzle at length over just what the phrase implied. Before signing, Mubarak asked Meade if under the agreement the British would protect his estates near Basra; Meade had no authority to make any such commitment, but he suggested that the general promise of good offices would "probably" cover the matter. Two of Mubarak's brothers who were present declined to countersign the agreement because it lacked such assurances. The Foreign Office, in order to prevent a split between Mubarak and his brothers and to ensure the silence of the latter, later authorized Meade to confirm to Mubarak that the British government would "do what they can to protect the family estates."[12] This pledge regarding the Al Sabah date gardens was to ripen in 1914 into a much more binding (and ultimately expensive) commitment.

Fourth, in obtaining Mubarak's promise "not to cede, sell, lease, mortgage or give for occupation or for any other purpose" any part of his territory, Colonel Meade exceeded his instructions, and he was later called on the carpet for it.[13]

Finally, requiring the shaikh to keep the agreement a secret, however prudent that may have seemed at the time, caused difficulties much later on, when Abdul Karim Qasim and then Saddam Hussein were to assert that Kuwait had been removed from the Ottoman Empire by stealth.

But it seems hardly accurate to call Britain's 1899 involvement with Shaikh Mubarak a "theft." The initiative had been the Shaikh's; he had tried more than once to throw himself into the British embrace. The legendary Arabist and explorer Harry St. John Philby put it this way: "In 1899, after long hesitation, the British had been forced by Turkish activities . . . to reconsider their hitherto platonic attitude towards the charms of Kuwait; and Mubarak had eagerly accepted their proposal of honourable marriage."[14] It could be argued that the British were guilty of nothing more than alienation of affections. Mubarak had simply seceded, very quietly, from the Ottoman Empire.

Qasim and his spokesmen in 1961, and their successors in 1990, complained that the 1899 agreement was "secret," as it certainly was, though not for very long;[15] they have also claimed that it was "forged," but for this there is no evidence whatever. Iraqis have likewise denounced the agreement as "illegal," by which they evidently mean that it was invalid because Mubarak, having accepted appointment as an Ottoman *qaimmaqam*,[16] was no more than a subordinate official in charge of a relatively minor section of an Ottoman vilayet, who had no business giving away rights to Turkish territory, much less entering into engagements with foreign governments. But the legal argument on this point is really circular: it depends entirely on whether Mubarak was an independent sovereign or not before he entered into the agreement. And to that question there is no satisfactory answer, only conflicting evidence and partisan interpretation. A leading authority summed up: "By the end of November 1897, the position was simply that no one, with the possible exception of Mubarak himself, really

understood the status of Kuwait."[17] The first element of the co-
nundrum that lies behind the struggle for Kuwait's identity re-
mains unresolved.

In entering into the 1899 agreement with Britain, Shaikh Mubarak had protected himself against annexation by the Ottomans;
he had also found an important and powerful ally in the continuing vendetta with his dissident nephews in Basra. But perhaps
equally significant, he had improved his internal political position:
the "good offices" extended by Colonel Meade in the name of
Her Majesty's Government were offered not only to Mubarak
himself but also to his "heirs and successors." Since the rules and
customs of succession did not provide for strict primogeniture—
the leadership was awarded, at least theoretically, on merit—the
reference to Mubarak's "heirs" amounted to a subtle amendment
to the tribal code. Mubarak's own line became legitimated by his
British sponsors. From the British point of view it was sensible to
restrict the array of political elements having potential claims to
the leadership; from the standpoint of Kuwait's own political and
social evolution, exclusive dynastic legitimacy for Al Sabah cast a
shadow over the system of government by mercantile consensus
that had hitherto prevailed. The political consequences of the
gradual consolidation of Al Sabah rule under Britain's aegis were
to become apparent only in the 1920s and 1930s, when the House
of Sabah segued imperceptibly from a *ruling* family into a *royal*
family. The consequences are apparent even today.[18]

Mubarak Runs with the Hare and Hunts with the Hounds

It took some time for Shaikh Mubarak himself to become fully
comfortable with his new status as a British protégé. He continued
to flirt with the Ottomans. In January 1900 he told a German
railway delegation that although he acknowledged Sultan Abdul
Hamid as "head of the Muhammadan world, [he] does not consider himself a subject of Turkey, and has not acknowledged
Turkish sovereignty over Kuwait territory." Yet he received another decoration from the sultan in June 1900 and was promised
an annual subsidy of 150 karas (225 tons) of dates. Later that year
it was reported that the sultan had awarded him "the gold and
silver medals of the Order of the Imtiaz," and soon the Constantinople press noted that Mubarak had built a new mosque in

Kuwait and named it after Abdul Hamid. Mubarak was seen at the telegraph office in Basra on November 19, 1900, "several hours communicating with Constantinople."[19] The British consul at Basra, A. C. Wratislaw, regarded the shaikh's movements as deeply compromising: "By his visit here [Basra] he has once more allowed the Turks to assert their suzerainty over Koweit, which, indeed, in his correspondence with the Valis and the Sultan since his accession to the Shaikhship, he has constantly admitted . . . Mubarak is undoubtedly a very able man, but he appears too much inclined to run with the hare and hunt with the hounds."[20]

In the meantime Mubarak found it almost impossible not to become entangled in the politics of the northern Arabian desert. For more than a decade the Sabah of Kuwait had played host to the exiled Shaikh Abdul Rahman ibn Faisal Al Saud and his entourage, including his young son Abdul Aziz ibn Saud. And the House of Saud was in a perpetual state of hostility with the Al Rashid, a powerful tribe closely affiliated with the Ottoman Empire which dominated the central desert from the town of Hail. In late 1900, when Mubarak's support of the Saudis in an attack on the Al Rashid came to the attention of the Turks, Mubarak's British handlers took alarm. It was one thing for Britain to support Kuwait as a bastion against potential outside interference in the Gulf; it was quite another to allow Mubarak to suppose that he could participate in the endemic desert infighting of northern Arabia and expect to be bailed out by His Majesty's Government. The political resident, Colonel Meade, warned Mubarak repeatedly to avoid getting involved in desert skirmishes that might draw unwanted attention from the Turks.[21] The increasingly firm British remonstrances finally seemed to take effect; on August 25, 1901, the shaikh addressed a contrite note to the resident: "I am agreeable to act according to your verbal orders that I should remain quiet and not do anything without instructions from you. As your eyes are on me, my heart is at rest."[22]

Mubarak's bond was still secret. With the signed agreement in his pocket in January 1899, Colonel Meade had sailed from Kuwait to Fao for a few more days' shooting, to throw the Turkish authorities off the scent before returning to Bushire. Consul Wratislaw at Basra gave the *wali* (governor) the "shooting excursion" story, as he said, to "tranquillize" him.[23] But the Ottomans soon sensed that the British had reached an understanding with Mubarak. In 1901 their suspicions were confirmed by the German government, which had learned about the shaikh's pledge when King Edward VII mistakenly gave a private Foreign Office briefing paper on the subject to his nephew, Kaiser Wilhelm II.[24] This embarrassing royal *faux pas* led to a fuller, franker discussion between Britain and the Porte, resulting in an exchange of diplomatic notes in September 1901 which set forth a proposed basis for British-Ottoman relations in regard to Kuwait.[25] Known to the diplomatic community as the "status quo," this understanding was to govern—in principle at least—the position of Kuwait for the next twelve years, when its main points were codified and elaborated in the Anglo-Ottoman Convention of July 29, 1913. The elements of the *status quo* were these:

1. Great Britain recognizes Ottoman "suzerainty" (a word carefully chosen) over Kuwait.
2. The Turks will keep hands off Mubarak and refrain from interference in the affairs of the shaikhdom.
3. Britain will not establish a "protectorate" in Kuwait.[26]

To Lord Curzon, the viceroy, the position was faintly ludicrous: "It seems to me that we are now in the quaint situation of having admitted and denied the suzerainty of the Sultan, both accepted and repudiated his sovereignty, and both asserted and given away the independence of the Shaikh."[27]

From now on, the touchstone for objection to any act or maneuver by either party was whether it could be claimed to have impinged upon the *status quo*. With an understanding so general there was of course much room for interpretation on both sides. In Delhi, Curzon was scornful: "When you hear a Foreign Minister say anywhere that all he wants is to defend the *status quo*, you may guess in nine cases out of ten that he has no policy at all."[28] Within weeks of the *status quo* exchange, reports reached the British in the Gulf that Turkish forces were on their way to come to the support of Amir Ibn Rashid of Hail, who was preparing to make a raid on Kuwait. On September 25, 1901, a British Indian naval force of four vessels descended on Kuwait Bay. Machine guns and cannon were offloaded into the town. As it turned out, no Turkish troops appeared, and it was assumed that they had been frightened away.

But the Turks persisted. On November 28, 1901, Mubarak

received an ominous ultimatum from the naqib, a high official of
Basra: either repair to Constantinople in honorable retirement as
a member of the Sultan's Council of State, or be removed from
Kuwait by force. Mubarak instantly appealed to the senior Indian
navy officer in the area, whose presence in the gunboat *Pomone*
was enough to deter the landing of the naqib, on his way from
Basra to demand Mubarak's reply to his ultimatum. News of the
incident was flashed to London and then to the British ambassador
at the Porte, who was instructed to make it clear that "if they insist
on raising these questions we may be driven to settlement less
favourable to their interests." A few weeks later the naqib embar-
goed food shipments from Basra to Kuwait, drawing a protest
from the British that the action was in violation of the *status quo*.
In both of these cases the Porte backed down, disclaiming any
knowledge of the naqib's actions.[29]

At the beginning of 1902 a new Turkish policy was adopted,
one that seemed far more menacing to the British in India. Turkish military detachments began to drift southward from Basra,
moving around Umm Qasr to a new outpost twenty miles south
of Safwan. In February 1902 they established a twenty-man garrison on the southeastern shore of Bubiyan Island at a point called
Ras al-Qaid and began to build a guardhouse, a position they were
not to abandon until the arrival of British-Indian Expeditionary
Force "D" in Mesopotamia at the beginning of World War I.[30]
During the intervening years the presence of Turkish soldiers on
Bubiyan was a thorn in the side not only of Shaikh Mubarak, who
claimed Bubiyan as his own, but also of the British. As a practical
matter there was little they could do without inflating the matter
into a major diplomatic incident, but they made no effort to
conceal their annoyance. Commander Kemp of the Royal Navy
reconnoitered the Turkish garrisons at Umm Qasr and Bubiyan
for several days in February 1902. Acting British Consul F. E.
Crow traveled from Basra overland to Umm Qasr at the end of
1903.[31] Britain protested repeatedly to the Porte that the Turkish
military establishments were a violation of the *status quo*.[32] There
were those, led by Lord Curzon, who would have been pleased to
dislodge the Bubiyan garrison by force; the viceroy indeed proposed that a military post be established at the northern end of
the island if the Turks persisted in their refusal to withdraw.[33] In
London cooler heads prevailed among those in charge at the

Foreign Office, weighing as they must the continuing railway negotiations and all the other factors in the swirling diplomatic tension that ultimately erupted in war. In any case, it was noted, the fact that Kuwait's boundaries had never been defined created uncertainty as to whether the presence of Turkish troops on Bubiyan actually constituted an infringement of the *status quo*. Responses to London's efforts to extract local information about the extent of Mubarak's jurisdiction were unsatisfactory. On January 29, 1902, Consul Wratislaw cabled from Basra: "There is no information to be got here as to the boundaries of Koweit territory. I consider Shaikh has no claim to Safwan, and think he would have difficulty proving title to much beyond immediate neighborhood of his town." The political resident at Bushire cabled: "Boundary of Koweit is quite uncertain . . . When I last saw Shaikh he told me that Safwan was his."[34] Ambassador O'Conor in Constantinople took the view that unless Great Britain were actually to declare a protectorate over the shaikhdom, it had no legal or diplomatic standing to raise the issue.

The 1902 incident thus brought into focus for the first time the question of who actually owned the desolate island of Bubiyan. Mubarak insisted that Kuwaitis regularly traveled in summer to the northeast shore of the island to catch fish by means of tidal weirs; Curzon considered this to be sufficient basis for lodging a protest, but London disagreed, sending instructions that Mubarak was to be supported only in Kuwait town and the bay. Ambassador O'Conor was cautionary: "To block, practically as far as Fao, all access to the Gulf would lead to trouble I fear."[35] Lord Lansdowne, the foreign secretary, expressed his candid view in a private memorandum of March 21, 1902; Shaikh Mubarak, he wrote, was "apparently an untrustworthy savage, no one knows where his possessions begin and end, and our obligations towards him are as ill-defined as the boundaries of his Principality . . . We once made him a present of 1000£ and promised him our 'good offices,' whatever that may mean."[36]

Who Owned the Islands?

From the British standpoint, the status of Bubiyan was a matter of great perplexity and growing concern. In October 1907 the cabinet's Committee of Imperial Defence (described by a student of British bureaucracy as "a kind of prototype national security council")[37] launched a full-scale investigation into Kuwait's boundary situation. For its part, the Foreign Office stated formally that "the limits of Koweit have never been accurately or, indeed, even approximately defined."[38] The particular problem about Bubiyan was what to do about the Ottoman military post that had been set up in 1902 at Ras al-Qaid on the southeast corner of the island. The conclusion of the Committee of Imperial Defence, reached in 1909, was that if Shaikh Mubarak could make out a plausible case that Bubiyan belonged to him, the Turkish post should be "neutralised" by the establishment of a British-guaranteed Kuwaiti outpost, either on Bubiyan itself, on neighboring Warba, or on both.[39] Because of the proviso, it was necessary first to find out just how good the shaikh's claims were. The evidence that could be adduced was not unequivocally persuasive. About little Warba there was nothing to be said. As for Bubiyan, Shaikh Mubarak spoke to his British interlocutors with great feeling about the Kuwaiti fishermen and the nets they stashed on the island during the off-season.

Even as the investigation was under way, there appeared in Calcutta (for official use only) the first issue of J. G. Lorimer's monumental *Gazetteer of the Persian Gulf,* an encyclopedic collection of information about the area that has been compared to the Domesday Book. Lorimer observed:

> The boundaries of Kuwait principality are for the most part fluctuating and undefined; they are, at any given time, the limits of the tribes which then, either voluntarily or under compulsion, own allegiance to the Shaikh of Kuwait. The northern and southern frontiers in the neighbourhood of the sea may however be regarded as fixed; on those sides the question is not between the Shaikh and nomadic Arab tribes, but between the Shaikh and the Turkish Government.

Lorimer then described, apparently for the first time ever, where Kuwait's northern boundaries were understood to lie. The description has scarcely varied in its essentials from that day to this, finding its most recent manifestation in United Nations Security Council Resolution 687 of April 3, 1991. Here is what Lorimer said:

On the north the most advanced Turkish outposts upon the mainland are at Umm Qasr and Safwan and the influence of the Shaikh of Kuwait is unquestioned up to the very walls of those places; we may therefore consider the frontier on this side to be a line running from Khor as-Sabiyah so as to pass immediately south of Umm Qasr and Safwan to Jabal Sanam and thence to the Batin.

When it came to the islands, however, Lorimer was more circumspect. He listed a number of smaller islands understood to belong to Kuwait (this list too has survived almost intact); but he found it impossible to say the same for Bubiyan, "which is claimed by the Shaikh of Kuwait but is at the present (1905) occupied by the Turks"; and Warba, "the ownership of which would naturally follow that of Bubiyan."[40]

The Committee of Imperial Defence reported to the cabinet that Mubarak had established his claim to Bubiyan but not to Warba. "In the circumstances," said an official historical summary in 1928, "His Majesty's Government decided that it was inadvisable to raise any question of the rights of the Shaikh to either island."[41] For the time being, nothing was done about "neutralising" the Turkish garrison on Bubiyan.

Although the British government was not prepared to commit land forces to oust Turkish troops from Shaikh Mubarak's problematical domains, it remained willing to come to his defense by sea. In September 1902, with the apparent backing of the Ottoman government, the refugee Yusuf al-Ibrahim (who had fled Kuwait with Mubarak's fatherless nephews in 1896) launched an expedition against Kuwait with two ships and 300 armed men, the apparent objective being to overthrow Mubarak and remove him from the scene. The British were ready for him. Yusuf and his cohorts were intercepted and pursued by the Indian motorship *Lapwing*. In the hand-to-hand combat that ensued, a British sailor and two Arabs were killed.[42] London once again declined to make formal diplomatic protest; Curzon, for the time being, could only fume: "We cannot," he wrote, "sit down and do nothing in a case where British sailors have lost their lives. In the old days there would have been a bombardment if not something stronger."[43]

Another aspect of Ottoman pressure on the House of Sabah, one that was to recur and persist until long after Mubarak, Curzon, Yusuf, Lansdowne, the naqib of Basra, and indeed all the Ottoman Turks had vanished from the scene, was the leverage represented by the family's landholdings in Iraq—those extensive "date gardens" along the Shatt al-Arab in the Basra vilayet. The two nephews, still under the influence of the vengeful Yusuf al-Ibrahim, brought suit in a court in Basra claiming title (through their murdered father) to a large portion of the properties. The revenues from the lands in question came to some 6,000 pounds sterling a year, a very substantial sum in those days.[44] (The revenues remained an important source of income for Al Sabah for many years; they became dwarfed by oil royalties beginning in the 1930s.) When Shaikh Mubarak failed to appear to respond to the claim, judgment was entered against him.[45] In this case there was very little Mubarak's British friends could do for him except to sympathize. Eventually the nephews' claim was settled out of court, but contention over the Al Sabah date gardens in Iraq had only begun. They were destined to play a significant part in the relations between the rulers of Kuwait and the British as long as the British were there.

Lord Curzon Visits Kuwait

The forceful and imposing Lord Curzon of Kedleston, one of the legendary figures of British imperial history, served as viceroy of India from 1899 to 1905, and it was largely through his influence that Britain's hold on Kuwait tightened in the years after the 1899 agreement. In his classic work *Persia and the Persian Question* (1892) he had set forth the blueprint for Great Britain's policy along the routes to India. Coastal Persia itself was already well within the British sphere of influence by the time Curzon arrived in Delhi in 1899. During his term he lost no opportunity to shore up Pax Britannica on the Arabian side. In the autumn of 1903 Curzon made a viceregal progress aboard an Indian mail steamer, R.I.M.S. *Hardinge,* accompanied by a flotilla of naval vessels, calling at all the key points of British concern and influence, making speeches here, entertaining potentates there, commanding thirty-one-gun salutes, inspiring awe, fear, and respect.[46] (Foreign Minister Lansdowne, for his part, ridiculed "Curzon's prancings in the Persian puddle.")[47] Curzon's address to an assembly of Arab chiefs gath-

ered on board H.M.S. *Argonaut* off the Trucial shaikhdom of
Sharjah on November 21 could hardly have been more explicit:

> We were here before any other Power in modern times had
> shown its face in these waters. We found strife and we have
> created order. It was our commerce as well as your security that
> was threatened and called for protection. At every port along
> this coast the subjects of the King of England still reside and
> trade. The great Empire of India which it is our duty to defend
> lies almost at your gates. We saved you from extinction at the
> hands of your neighbours. We opened these seas to the ships of
> all nations and enabled their flags to fly in peace. We have not
> seized or held your territory. We have not destroyed your in-
> dependence, but have preserved it. We are not now going to
> throw away this century of costly and triumphant enterprise; we
> shall not wipe out the most unselfish page in history. The peace
> of these waters must still be maintained; your independence will
> continue to be upheld; and the influence of the British Govern-
> ment must remain supreme.[48]

At the top of the Gulf lay Kuwait, where in late November Shaikh
Mubarak and his fellow townsmen greeted the viceroy with
warmth and respect. Curzon painted the scene himself:

> When I landed at Koweit the Sheikh gave me a great reception.
> His forces, cavalry, camel-cavalry and foot, had been marshalled
> on the plain outside the town; the solitary vehicle of Koweit was
> pulled out for the accommodation of the Sheikh and myself—
> later in the day it was kicked to pieces by the two Arab horses
> who drew it and who were not accustomed to such employment;
> and surrounded by a shouting, galloping crowd, firing guns with
> ball cartridge into the air or onto the ground, and careering in
> every direction, we made our state entry into the town.[49]

When Mubarak was tendered a handsome ceremonial sword from
the viceroy's own hands, he asked for a belt as well, "so that he
might buckle it on at once to show that he had become 'a military
officer of the British Government.'"[50] If any Turkish officials
heard about these festive proceedings, they may well have wondered what sort of *status quo* they had bargained for. Curzon
himself was pleased with the shaikh, calling him "by far the most
masculine and vigorous personality whom I have encountered in
the Gulf."[51]

Before he left the area Curzon steamed up the Khor Abdullah toward Umm Qasr, where he could see for himself the spot where European railway promoters were still planning their terminal. On his way past Bubiyan Island he could not have failed to notice the little Turkish garrison (now occupied by only half a dozen men) which had been established the previous year.[52]

After the viceroy departed, Mubarak moved quickly to mend his fences with the Ottomans. Ambassador O'Conor reported from Constantinople: "The Shaikh of Koweit readily assures us that he is the warm partisan and faithful subject of His Majesty's Government, but he gives equal, if not more fervent, assurances to the Sultan in a contrary sense, and Mr. Crow [acting consul, Basra] has reported that Lord Curzon had hardly left Koweit before Mubarak hastened to send a propitiatory telegram to His Imperial Majesty at Constantinople."[53] When O'Conor next called upon the grand vizier he learned the gist of what Mubarak had said in his propitiatory telegram: "An important Indian official, having been on a pleasure trip round the Persian Gulf, in the course of which he visited Koweit, Mubarak had accorded to him the reception due to his rank; but that he remained, as before, the faithful servant of the Caliphate." O'Conor's informant (presumably the grand vizier himself) "declared that the Turkish authorities attached little value to the Shaikh's protestations, realizing that Koweit was lost to them. In proof of which, he added that a question had more than once been raised of dismissing Mubarak and nominating some one else as Qaimmaqam of Koweit; but the idea had been abandoned as futile."[54] If this was indeed the immediate result of Curzon's visit to Kuwait, he must have felt that the time and effort had been well spent.

Until now, Britain's surveillance of Mubarak had been in the hands of the political resident in Bushire. One almost immediate result of Curzon's visit was the appointment in 1904 of the Indian government's first resident political agent in Kuwait, Capt. Stuart George Knox. Captain (later Major) Knox arrived on August 6, 1904, to the accompaniment of some characteristic London-Delhi fuss over whether the appointment was to be permanent or only temporary. London foresaw objection by the Porte that the appointment of a permanent agent constituted an infraction of the *status quo,* and in fact Knox was withdrawn briefly early in 1905. Soon after, though, the threat of adverse Turkish reaction was deemed to be outweighed by the manifest advantages of having a British officer continuously in residence. The agency was made permanent, much to the gratification of Curzon and his colleagues in India.[55]

Kuwait quickly fell into the prevailing pattern of treaty arrangements that the British had developed elsewhere in the Gulf. In 1900 Shaikh Mubarak had undertaken not to engage in arms trade; now he agreed not to allow anyone to establish a post office (1904), nor grant pearling or sponge fishing concessions (1911), nor erect a telegraph station (1912), nor award oil concessions (1913) without British consent. One further agreement outweighed all the others because it provided an important weapon in Britain's arsenal in connection with the still-uncompleted negotiations about a railway to the Gulf. By now it was becoming apparent that the prime location for a railway terminal might well be Kuwait Bay itself. Britain had no reason to oppose the site, provided that British interests were allocated a major share in the railway enterprise. Much of the negotiation between the British and other interests, especially German, concerned the percentage of ownership and control of the line that would be held by Britain. British negotiators perceived that if they were in a position to withhold consent to locating the Gulf terminal of the line in the most propitious spot, they would have achieved a most significant tactical advantage. Thus early in 1907 Major Knox was instructed to approach Shaikh Mubarak with a proposal to lease from him an extensive tract along the southern shore of Kuwait Bay, just where it was supposed the railway experts and engineers would plan to build their terminal. The shaikh responded readily to Knox's overtures, and a deal was soon struck. Like the 1899 agreement, the 1907 Lease Agreement was secret; in fact its text was never published until it was located by two enterprising German researchers in the India Office files and printed as an appendix to their seminal work *Die Grenzen des Irak* (Iraq's Boundaries) in 1963.[56]

The 1907 Lease Agreement

The 1907 Lease Agreement was in fact far more than a lease. Its essential provisions, listed below, were seen to bind Great Britain more closely than ever to Kuwait and its rulers.

1. Great Britain obtained a lease in perpetuity over a shorefront tract described as a rectangle 7,500 by 600 cubits (Knox said that Mubarak had a preference for expressing the dimensions in *thera'as*—about 18.75 inches—and this was translated as "cubits"),[57] or about 3,750 by 300 yards. The yearly rent was 60,000 rupees, or 4,000 pounds sterling.

2. Britain could relinquish the lease and stop paying rent at any time without penalty. (In fact, the land was relinquished in 1922, and the question then for Whitehall lawyers was whether the entire agreement was thereby extinguished; they came to the conclusion that it was not, and that the remaining provisions of the 1907 agreement were still in effect.)

3. Britain also got a "right of pre-emption" to take up a great deal of other land, including the strategic island of Warba (though not, significantly, Bubiyan), and a priority in the event the ruler received an offer from another prospective lessee.

4. Shaikh Mubarak agreed that neither he nor his successors would grant, sell, or lease *any* of his or their land "within Koweit boundaries or around it" to any foreign government or subject thereof, including the Ottoman government, without British permission. Meade's unauthorized insertion in the 1899 agreement was thus confirmed.

5. Knox emphatically promised on behalf of the British government that "the town of Koweit and its boundaries likewise" belonged to the shaikh and his heirs, that all the shaikh's "arrangements" would remain in his hands, and that Britain would not collect any customs duties on anything in the leased lands. The shaikh in turn promised preferential tariff terms for British goods.

6. In "Twelfthly," a sort of catchall, Mubarak promised that he would not allow other parties to interfere even if they offered him more rent, that he would not allow others "to possess authority in his dominions," and expressed his hope "for the permanence of the care of the precious Imperial English Government and its kindness on him and on his heirs after him." Knox, for the British government, disclaimed any wish to interfere in the affairs of Kuwait except beneficially, and expressed the "desire" that "the friendship and agreement between the English Government and the Sheikh of Koweit may be perpetual."

7. Finally, Mubarak promised to keep the new agreement "ab-

solutely secret" until the British government gave permission for its release.

The 1907 Lease Agreement is a rather odd document, given the traditional precision of Britain's diplomatic correspondence. Major Knox was something of an Arabic scholar, and the agreement was drafted in that language with a good many ruffles and flourishes.[58] But whatever its deficiencies of draftsmanship, the agreement meant that the British were now more involved than ever before with Kuwait and its ruler, and they did not want anyone else to know about it. For a tactical advantage in the railway negotiations, they had committed themselves very deeply.

Cox, Knox, and the Shaikh

Percy Zachariah Cox was one of the most extraordinary in the long line of civil servants who devoted their lives to the administration of the British Empire. Born in England in 1864, he showed early promise in several sensitive assignments for the Indian Civil Service. There he caught the eye of the viceroy, Lord Curzon, who (according to his biographer) selected Cox "to carry out his policy in the Gulf." Curzon's approach to Persian Gulf statecraft is exquisitely crystallized in the instructions he gave Cox before sending him on a delicate mission in 1899: "I have had Cox up at Simla," he wrote the Secretary of State for India, "and have coached him carefully for Muskat. My advice has been summed up in this precept: make the Sultan understand that every consideration of policy, of prudence, of past experience, of future hopes compels him to be on our side—not necessarily against anybody else, but to recognise that his interests are bound up in loyalty to Great Britain."[59]

1904 was a year of consolidation and also transition in Britain's management of Kuwait. Curzon left India after five years as viceroy, but not before he had installed his brilliant protégé as political resident at Bushire.[60] Cox was just the man to take charge of the Indian Lake, and he relished his task. "Having now put our hand to the plough in Koweit," he wrote Curzon, "it is important that we should make our position there as strong as possible and that without delay." He recommended connecting Kuwait into the Bushire-Fao cable, and having fast British-Indian mail steamers call weekly.[61] On August 4, Cox wrote Mubarak to explain that Captain Knox was being sent to represent the British government, to look after the shaikh's interests, and to help him in his affairs. He requested Mubarak's assistance in finding Knox a place to live. The shaikh replied with a pledge of cooperation and a warning:

> I entertain friendship for you [Cox] and no one else from my heart . . . Till now, however, I have not received relief from your Government as to the losses which I suffer at the hands of the Turks . . . only on account of my friendship with you. . . . I at present am paying all honor to Captain Knox, as I thereby see that I will have peace and secure protection of my rights. If I will not get the same, no good will result from the stay of Captain Knox.[62]

Cox's reply was soothing: "My friend, I am glad that you should express to me freely what is in your heart, for it is by the closer knowledge of your feelings and difficulties that we shall be able to help you more and more fully as time goes on."[63]

Knox lodged at first as a guest of the shaikh, who took him to inspect a house he had selected for Knox to live in and use as an office. "Quite unfitted for the permanent residence of a European," Knox sniffed. "Toward the sea, it looks out on a shipbuilding yard, with a very unpleasant smell of tallow. On all the other three sides it is shut in by unsanitary surroundings." The captain was then shown a possible building site at the east end of the town, facing "a long stretch of sand and slime." Eventually he found temporary quarters pending the construction of a permanent office and residence. He engaged one Abdullah as an Arabic instructor. With Mubarak's approval he hoisted the British flag over his home, provoking yet another protest from the Turks about upsetting the *status quo*.[64]

Shaikh Mubarak thrived under the agency arrangement. By the end of 1908 he had bought himself an automobile; he had been given a steam yacht in connection with the 1907 lease; and he built a large new palace. Perhaps his own self-esteem also expanded. Knox fretted over "the hundred little ways in which

Shaikh Mubarak seeks to impress upon me that I must play second fiddle." He also worried about Mubarak's subjects: "It will be an unpleasant moment for us when they arrive at a juster view of the situation and realize that it is our support chiefly that has enabled and will enable Shaikh Mubarak's despotism to flourish."[65] (Mubarak's "despotism" included heavier financial calls on the merchant community; they were an early strain on Kuwait's historic mercantile consensus.)[66]

The shorefront Agency compound established by Knox was improved by his successor, Captain Shakespear, who arrived in 1909. It was described by a traveler in 1912:

> A few hundred metres northeast of the *serai* [palace] is the British Agent's house, a conspicuous building before which the flag of Great Britain waves from a mighty mast. At night, a red lantern is hoisted on this mast to guide sailors. England . . . is the only state which has an envoy in Koweit. Of Turkey there is no visible sign. Koweit being officially Ottoman territory, the Turks cannot very well put a consul there, but more than that, one finds no other Turkish functionary in Koweit. Turkish pretension is only supported by Mubarak bearing the title Qaim-maqam of Kuwait, and by the fact that the Government flag on the staff at the *serai* is red, with white crescent and star.[67]

The Anglo-Ottoman Convention of 1913

By early 1911 the wheels of diplomacy had turned to the point where a comprehensive agreement about the Baghdad Railway was distinctly in prospect, involving Germany as well as Great Britain and the Ottomans. Since Kuwait was still in the forefront as a potential terminus on the Gulf, it was time for Britain to shore up and codify its status in Kuwait as far as the Ottomans were concerned. The British negotiating objectives, essentially, were to regularize the 1901 *status quo* along the lines of earlier understandings, with the added refinement of a clear definition of Kuwait's boundaries. On July 29, 1911, the Foreign Office sent a careful proposal to the Turks. Britain was prepared, it said, to acknowledge Ottoman suzerainty, but in return would require three things:

1. recognition by the Ottomans of "the validity of certain agreements which the Shaikh has concluded with the British Government"
2. recognition that Warba and Bubiyan belong to Kuwait, and withdrawal of Turkish troops from Bubiyan
3. for the shaikh, "full and undisturbed enjoyments of any properties he may own or hereafter purchase on Turkish territory"[68]

With regard to the first point, Turkish negotiators quickly asked for copies of the "certain agreements" referred to, and for the first time they were given the 1899 "bond," the 1900 commitment about arms control, and the 1904 post office agreement.[69] The British did not disclose the 1907 Lease Agreement. This was not exactly an oversight: it was withheld because the provision relating to preemptive rights to Warba and other coastal areas might yet prove controversial (as a departure from the *status quo*) and also because it was felt that the agreement could not be turned over without first informing Mubarak. This the British officials were loath to do, inasmuch as up until now the shaikh had been told very little about even the general nature of these railway and boundary negotiations going to the very heart of his status and sovereignty.[70]

The Turkish Porte took its time in responding to the British initiative, and when the response came on April 15, 1912, it was not encouraging. For a start, they pointed out when they accepted the *status quo* in 1901 they had not been aware of the secret 1899 bond. They noted that Al Sabah shaikhs (including Mubarak himself) had been honored with the office of *qaimmaqam* since the days of Abdullah II, and that they flew the Turkish flag. Mubarak, they said, had written letters to officials in Basra describing himself as a loyal subject of the sultan and had recently applied to the Basra vilayet for Turkish citizenship for his sons. In fact, the only thing the Ottoman negotiators would agree to in the British note was that they would, of course, guarantee the shaikh's property interests in Turkey, inasmuch as he was a Turkish subject![71]

The negotiations were headed for deadlock. The chief negotiator at the Foreign Office, Alwyn Parker, was perturbed at the prospect of failure:

For five reasons I think it is urgent that our negotiations with Turkey should not fail—

(1) Turkey's military striking power at Koweit is increased by the advent of the railway.

(2) Our own power is decreasing owing to our virtual naval withdrawal from the Mediterranean.

(3) Turkey may be driven into the German combination.

(4) The private fortunes of the Sheikhs of Mohammerah and Koweit are derived from Turkish properties.

(5) Our diplomatic and historical claim to Koweit is, to my mind, very vulnerable.[72]

The Foreign Office and India Office, as so often, saw things somewhat divergently, and it took several weeks to hammer out a further response to the Turks. This took the form of a counteroffer:

1. The actual boundaries of the shaikhdom of Kuwait would be limited to Kuwait town and bay and their immediate surroundings.
2. However, the *status quo* would apply to a much wider peripheral area to which Mubarak laid claim (thereby, according to a private Foreign Office note, preserving the fiction of Ottoman authority but allowing British interference if this pledge should be broken).
3. The Turks would be permitted to station an agent at Kuwait.[73]

The Turks, now engaged in another Balkan war, were again slow to respond. Their reply, in February 1913, showed enough flexibility that the British were encouraged to send them the draft of a treaty. The Turks produced a counterdraft, and the negotiators initialed a compromise on May 6. The Convention was finally signed on July 29, 1913. It could not go into effect until it was ratified, however. There were other matters to be settled first, notably the three-way arrangement among Turkey, Britain, and Germany about the railway.

The final negotiations were overtaken by events. World War I preempted diplomacy for four years. Ratification of the 1913 Anglo-Ottoman Convention never came.

The Importance of the 1913 Convention

Although the Anglo-Ottoman Convention of 1913 never went into effect, parts of it figured in subsequent affairs involving Kuwait, Britain, and the newly created state of Iraq, which emerged as the successor to Turkish Mesopotamia when the war was over. The key features involving Kuwait were these:

1. "The territory of Koweit . . . constitutes an autonomous *qaza* [subprovince, district] of the Ottoman Empire." These twelve words are at the heart of every later Iraqi claim that Kuwait is part of Iraq. Sir Percy Cox, who had not been involved personally in the negotiations and was free to criticize them, wrote to a journalist in September 1913: "I think we came off worst in the Koweit part, as they [Foreign Office] have recognized Turkish sovereignty, and I think they might at any rate have secured suzerainty only."[74] The Foreign Office negotiators thought that the distinction between "sovereignty" and "suzerainty" was not material.[75] Neither word appears in the Convention.

2. The territories of Kuwait are identified as two different regions,[76] with separate provisions applying to each:

a. The shaikh is to have "complete administrative autonomy" in a region described by a semi-circle with Kuwait town at the center, Khor al-Zubair at the northern extremity and al-Qurayyin at the southern extremity. The region incorporated all of the islands listed in Lorimer's *Gazetteer* as belonging to Kuwait, plus Warba and Bubiyan.

b. The tribes situated in a much larger area "are recognized as within the dependence of the Shaikh," who will exercise administrative rights as *qaimmaqam* free of all Ottoman interference or control. The description of this second region was of importance for the future because it set out for the first time the basis for the established frontiers of modern Kuwait:

> The demarcation line begins on the coast at the mouth of Khor al-Zubair in the northwest and crosses immediately south of Umm Qasr, Safwan, and Jabal Sanam, in such a way as to leave to the vilayet of Basra these locations and their wells [note the correspondence to Lorimer's description]; arriving at the al-Batin, it follows it toward the southwest until Hafr-al-Batin which it leaves on the same side as Kuwait; from that point on the line

in question goes southeast leaving to Kuwait the wells of al-Safah, al-Garaa, al-Haba, al-Warba, and Antaa, reaching the sea near Jabal Munifa.

3. A boundary commission will be set up to fix on the ground, as soon as possible, the boundaries described above. (This is a very salutary provision in any international agreement about boundaries, as the Kuwaitis were to learn to their regret in a later context.)

4. The Ottoman Government may appoint a *commissaire* (or "agent" in British parlance) to the shaikh to protect Ottoman interests.

5. The Ottomans recognize the validity of the 1899 bond and the 1900 and 1904 agreements (arms and post office, respectively), as well as the validity of land concessions to the British (unspecified, but encompassing the secret 1907 Lease). The British negotiators decided against including a reference to the right of preemption over Warba Island contained in the Lease Agreement, judging that "it would be very impolitic to introduce it at the eleventh hour unless it was absolutely necessary."[77]

6. Britain promises not to alter the *status quo* in Kuwait, and not to establish a protectorate.

7. The shaikh's property rights in the Basra vilayet will be protected, subject to normal Ottoman taxes and other laws. (Article 9).[78]

The Meaning of the Green Line

One might ask why the Ottoman negotiators were willing to accept such an expansive description of Kuwait's jurisdiction to the north, marked in green on a map included with the draft Convention, and accordingly known as the "green line." Perhaps in the waning days of their empire it seemed important, possibly for internal political reasons, to have Great Britain recognize that Kuwait was part of the empire, even if this status was to be more symbolic than real. With the shaikhdom designated as an Ottoman *qaza*, the location of the border became less important to the Turks; Kuwait would be juridically part of the Basra vilayet whatever its dimensions.[79] The British, on the other hand, working from en-

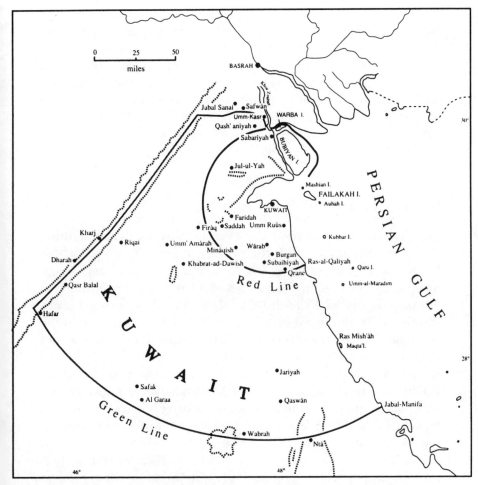

Map 1. These lines show the territories of Kuwait as described in the unratified Anglo-Ottoman Convention of July 29, 1913. Much of the region south and west of the Red Line was given by Sir Percy Cox to Abdul Aziz ibn Saud at the Uqair Conference in 1922.

tirely different premises, were concerned that Kuwait's perimeter to the north be ample enough to serve its strategic interests; they were willing to concede the *qaza* point in return for assurances that the Turks would not interfere in the affairs of the shaikhdom to the disadvantage of the British. It may be conjectured that if Britain had *not* acceded on the *qaza* matter, getting agreement from the Turks on the boundary would have not have proved so easy (and the line could conceivably have been drawn to the south, rather than to the north, of Bubiyan Island). It is worth keeping in mind, then, that in 1913 the northern islands were apparently allocated to Kuwait as part of a *quid pro quo* for the recognition by Britain that Kuwait constituted part of the Basra vilayet. Although the 1913 Convention was never ratified, independent Iraq would claim to the world that as a successor to the Ottomans it was entitled to the benefit of that bargain.

"We Have Used Kuwait as a Pawn"

Once the draft Convention had been initialed by Britain and the Ottomans on May 6, 1913, the delicate job of telling Shaikh Mubarak about the outcome fell to Capt. William Henry Irving Shakespear, the political agent who had replaced Knox in 1909. Shakespear outlined the draft to Mubarak, whose chief concern was the reference to a Turkish agent. "He was so surprised at the possibility," Shakespear reported, "that he asked me to repeat and explain the matter to him more than once, and when I had done so, he became most vehement in his opposition to the idea." Having a Turkish agent, declared Mubarak, would outweigh any other value the treaty might have; for fourteen years, he insisted, he had faithfully observed the 1899 bond, which had been directed precisely against such measures.[80]

Captain Shakespear, an Arabic-speaking officer of tremendous promise and great personal courage, who would perish in a desert battle at the side of Abdul Aziz ibn Saud in early 1915,[81] thoroughly sympathized with the shaikh's outraged protests:

> The Agreement, as it stands in the draft, will in reality give nothing whatsoever to the Ruler of Kuwait or his people which they have not enjoyed for years, while to them it will appear— owing to the clause permitting a resident Turkish Agent—rather as a formal delivery of Kuwait into the hands of Turkey by the Power which has hitherto safeguarded them from the menaces of that very Power. I confess even I find it difficult to avoid such conclusion . . .
> No amount of explanation will ever remove the impression

that we have used Kuwait as a pawn to secure other advantages for ourselves.[82]

Shakespear had gone about as far as he could in trying to sell the treaty to Mubarak. Concerned about the shaikh's displeasure as revealed in Shakespear's report, the Foreign Office asked the India Office to send Cox from Bushire to pacify him. "Mubarak made a great fuss," the political resident reported later, "and I had to make a special pilgrimage." Cox thought that the ruler was making rather heavy weather over having to accept a Turkish agent: "The Shaikh will either subsidise the individual and keep him in his pocket, or else he will make things so uncomfortable for the agent that the Turks will not bother to send him." On July 6 Cox spent four hours with Mubarak, who finally said with resignation: "What can I do but put my faith in you and your government and do as you ask; but it is with great trembling of heart that I do so." Cox left behind this letter of comfort:

The points which you [*sic*] have conceded in the course of this agreement—which was on a give and take basis—you must regard as the price paid in exchange for the great advantages which you derive from it. Among them [are] the confirmation of your independence on the basis of this Convention, and the formal recognition of your extensive claims. Further, it is not hidden from Your Honour that the Sublime Porte undertakes not to interfere in the question of succession or in the internal or external affairs of your administration, and you are aware that there will always be an Agent of the British Government accredited to you at Kuwait; again, it is established in your mind that you have the formal assurance of the British Government to support you in your affairs, so long as you faithfully observe your engagements to us as you have done in the past.[83]

Of course Mubarak gave in; he had no other choice, and he had no leverage. Shakespear was right: Kuwait was a pawn. The British briefly considered bestowing upon the shaikh "some fresh decoration," but decided that a picture of Britain's new King George V would suffice.[84]

3. Britain Takes Charge in Iraq and Kuwait

Kuwait Shakes Off the Ottomans

Soon after the European war broke out in the summer of 1914 it became apparent that Turkey would be drawn in on the German side. The Indian government quickly organized and dispatched a considerable army (Expeditionary Force "D") to occupy Basra and the Shatt al-Arab. The first detachment left Bombay on October 16 with sealed orders. On October 23 it reached Bahrain, where it waited until war was declared between Great Britain and Turkey on November 5; the following day the first troops stepped ashore at Fao. Mesopotamia had seen many incursions in its long history, but according to a British military handbook this was its first invasion by sea.[1]

Kuwait's strategic position at the head of the Gulf was not lost on Anglo-Indian military planners. Sir Percy Cox, still the political resident in the Persian Gulf but shortly to become the political adviser to the commanding general of the Mesopotamian campaign, moved swiftly to bring Mubarak in on the British side. On August 21, 1914, Mubarak declared his loyalty to the British, placed "his efforts, his men and his ships" at Great Britain's disposal, and expressed a desire to eject Turkish forces from areas he claimed as his own.[2] Cox wrote him a letter asking him to attack and occupy Umm Qasr, Safwan, and Bubiyan and afterward to assist in the liberation of Basra. In return, Mubarak was promised three things on behalf of the British government: (1) "Your gardens which are now in your possession, *viz.*, the date gardens situate between Fao and Qurnah shall remain in your possession and in possession of your descendants without being subject to the payment of revenue or taxes." (This pledge of tax exemption, which went further than article 9 of the 1913 Convention, was to cause enormous difficulty for both Britain and the shaikh.) (2) "If you attack Safwan, Umm Qasr and Bubiyan and occupy them the British Government will protect you from any consequences arising from that action." (3) "The British Government does recognise and admit that the Shaikhdom of Kuwait is an independent Government under British protection."[3] At long last, in that final paragraph, Mubarak had what he had always sought: a clear statement from the British government recognizing his independence under British protection.

As for the date gardens, they had never been far from Mubarak's thoughts, and Cox knew it. During a conversation between them in August 1910, recorded by Political Agent Shakespear, the ruler himself had hinted at an indemnity arrangement:

> The Shaikh said he was prepared to do anything the British Gvmt. desired, even to flying a British flag over his palace, but the inevitable consequence of any open declaration that Kuwait lay within the sphere of British influence would not be tolerated, would at once lead to Turkish reprisals on the Shaikh's properties on the river . . . If the British Govt would take upon themselves that these properties should not suffer the Shaikh was prepared to accept any demand we should make.[4]

Grateful as they may have been for Mubarak's offer of assistance in 1914, it is not clear why Cox and his superiors thought it necessary to enter into such an open-ended financial commitment.[5] At this early stage of the war, of course, the future status of the Basra vilayet was quite indefinite. Cox and some of his colleagues from British India seem to have been contemplating outright annexation (which would have made it feasible administratively to grant the shaikh a tax exemption); as it turned out, the pledge of tax immunity ultimately had to be redeemed by Britain when the government of an independent Iraq declined to honor it.[6]

Historians of the war have not been particularly impressed by Mubarak's contribution to the Allied effort. The British official history makes no reference to Kuwait in any military context. Apparently alone among contemporary observers, Col. H. R. P. Dickson credits Mubarak with a substantial contribution: "His presence with a large Bedawin force in the hinterland created a most useful diversion and was of material assistance to General Sir Arthur Barrett and his army (I.E.F.'D') . . . on the Shatt al-Arab."[7] The islands mentioned in Cox's letter were indeed occupied by Mubarak's men,[8] but the Turkish garrisons had withdrawn before any opposing forces could reach them. Nevertheless, Mubarak demonstrated his allegiance to the British cause in various ways: he contributed 50,000 rupees to the British Red Cross, he suppressed anti-Allied propaganda in the shaikhdom, and he sent boats at his own expense to Bushire to help with troop movements.[9] The Indian army's official *Handbook of Arabia*, prepared for use by British officers, characterized Mubarak as a "mediatized independent ruler," an expression dating from the days of the Holy Roman Empire to describe a prince who had been taken over without depriving him of all vestiges of his authority and prestige.[10]

But Mubarak died on November 28, 1915, when the war was hardly a year along. He was succeeded by his son Jabir, who within the hour sent word to the Political Agency "promising to be even more devoted to British interests than his father had been."[11] In a formal letter the viceroy of India assured Jabir II that "so long as you act up to existing arrangements with the British Government you may expect the same support as was enjoyed by your father."[12] Jabir was an amiable man by all accounts, anxious to please not only those by whom he had been mediatized but also some of the Kuwaiti merchants who were being pinched by British wartime restrictions on trading with the Turks. British authorities in London, distressed that supplies were still slipping through, urged Sir Percy Cox to try to persuade his Arab "protégés" (who included not only Jabir but also Abdul Aziz ibn Saud, then expanding his influence in northern Arabia, and also Shaikh Khaz'al of Muhammarah) to do a little more for the war effort.[13] Cox sought to rectify the situation by convening a mighty "durbar," an Indian-style festive and ceremonial convention that took place in Kuwait in November 1916. The centerpiece of his extravaganza was a display of camels captured by Ibn Saud from bedouin allies of the Turks. There were also stirring orations in praise of the British, followed by gifts and the award of decorations. Knowing Cox's management techniques, one may also conjecture that some hard currency changed hands. The three Arab chieftains "swore together to work [with Britain] for the achievement of a common end."[14] Ibn Saud went away from the durbar as a Knight Commander of the Most Eminent Order of the Indian Empire (K.C.I.E.); Jabir, still on probation for evading the blockade of Turkey, was made only a Companion of the Most Exalted Order to the Star of India (C.S.I.).[15] Some British officials clearly never trusted Jabir: reports complained of his "shilly-shallying evasions" and the fact that he "gave us little or no real assistance."[16]

Jabir died on February 5, 1917, of acute gastritis, despite having been "cupped and branded," according to the political agent's report.[17] He was succeeded by a brother, Salim I, described in the British official historical summary as "narrow in outlook, bigoted in religious matters, [and] tactless in his personal relations."[18] Among other things, Salim summoned Kuwait's Jewish leaders and told them that the distillation of spirits must cease. Moreover, he forbade prostitution, at least inside the town walls.[19] Lt. Col. Robert Hamilton, who served as political agent from June 1916 to March 1918, described Salim as "small in stature, close-fisted, secretive, calculating and shy. He . . . manages to get hold of many of the pretty girls of Kuwait, but all is done quietly and with the greatest circumspection."[20]

Throughout the war the merchants of Kuwait did well by supplying provisions to the British army commissariat: in 1917 alone 4,700 camels, 19,975 sheep, 1,111 cattle, and 3,000 tons of other stores.[21] But Shaikh Salim and some of his fellow citizens also found it impossible to resist the temptation to supply the Turkish forces across the desert in Syria. In February 1918 there was a serious clash between the shaikh and Colonel Hamilton over the unloading of a large steamship with cargo destined for the Turks. On July 5 Salim got a stern warning in writing from Hamilton's replacement, Capt. Percy Loch. Salim was reminded of the British pledge to Mubarak of November 3, 1914, which had been renewed in specific terms upon the accessions of Jabir and Salim himself, in the form of a "kharta" in the name of the viceroy, forwarded through the resident. Captain Loch's letter went on:

Should you show to Government the same friendship and assistance which they have experienced for many years in their dealings with the rulers of Kuwait, they will continue to you the assurances given to your illustrious father [Mubarak] . . . especially that the town of Kuwait and its boundaries likewise belong to Shaikh Mubarak as-Sabah, ruler of Kuwait, and to his heirs after him [the reference is to article 9 of the 1907 lease] and will extend to you the friendship and protection and assistance which they gave to him.

On the other hand, "it is the plain duty of the ruler of a state which is on terms of friendship with Government to prevent all acts, either by his own subjects or by other persons in his territory, which may be contrary to interests of Government . . . Government will be compelled to hold Your Excellency personally responsible should any such act unfortunately be committed in future."[22]

Shaikh Salim was now on notice that the status of Kuwait as an independent shaikhdom under British protection was at risk; he was to be held personally responsible for any act construed by the British to be anti-British, committed by anyone in Kuwait, whether Salim knew about it or not. Even granting the exigencies of war, this was a dire warning indeed. For anyone seeking to argue later that before the war Kuwait had been a sovereign state independent of the Ottoman Empire, this letter contained a trap, because it appeared to show that British recognition of Kuwait's independent status vis-à-vis the Ottomans was actually conditioned on how some British official might interpret an alleged failure by the shaikh to prevent some supposedly subversive act. For Britain itself, Kuwait's independence was evidently not unconditional and absolute, but depended on Britain's estimate of the shaikh's good behavior.

Apparently the warning to Salim was effective. According to a postwar India Office memorandum, "the Shaikh for the remainder of the war maintained a less unsatisfactory attitude to His Majesty's Government, and his cooperation was recognized at the end of 1918 by the grant of the C.S.I. [Star of India] and of a lump sum of 3 lakhs of rupees [300,000 rupees, equivalent to £20,000], and by the cancellation of the claim of the Government of India in respect of the loan of £12,500 made in connection with the Kuwait water supply in 1914."[23]

Long before the end of the war in Europe, the Turkish army

in Syria had been pushed far to the north by the advancing British forces under General Allenby, with support from T. E. Lawrence's Arab irregulars. In Mesopotamia itself, after some of the most difficult fighting of the entire war, the British entered Baghdad in March 1917. On October 30, 1918, the Turks surrendered to the Allies and signed the Armistice of Mudros. Shaikh Salim's inadequacies were forgotten or forgiven. The British lifted their blockade in February 1919.[24]

Trouble with the Saudis

With the Ottoman Turks out of the way, and with the new country of Iraq still only in the process of formation, Kuwaitis might now have been in a position to hope for some relative peace and quiet. But if they did, they reckoned without the growing stature and influence of Abdul Aziz ibn Saud, that extraordinary Arab leader who spent his youth as a refugee in Kuwait and eventually consolidated most of the Arabian Peninsula under his own banner as the Kingdom of Saudi Arabia. Having swept through much of the northern Arabian desert, spearheaded by the puritanical and ruthless Wahhabis (also known as "Ikhwan" or brothers), Ibn Saud was now probing at the fringes of Kuwait. He would not (or could not—it was not always clear which) put a stop to the incursions of the Wahhabis for another decade. Throughout the 1920s it was the British who drew the line against Saudi northern expansion, all the way from Trans-Jordan to the Gulf.

The trouble with the Saudis involved, among other things, the question of how far the borders of Kuwait extended to the south and southwest. In Britain's bargain with the Ottomans, codified in the unratified 1913 Convention, Kuwait had been allocated a wide expanse of territory stretching far to the south and west. Ibn Saud now pointed out that the 1913 line had been drawn without *his* knowledge and consent, and he did not propose to be bound by it. In those prewar days, he added, Kuwait had been ruled by the powerful Shaikh Mubarak, who commanded respect and allegiance from various far-flung tribes. These tribes, declared Ibn Saud, owed no allegiance to the present Kuwaiti ruler, Salim; they had turned to Ibn Saud as their leader. It only made sense to include those tribes within the domains of the House of

Saud. In any case, Ibn Saud pointed out, the 1913 Convention had never been ratified.[25]

In May 1920 a party of Ibn Saud's Ikhwan raided a recently constructed Kuwaiti fort that had been somewhat aggressively sited by Shaikh Salim far to the south of Kuwait town in an area contested by the Saudis. The Kuwaitis were soundly trounced.[26] Some months later a larger force of Kuwaitis under the leadership of Shaikh Salim himself was defeated at Jahra. Fearing for the shaikhdom and for their lives, a group of merchants and notables approached Shaikh Salim and insisted that he appeal to the British for assistance; he did so. The British responded with a display of aircraft, naval vessels, and armored cars, causing the Wahhabis to withdraw.

The Kuwaiti merchants' approach to Shaikh Salim marked the first time on record that Kuwait's consensus system of governance was brought to bear in a situation that threatened the very existence of the shaikhdom. Owing in large measure to Salim's own ineptitude in dealing with Ibn Saud, Kuwait had faced obliteration at the hands of the Wahhabi warriors from the desert. The common interest demanded prompt and decisive action; the remedy sought and obtained was a police action by Salim's British sponsors. Alarmed by the continuing strife, the British authorities tried diligently to bring the Saudis and the Kuwaitis together to compromise their differences. Early in 1921, during a meeting arranged by Sir Percy Cox to try to sort out these intractable and conflicting claims, word was received that Salim had suddenly died in Kuwait. On hearing this news, Ibn Saud unexpectedly declared that there was no longer any quarrel to settle, or any further need for a boundary between his territory and that of Kuwait. Although the territorial problem had not yet been resolved, at least the crisis had eased.[27]

In Kuwait, nevertheless, momentum had gathered for wider participation in decision making. Salim's death meant that a new leader must be named. The group of notables who had earlier petitioned Salim to ask the British for military aid now made it clear to the most promising candidate, Salim's nephew Ahmad, that they would support him only if he would accept the formation of a permanent forum where their voices could be heard. Ahmad agreed in writing to the formation of a Council of Advisors (al-

Majlis al-Istishari) comprised of twelve representatives of the merchant community, including members of Al Sabah.[28] Ahmad was thereupon recognized as shaikh of Kuwait. Although the Council itself was ephemeral, it would be remembered in 1938 when Kuwait faced an equally serious threat from another direction: newly independent Iraq.

The Beginnings of the Mandate in Iraq

The war was over, and a new era was about to unfold in Mesopotamia. The defeat of the Ottoman Empire meant that its former constituent parts were to acquire new identities. The carving up of the former empire inevitably fell to the victors. Even during the war Britain and France had reached a general understanding (the secret Sykes-Picot agreement) whereby France would have a "sphere of influence" in Syria and Lebanon, while Great Britain would enjoy the same in Palestine and Mesopotamia. Somewhat to the dismay of the old-time colonialists, however, new notions were in the air: the twelfth of President Woodrow Wilson's Fourteen Points, announced on January 9, 1918, stated that nationalities under Turkish rule "should be assured an undoubted security of life and an absolutely unmolested opportunity of autonomous development." (Baghdad's press, still under British wartime censorship, withheld the news of the Fourteen Points for another nine months.)[29] Moreover, the European Allies had made certain expedient wartime promises to the Turks' Arab subjects in return for their cooperation in defeating their Ottoman masters. On November 8, 1918, just before the armistice in Europe, an Anglo-French statement declared that the two governments intended to establish in the former Ottoman territories "national governments and administrations drawing their authority from the free choice of the populations . . . and to assure by . . . [Allied] support and effective aid the normal working of the governments and administrations which they have adopted of their own free will."[30]

Under the Sykes-Picot understanding, however, Great Britain was entitled to a sphere of influence in Iraq. Accordingly, the former Ottoman vilayets of Baghdad and Basra were established as a British mandate under Article 22 of the Covenant of the newly formed League of Nations (Mosul's status was uncertain; it became the third piece of Iraq only in 1926). The mandate arrangements were set in place at a conference at San Remo, Italy, in April 1920, to which no Iraqi—perhaps needless to say—was invited. When news of the proposed mandate reached Baghdad in May, the country erupted in a furious insurrection, a major setback for the British plans and an event remembered in Iraq as "the Great Iraqi Revolution." Unable to establish the formal mandate in the face of such violent opposition, Britain proposed a substitute: a treaty between Great Britain and a new Iraqi government, which up to this point had not yet been formed. To the League of Nations and the European-American community the British made it clear that the treaty would simply embody its rights and responsibilities as a mandatory power under Article 22 of the Covenant, while it was presented in Iraq as a giant step forward toward independence and nationhood. The treaty, drafted mainly in London by British government lawyers, was specifically designed to cover the same ground covered by Article 22 of the League of Nations Covenant.[31]

Curzon, Churchill, and Cox

In power in Britain throughout these events was a coalition government led by the Liberal David Lloyd George, who had been prime minister for much of the war. The foreign secretary was Lord Curzon, who had seen many years of service in India and the Middle East, and of whom it had been said that he regarded himself as the leading expert on any place he had ever been. Winston Churchill, already a controversial figure as secretary of state for war, was offered the Colonial Office at the end of 1920. He accepted the position only after some hesitation: "I look forward only to toil and abuse," he wrote Curzon privately on January 8, 1921.[32] The Colonial Office was the designated repository for some of the most intractable and thankless situations that Great Britain had ever faced: notably Ireland, Palestine, and Mesopotamia. Moreover, Churchill and Curzon were natural political competitors in the cabinet, by temperament as well as by their somewhat overlapping portfolios.

During the Mesopotamia campaign Sir Percy Cox served as chief political officer of Expeditionary Force "D." Here he became in effect the head of Iraq's civil administration. T. E. Lawrence, sent in 1916 by the Arab Bureau in Cairo to assess Anglo-Indian intelligence capabilities in Basra, reported with considerable prescience: "Sir Percy Cox is High Commissioner except in name. He is absolute dictator in the Gulf, and will remain so as long as he is there."[33] Cox was known in Whitehall as a sort of one-man fire brigade for the Middle East. In the middle of 1918, having just been appointed civil commissioner for Iraq, he was dispatched urgently by Curzon as Minister to Persia for two years. Until October 1920 he also retained his title as political resident in the Persian Gulf.[34] In his absence from Baghdad the acting civil commissioner, Sir Arnold Wilson, found it a daunting challenge to fill his old boss's shoes. Wilson, a totally unreconstructed imperialist of the old Indian school, felt unjustly criticized when civil unrest over the proposed mandate erupted into the major insurrection in June 1920.[35] His respect for Cox was enormous, however, and he recommended as strongly as anyone else that Cox be recalled from Tehran to take charge in the Iraqi capital. On October 4, 1920, Cox returned as high commissioner for Iraq. His new title (he had previously been civil commissioner) signified that military government in Iraq had been replaced by civilian government.[36]

Even before taking over the Colonial Office, Churchill was dubious about the way things were going in Mesopotamia. On August 31, 1920, in the middle of the disturbances of that summer, for which he had some responsibility at the War Office, he drafted (but did not send) a letter to Curzon at the Foreign Office: "It is an extraordinary thing that the British civil administration [under Sir Arnold Wilson] should have succeeded in such a short time in alienating the whole country . . . I hope Percy Cox will be able to get things on to better lines, but I must confess that I do not feel any complete sense of confidence in him. His personality did not impress me."[37] On January 8, 1921, before his new appointment as colonial secretary had been announced, Churchill fired off a telegram to Cox in Baghdad, setting out some ill-informed observations and inquiries focused mainly on the expense of the British-run administration and the need for reduction in troop strength. Churchill demanded an immediate response. Cox, unaccustomed to this sort of message, replied coolly that if Churchill's telegram was designed merely as a basis for discussion, all well and good, but if he was supposed to construe it as settled government policy, he would resign with regret.

Sir Arthur Hirtzel, permanent under secretary at the India Office, had the delicate task of forwarding Cox's response to Churchill: "It may be that you would not be unwilling for him to resign. I should be sorry if that were the case . . . Cox has a wonderful hold over most of the very disparate elements of the Mesopotamian population, and they will take things from him which they will take from no one else."

Although Churchill accepted Hirtzel's advice, it was not in his nature to give ground. He wrote Cox:

> I quite understand your difficulties, and you in your turn ought to try to realise the difficulties which exist at home . . . I do not think there is the slightest chance of the Cabinet or Parliament agreeing to expenditure on such a scale [12 to 14 million pounds a year] for a country which we only hold under the League of Nations and are pledged to return to the Arabs at the earliest possible moment . . . You would take a great responsibility if . . . you deprived His Majesty's Government of your local knowledge and influence and thus diminished gravely the chances of a satisfactory solution.[38]

Cox tacitly withdrew his threat to resign, and over time relations between the two men seem to have mellowed somewhat. Churchill's respect for Cox's abilities grew. Late in 1921 he proposed to Curzon, and it was agreed among the Foreign Office, the India Office, and the Colonial Office, that "so long as Sir P. Cox held the post of High Commissioner in Iraq, he should be in charge of the political affairs of Kuwait also."[39] Cox and Churchill worked together on Iraq until the latter left office with the fall of the coalition cabinet on October 23, 1922; Sir Percy Cox retired from government service early in the following year.

The Faisal Formula

Churchill began his tenure as colonial secretary by convening a conference in March 1921 in Cairo, to be attended by all the most important British officials with knowledge of and responsibility in the area. Cox was summoned, of course; he brought with him from Baghdad Miss Gertrude Bell, by then a well-known Orientalist and travel writer, who was serving as oriental secretary to the high commissioner. The Cairo Conference was a crucial step in the establishment of the Hashemites on thrones in Jordan (then called Trans-Jordan) and Iraq, very much as Britain's chosen instruments. Emir Abdullah was installed in Amman. There was much discussion about Iraq: should there be a king at all? If so, who? The choice fell on Abdullah's brother Faisal, who had previously been installed as king of Syria but had been dismissed by the French.

Cox wrote later to Curzon, his career mentor: "The Conference at Cairo was useful . . . I thought he [Churchill] was very good [at running it]."[40] Cox's favorable assessment was perhaps colored by the fact that at Cairo Churchill entrusted to Cox the installation of Emir Faisal as king of Iraq, following a "formula" devised and articulated by Cox with the assistance of Gertrude Bell and Col. T. E. Lawrence, already famous as "Lawrence of Arabia." How the formula evolved at Cairo was reported in several messages from Churchill to the prime minister in London. On March 14, two days after the Conference opened, he cabled Lloyd George that all the experts were agreed that "Faisal offers hope of best and cheapest solution . . . Formula would be: 'In response to enquiries from adherents of Emir Faisal the British Government have stated that they will place no obstacles in the way of his candidature as Ruler of Iraq, and if he is chosen he will have their support' . . . I have no doubt Faisal offers far away best chance of saving our money."[41] Two days later he described the formula in more detail:

> Sir Percy Cox to arrive in Basra early April . . . Faisal, as soon as possible, to proceed to Mecca and thence to telegraph on about 23rd April to his friends in Mesopotamia saying that British Government had informed him, in response to their enquiries, that they would place no obstacle in the way of his candidature as ruler of Iraq, and that he would have their support if he were chosen; that he, after discussion with his father and brothers, had decided to offer services Iraq.

Churchill explained further particulars to be managed by Cox from Baghdad, including what Faisal was to say about the man-

date, and how he was to dissolve the existing provisional government and ask a senior Muslim notable, the naqib of Baghdad, to
form a cabinet. "The foregoing recommendations have been
unanimously adopted," Churchill told his prime minister, "and I
urgently request you to obtain Cabinet sanction for them in time
to allow me to concert final details with Cox before he leaves
Cairo."[42]

Lloyd George hesitated: would it appear that the Iraqi initiative
for Faisal was spontaneous? Churchill's next message was extraor-
dinarily blunt, even for him:

> I am very anxious no misunderstanding should exist between us
> . . . This procedure, which was devised by Cox, Miss Bell and
> Lawrence, carries with it unanimous opinion of all authorities
> here. We are quite as fully conscious as you are of desire for
> securing a spontaneous movement for Faisal in Mesopotamia as
> a prelude to his being countenanced by us . . . All my proposals
> which were sent you on 16th hang together, and you reject my
> policy . . . I do hope you will give me personally the support to
> which I am entitled in a task which I certainly have not sought
> . . . I hope for dispersal of conference on 24th, so early reply is
> requested.[43]

The prime minister met with his cabinet on March 22, and the
same day cabled Churchill that the Faisal formula had been approved.[44] Faisal arrived in Iraq in June and was "elected" king by
a hand-picked Council of Ministers in July. By July 23, Cox was
able to write Churchill: "I hope that before this reaches you I
shall have been able to let you know that our Royal fish is safely
ashore."[45]

"Has He Not Got Some Wives to Keep Him Quiet?"

Emir Faisal was duly crowned in Baghdad as the first king of Iraq
on August 23, 1921. In that sense he was "safely ashore." But
Cox's worries—and Churchill's—were not over. Part of the formula worked out at Cairo was to make sure that Faisal thoroughly
understood (by way of a very personal and confidential briefing
from his old friend and wartime ally, Colonel Lawrence) that Iraq
under his regime would still be controlled by Great Britain under

its mandate from the League of Nations. In order to accommodate nationalist sentiment in Iraq, which had already convincingly displayed its explosiveness in the June 1920 insurrection, Britain was willing to couch the mandate in the form of a treaty, provided that the essential terms of the mandate remained in effect. Perhaps Lawrence, already suffering remorse over his role in the betrayal of the Sharifeans after the war, found difficulty in making the point entirely clear to Faisal; perhaps Faisal merely affected not to have understood him.[46] At all events, complications arose as drafting of the treaty went forward during the summer of 1921. "I do not think," Churchill wrote his undersecretary impatiently, "we ought to bombard the High Commissioner with these elaborate instructions . . . I think it much better to leave matters to Sir Percy Cox, who alone knows the local situation and who has the greatest possible interest in bringing out a satisfactory result. There is also too much talk about 'Mandates,' 'Mandatories' and things like that. All this obsolescent rigmarole is not worth telegraphing about."[47]

In August Churchill assured the cabinet: "The government of the country will be conducted by an Arab administration under King Faisal, who will act in general accordance with the advice tendered him by the High Commissioner, Sir Percy Cox."[48] But it still was by no means certain that Faisal himself saw things that way. Churchill instructed Cox on August 15: "You should explain to Faisal that whether under mandatory or Treaty arrangements we must expect to be consulted so long as we are meeting heavy financial charges in Mesopotamia . . . You should tell Faisal that we regard his promise to accept the mandatory system, subject to Treaty modification, as binding."[49] In a message drafted by Churchill but not sent to Cox, he was even more direct: "The position was most clearly explained to him by Lawrence . . . It seems to me early days for Faisal to begin making difficulties . . . I am quite sure that if Faisal plays us false a policy founded on him breaks down Br Govt will leave him to his fate & withdraw immediately all aid & military force."[50]

In November, after the enthronement, Churchill was still vexed. "This is what I think ought to be said to Sir Percy Cox," he instructed his senior advisors: "I am getting tired of all these lengthy telegrams about Faisal and his state of mind. There is too much of it. Six months ago we were paying his hotel bill in London, and now I am forced to read day after day 800-word messages on questions of his status and his relations with foreign Powers. Has he not got some wives to keep him quiet? He seems to be in a state of perpetual ferment, and Cox is much too ready to pass it on here."[51]

Work on the Anglo-Iraqi treaty proceeded into the winter. A draft circulated to the British cabinet on February 17, 1922, was approved in principle four days later. At the end of March, Churchill had to advise the cabinet that King Faisal was not satisfied with the preamble, insisting on the inclusion of a declaration that the mandate was abrogated; without such a provision he would negotiate no longer. Churchill was certain that the inclusion of any such statement would make the treaty fatally unacceptable to the Council of the League of Nations. He speculated that Faisal's attitude could reflect in part "a misunderstanding of a message delivered to him by Colonel Lawrence in April 1921, just before he went to Iraq." Churchill proposed to send Lawrence to Baghdad to explain matters once again, but someone (perhaps Cox, who had no use for Lawrence) killed the idea.[52] Matters remained at a stalemate throughout the summer of 1922, while Sir Percy Cox tried to coax the king into signing the treaty. By September Churchill was very discouraged; he wrote the prime minister: "I am deeply concerned about Iraq. The task you have given me is becoming really impossible . . . Faisal is playing the fool, if not the knave . . . There is scarcely a single newspaper—Tory, Liberal or Labour—which is not consistently hostile to our remaining in this country . . . At present we are paying eight millions a year for the privilege of living on an ungrateful volcano."[53]

Foreign Secretary Curzon wrote his colleague with considerable sympathy: "May I express my admiration of the patience and resource you have shown in a very difficult situation. But I am afraid that Faisal is a 'bad hat.'"[54] Churchill seized this opening to appeal for Curzon's support: "Before I bring the Iraq position to the Cabinet I should be glad to have a talk with you, in order that we may if possible speak with one voice. You must remember that my task has been to make bricks without straw and to blow bubbles without soap."[55]

But in the end King Faisal of Iraq came to accept that he had no choice but to put his name to the treaty linking the fortunes of his adopted country so closely to Great Britain. He and Cox signed the treaty on October 10, 1922; ratifications were exchanged in Baghdad on December 19, 1924. The treaty-mandate arrangements were to remain in effect for almost eight years. On October 3, 1932, Iraq itself, under British sponsorship, became a member of the League of Nations—the first Arab country to achieve that status. But in the intervening period Great Britain was in a commanding position as far as Iraq's relations with Kuwait and its other neighbors were concerned.

4. First Lines in the Sand, 1923

The desert had always been as free as the Atlantic
Ocean, Iraq and Syria normally limiting their administration to the edge of the cultivation. The ruler of
Najd, however . . . being the only great 'sea power,'
controlled all deserts.

— *John Bagot Glubb*

There are those who say, and who said at the time, that the whole
idea of drawing boundary lines in the Arabian desert after World
War I was ill-conceived. Some geographers are wont to compare
the desert to the ocean, whose vast interiors belong to no man,
whose routes may be traversed with total freedom from any human interference. Just as the law of the sea has arisen out of these
concepts of freedom of navigation, so has the customary law of
the desert.

Once in a while a very great leader arises out of the desert to
command the respect and fealty of many tribes and clans, and
one of these was Abdul Aziz ibn Saud. An American physician
with years of experience in Kuwait pointed out the difference
between Ibn Saud and Mubarak:

> A man can hardly be a great shaikh unless his followers welcome
> the chance to die for him. Not every chief in Arabia is cast in
> this mold, but the great ones are. The difference between Mu-
> barak of Kuwait and Ibn Saud of Riyadh is just this difference.
> Mubarak . . . was a shrewd man and a very able ruler. The justice
> and strength of his government in Kuwait were renowned all
> up and down the Gulf, but no one loved him. His dominion
> never extended beyond the territory that was naturally tributary
> to Kuwait.[1]

From the point of view of Ibn Saud, the northern Arabian desert
belonged to whoever controlled the allegiance of the tribes who

lived there, and any tribe whose adherence to some other chieftain was problematical could be reckoned as fair game.

South of the Euphrates, clearly within the area from which the British had ousted the Ottomans, the desert was inhabited by bedouin whom the British hoped to integrate into the new Iraqi nation. With Ibn Saud continuing to stretch the limits of his own jurisdiction, often with the warlike and puritanical Wahhabis in the van, clashes with the new British mandatory administration in Iraq were inevitable. The British decided that a definite frontier was required to stabilize Iraq. For similar reasons there was need for a better-defined boundary between Ibn Saud and Kuwait. And Britain had another, even more compelling, reason for having acceptable frontiers, one that had nothing to do with nomads: with its mandate over Iraq and similar ones over Trans-Jordan and Palestine, there was much to be said from the military and strategic standpoint for having an overland corridor across the northern desert all the way from the eastern Mediterranean to the Persian Gulf.[2] It fell to the high commissioner for Iraq to see that all these objectives were accomplished.

The Uqair Conference, 1922

Early in 1922 Sir Percy Cox arranged a conference at Muhammarah (on the Persian side of the Shatt al-Arab) between representatives of King Faisal of Iraq and Ibn Saud of Najd, to sort out their conflicting tribal claims. Cox himself did not attend. The Muhammarah meeting was useful in bringing the parties together, but it left open the question of just how far their jurisdictions extended. In the middle of the year Cox sent word to Ibn Saud that he would like to meet with him personally to settle his frontiers with both Iraq and Kuwait. The result was a conference from November 28 to December 3, 1922, at the undistinguished Persian Gulf port of Uqair, in Saudi territory opposite the island shaikhdom of Bahrain.

Sir Percy Cox's Uqair Conference was unusual on a number of counts. In the first place, he was armed with authority to deal on behalf of two (Iraq and Kuwait) of the three parties involved; thus Cox and Ibn Saud were the only real negotiators.[3] At one point, according to an eyewitness, Cox reduced the formidable Ibn Saud to tears. Yet he gave to the Saudis about two-thirds of the territory claimed by the ruler of Kuwait, later presenting the result to him in such a way that Ahmad I expressed gratitude and praise. The only published firsthand account of the Uqair negotiations is the one by Colonel Harold R. P. Dickson in his sprawling lifework, *Kuwait and Her Neighbours,* published only in 1956, after most of the principals had died.[4] Dickson was another in the line of Oxford men who made their careers in the Indian army or civil service. He was born in Beirut in 1881, son of the British consul-general in Jerusalem. At the time Cox was preparing to meet Ibn Saud, Dickson was serving as political officer at Hilla in southern Iraq. He was a conscientious administrator with a knack for gaining the confidence of independent-minded Arab tribal leaders. St. John Philby wrote years later of "the unstudied ease with which he fitted into an Arab setting."[5] Though never trained as an Arabic scholar, Dickson had learned the spoken language in his childhood. More than many other British administrators in his position, he enjoyed being with the bedouin in their tents, drinking endless rounds of coffee, swapping yarns, winning their respect, becoming their friend. When Dickson spoke of going to see his "friends," he was invariably referring to the bedouin tribesmen, and the appellation was sincere.[6]

Cox, who knew Dickson as a seasoned and reliable hand, recruited him to prepare for the Uqair Conference. He was to go to Bahrain, which he knew well from a tour as political agent in 1918–1920; get in touch with Ibn Saud; and keep him interested in the projected meeting with Cox until Cox was ready to see him. (Cox was deeply involved in crucial matters that year in Iraq.) Harold and Violet Dickson arrived in Bahrain on September 16; Cox did not appear until November 21.[7] It is a tribute not only to Cox's eminence and prestige but also to Dickson's gift for patient palaver that the meeting ever took place at all. Violet Dickson herself had a role in preparing for the conference. Her husband had told her that "Sir Percy loathes Arab food . . . and it always makes him in a very bad temper!" Mrs. Dickson accordingly packed boxes of proper English provisions, including kippered herring and sausages.[8]

The main business of the conference was to settle finally the frontier between Iraq and Najd on the basis discussed earlier at

Muhammarah. King Faisal of Iraq was represented nominally by a Baghdad official named Sabih Beg, a former minister of works,[9] not an experienced negotiator but well known to British administrators: "A good raconteur," wrote one of them, "always bubbling over with fun and nonsense of some kind."[10] When it came time to sign on behalf of Iraq, Sabih Beg did so, but he evidently did very little else during the six days of the conference. The Najdi delegation was headed by the redoubtable Ibn Saud himself.

Progress was slow, according to Dickson. "The talks were a wonderful example of the bargaining methods employed when representatives of two great oriental states get together and try to settle a problem. There was no give and take whatever . . . both sides making ridiculous demands all the time . . . The arguments went on for five whole days." On the sixth day, Cox had had enough. He took Ibn Saud aside for a final chat, the two of them attended only by Dickson as interpreter. "[Cox] lost all patience over what he called the childish attitude of Ibn Saud . . . It was astonishing to see the Sultan of Najd being reprimanded like a naughty schoolboy . . . Ibn Saud almost broke down, and pathetically remarked that Sir Percy was his father and mother . . . and that he would surrender half his kingdom, nay the whole, if Sir Percy ordered." Meeting once more in plenary session, the conferees watched in awe as "Sir Percy took a red pencil and very carefully drew in on the map of Arabia a boundary line . . . This gave Iraq a large area of the territory claimed by Najd. Obviously to placate Ibn Saud, he ruthlessly deprived Kuwait of nearly two-thirds of her territory and gave it to Najd."[11]

Later that evening, Dickson witnessed what he called "an amazing sequel:"

> Ibn Saud asked to see Sir Percy alone. Sir Percy took me with him. Ibn Saud was by himself, standing in the centre of his great reception tent. He seemed terribly upset.
>
> "My friend," he moaned, "you have deprived me of half my kingdom. Better take it all and let me go into retirement."
>
> Still standing, this great strong man, magnificent in his grief, suddenly burst out into sobs. Deeply disturbed, Sir Percy seized his hand and began to weep also. Tears were rolling down his cheeks. No one but the three of us was present, and I relate exactly what I saw.

The emotional storm did not last long. Still holding Ibn Saud's hand Sir Percy said:

"My friend, I know exactly how you feel, and for this reason I gave you two-thirds of Kuwait's territory. I don't know how Ibn Sabah [Shaikh Ahmad al Jabir, ruler of Kuwait] will take the blow." . . .

Sir Percy was a very great man. Abdul Aziz Al Saud was a very great man too—and a very great actor besides.[12]

Kuwait's interests at the conference were supposed to have been looked after by Maj. James Carmichael More, the political agent in Kuwait from 1920 to 1929.[13] Yet throughout the talks, according to Dickson, More said nothing: "Sir Percy had dominated everything and everybody. He won the day, and I doubt if any other person in the world could have succeeded as he did, but he grievously harmed a great reputation for fair dealing among the Arabs, which he had justly acquired over a long period of years; and the young Shaikh Ahmad al Jabir, scarcely a year on the throne [of Kuwait] and very impressionable, received a blow to his faith in Great Britain from which he never really recovered."[14]

The Uqair Conference wound down. After the raucous and emotional negotiations over the Najd-Iraq boundary, the frontier between Najd and Kuwait was laid down in a day. (In both cases Cox provided for lozenge-shaped "neutral zones.") Documents confirming both boundaries were signed on December 2, 1922. There was one piece of unfinished business: to tell the ruler of Kuwait what had been done to his domains. Rather than leave this touchy matter to Major More, Cox stopped in Kuwait on the way back to Baghdad to break the news in person. He took Dickson along, as well as Major More. Dickson described the scene:

Both Major More and myself, I only in a secretarial capacity, were present when Sir Percy broke the news . . . Shaikh Ahmad pathetically asked why he had done this without even consulting him. Sir Percy explained that, on this unfortunate occasion, the sword had been mightier than the pen, and that had he not conceded the territory, Ibn Saud would certainly have soon picked a quarrel and taken it, if not more, by force of arms. As it was, he (Sir Percy) had placated Shaikh Ahmad's powerful neighbour and brought about a friendly feeling for Kuwait. Shaikh Ahmad then asked if Great Britain had not entered the war in defense of the rights of small nations. Sir Percy admitted that this was correct.

"If some day," said Shaikh Ahmad, "Ibn Saud dies and I grow strong like my grandfather, Mubarak, will the British Government object if I denounce the unjust frontier line and recover my lost territories?"

"No!" laughed Sir Percy. "And may God bless your efforts."

There was nothing young Shaikh Ahmad could do but add his signature to the agreement. To the end of his days he would tell friends: "I trusted Sir Percy as my father, and would certainly not have minded if a few miles of my territory had been taken from me, but to be robbed of two-thirds of my kingdom without a say in the matter, and to see it given to another, was hard indeed."[15]

Colonel Dickson was a life-long partisan of Kuwait and the House of Sabah, so some correctives to his account are in order.[16] First, the territories to which Dickson refers as two-thirds of the shaikhdom fell entirely within the peripheral area described in Article 7 of the unratified Anglo-Ottoman Convention of 1913, an area from whose inhabitants the ruler was to be entitled to exact tribute and allegiance free of interference from the Ottomans; this region was quite distinct from the much smaller area around Kuwait town and bay which Britain (in the 1907 Lease Agreement and the letter to Mubarak of November 3, 1914) had declared to belong to Kuwait and which it was pledged to protect. Moreover, there was something to be said for Ibn Saud's point that in the years since 1913 Saudi influence with the tribes had displaced Kuwait's throughout much of this region. Although perhaps these were distinctions that could not have been very easily explained to Shaikh Ahmad, they provide some extenuation for Cox's high-handed action. Second, although the shaikh made much of the fact that he had not been kept informed about what was going on at Uqair, this was not entirely Cox's fault. He wrote later to the Colonial Office: "Previous to proceeding to Ojair [Uqair], I had invited the Shaikh of Kuwait to send a representative but he replied that the Political Agent, Major More, was aware of his views and interests and he left himself in the latter's hands."[17] To be sure, Major More had proved to be a slender reed for Shaikh Ahmad. Because of Whitehall's decision that Cox should retain administrative control over Kuwait in addition to his position in Iraq, More was his de facto subordinate. He knew when to keep his peace.

As it turned out, Shaikh Ahmad never had occasion, even with the parting blessing of Sir Percy Cox, to "denounce the unjust frontier line and recover my lost territories." In fact, that is more or less what happened in reverse to Ahmad's descendant, Jabir al-Ahmad, when Saddam Hussein made his move in the summer of 1990.

"Settlement" of the Iraq-Kuwait Border, April 1923

Nothing had been said at Uqair about Kuwait's other frontier, the one facing Iraq. A line agreeable to Great Britain and the Ottoman negotiators had been laid down in the 1913 Convention, but that document had never been ratified and consequently had no binding effect. This frontier, various modern commentators notwithstanding,[18] was not even on the Uqair agenda, where the principal purpose was to come to terms with Ibn Saud, who had no direct interest in the boundary between Kuwait and Iraq. It was not that the question of Iraq's boundary with Kuwait had gone unnoticed by British officials in the Middle East. As early as December 1918, the acting civil commissioner in Baghdad, Arnold Wilson, had been asked to draft a definition of the frontiers of the new state to be carved out of the former Ottoman provinces in Mesopotamia. He replied that it would not be feasible to delimit the Iraq-Kuwait frontier without the concurrence of the shaikh of Kuwait.[19] In 1919 the British political agent in Kuwait, Capt. Daniel Mc-Callum, seems to have told Shaikh Salim that Britain recognized the 1913 "green line," and apparently Salim laid claim to that line on September 17, 1920.[20] The subject may well have been mentioned by Cox during his visit to Shaikh Ahmad on the way back to Baghdad after Uqair, although Dickson makes no reference to it. Perhaps it was simply that the matter of Kuwait's borders had by now become a sore subject with Ahmad, best left to be dealt with at a more propitious time.

Sir Percy Cox, in any case, had not forgotten about the need to set the frontier between Kuwait and Iraq. Shortly after his return to the high commissioner's office in Baghdad on December 11, Cox's personal secretary, B. H. Bourdillon, forwarded to the Colonial Office the texts of the two boundary agreements (Najd-Iraq and Najd-Kuwait) signed at Uqair.[21] In a companion message on December 20 Bourdillon wrote: "It would be convenient if we could at the same time arrive at a decision as to the frontier which we can advisedly recognise as between Iraq and Kuwait." Bourdillon, on behalf of the high commissioner, suggested that "the said frontier should start in the south from the point on the green line of the Anglo-Turkish Agreement of 29th July 1913, where the Wadi-el-Aadja intersects with the Batin, and from thence follow the said green line along the Batin to its termination at the mouth of the Khor Zubeir just south of Jebel Sanam, Safwan and Umm Qasr, leaving them to Iraq."[22] On February 2, 1923, the new colonial secretary, the Duke of Devonshire, replied approving the description.[23]

In the meantime, on January 26, 1923, Shaikh Ahmad returned to Major More the two copies of the Najd-Kuwait agreement that Sir Percy Cox had left with him for signature. "I have checked these, and I thank His Excellency the High Commissioner from the bottom of my heart for the laudable action he has taken, and I agree entirely with him regarding the terms of the Agreement."[24] On March 31, 1923, he wrote again to Major More: "I know now that the frontier between Najd and Kuwait is as laid down in the [Uqair] Agreement. I still do not know, however, what the frontier between Iraq and Kuwait is, and I shall be glad if you will kindly give me this information so that I may know it."[25]

More, who had received copies of the December 20–February 2 correspondence between Baghdad and London on this subject, knew what had already been agreed upon between Cox and the Colonial Office. Even so, before referring the ruler's question to Cox, he replied to Ahmad that it would be a good thing if the shaikh would let him know for the high commissioner's information "what line he himself claimed." More's cautious ploy evoked an immediate response, which More paraphrased for Cox: "His reply amounts to the fact that he claims the northern portion of the green line on the map attached to the Draft Anglo-Turkish Agreement dated the 29th July 1913 as the boundary between Kuwait and Iraq. He also specifically claims the islands [including Warba and Bubiyan] as belonging to Kuwait."[26]

Such was the background to Cox's problematical memorandum to Major More on April 19, 1923, a document still very much on the minds of many proponents of Saddam Hussein's claims today. Here is Cox's memorandum:

> Please see your memorandum No. 52-S., dated the 4th April 1923, giving cover to a letter from the Shaikh of Kuwait, dated 17th Shaaban 1341 (4th April 1923) in which he is understood to claim the frontier of Kuwait with Iraq to be as follows:—
>
> From the intersection of the Wadi El Audja with the Batin and thence Northwards along the Batin to a point just south of the Latitude of Safwan; thence Eastwards passing south of Safwan wells, Jebel Sanm and Um Qasr, leaving them to 'Iraq and so on to the junction of the Khor Zobeir with the Khor 'Abdullah.
>
> Shaikh Ahmed at the same time claims as appertaining to Kuwait the Islands of Warbah, Bubiyan, Maskan (or Mashjan), Failakah, Auha, Kubha, Qaru and Um-el-Maradim.
>
> The Shaikh can be informed that his claim to the frontier and islands above indicated is recognised in so far as His Majesty's Government are concerned.
>
> As you are aware it is, in so far as it goes, identical with the frontier indicated by the Green line of the Anglo-Turkish Agreement of July 29th, 1913, but there seems no necessity to make special allusion to that document in your communication to the Shaikh.[27]

The Cox-More Memorandum raises several puzzling questions. First, why did More write directly to Cox, and why did Cox respond directly to him, rather than going through established channels—namely, More's immediate superior, Col. A. P. Trevor, the political resident in the Persian Gulf? (Nine years later, in a reprise of this very question, the official lines of communication were scrupulously observed; see Chapter 5.) Presumably this had to do with the 1921 decision to keep Cox in control of Kuwait as long as he remained as high commissioner in Iraq; even so, it would have been normal and more orderly to make the political resident a party to the correspondence. Another explanation may be a more human one: Cox at this time was only weeks away from retirement and departure from the Middle East forever, and time may have been closing in on him; it was quicker to correspond directly between Baghdad and Kuwait than to route papers through Bushire.

Second, why did Cox caution More that "there seems no necessity to make special allusion to that document [the Anglo-Ottoman Convention of July 29, 1913] in your communication to the Shaikh"? The explanation is probably just that Cox feared a reprise of Shaikh Ahmad's outrage at having been deprived of "two-thirds of my kingdom" at Cox's hands at Uqair—territories that had been allocated to Kuwait by the 1913 Agreement. True, Cox did not *forbid* More to mention the 1913 Convention, but More too had been present when Ahmad got the bad news, and Cox's injunction would not have gone over his head.

Third, and more important for the future, why did Cox so conspicuously avoid committing the government of Iraq to the boundary as described? Why did he couch recognition of the frontier as extending only "as far as His Majesty's Government are concerned"? As far as the Iraqi government was concerned, the question of the boundary with Kuwait had lain dormant since the 1913 Convention between Great Britain and Iraq's predecessor state, the Ottoman Empire. But the fact of the matter was that in the spring of 1923 the Ottoman Empire was not yet entirely out of the picture. A first attempt to lay to rest any possible claims Turkey might have to her former Ottoman provinces was incorporated in the imposed Treaty of Sèvres between Britain, France, and Turkey, signed under protest by the Turks on August 10, 1920, but never ratified. A second attempt was embodied in the Treaty of Lausanne, but this treaty was still under negotiation at the time of the Cox-More Memorandum and was not signed until July 24, 1923. (It was ratified in 1924.) Until the Lausanne Treaty came into effect, the Turks had not yet signed away any rights or claims to the Ottoman Arab regions, including Mesopotamia (with or without a claim to Kuwait, depending on one's view of prewar events).[28] At the time of Cox's memorandum to Major More, therefore, Iraq had not yet legally succeeded the Turks as sovereign of its own territories, despite the fact that by this time Iraq had a king, a provisional government of its own, an internationally recognized status as a mandated territory under the League of Nations, and a signed treaty with Great Britain implementing that mandatory status. Although Cox was no international lawyer, he had access to competent legal advice to guide him, both in Baghdad and in London. If he had sought advice, he might well have been told that the time was not quite ripe for Iraq to enter into a formal treaty involving boundaries of the not-quite-in-place Iraqi state.

On the other hand, if mere lawyerly caution was behind the reluctance to formalize the boundary description in the name of Iraq, it is hard to account for the form of the boundary agreement made at Uqair involving Ibn Saud's kingdom of Najd and the government of Iraq. That agreement, designated "Protocol No. 1," was signed "Subih [Sabih Beg], Representative of His Majesty the King of Iraq."[29] Whoever authorized that formulation, presumably Cox, was not concerned about some legal quibble over vestigial Ottoman rights. Who would be so bold as to contest a sovereign act by King Faisal of Iraq on the ground that it was *ultra vires*—beyond his authority?

So we are left with a little puzzle: for whom was Sir Percy Cox acting when he wrote the celebrated April 19, 1923, memorandum to Major J. C. More?

Not for the government of Iraq, nor for its monarch.

For the British government? Yes, but in what capacity? One possibility is that Cox purported to act in his capacity as high commissioner for Iraq under the League of Nations mandate as implemented under the as-yet-unratified Anglo-Iraqi treaty of 1922. But the mandate for Iraq (Article VIII) provided that "the Mandatory shall be responsible for seeing that no Iraqi territory shall be ceded or leased to, or in any way placed under the control of, the Government of any foreign Power."[30] The rapporteur of the Council of the League of Nations once underscored the importance of this provision by stating that the plenary authorities of a mandatory power over the foreign relations of the mandated territory "do not include power to cede or lease on its own authority, any part, however small, of the territory."[31]

In the case of the Najd-Iraq Protocol, care was taken to leave Great Britain ("the Mandatory Power") out of the document, a neat way of steering clear of any infringement of the mandate. It seems unlikely that Cox, in the case of Iraq-Kuwait just a few months later, would carelessly fall into the trap that he had avoided at Uqair. No, Sir Percy clearly did not have his high commissioner's hat on when he wrote to More on April 19; he was acting, as he said, only "as far as His Majesty's Government are concerned." His authority was simply administrative: it came directly from the Secretary of State for the Colonies, Lord Devonshire, who on February 2, 1923, had approved in writing the border description recommended by Cox.

In short, the Cox-More Memorandum did not bind the government of Iraq, the state of Iraq, or the king of Iraq. Moreover, it did not even purport to do so. Had it purported to do so, it could have come under legal challenge as being beyond Cox's authority and in contravention of the mandate. As far as Iraq's eventual legal position with regard to the status of Kuwait and its frontiers was concerned, the Cox-More Memorandum was entirely beside the point.

Finally, the way the Cox-More Memorandum has been treated over the years by British officialdom and by historians and chroniclers is curious in light of what we now know about it:

1. Great Britain, as the mandatory power in Iraq, filed reports regularly with the Permanent Mandates Commission of the League of Nations in Geneva. Britain's reports, written at the start by Gertrude Bell (who died in Baghdad in 1926), are worth reading even now as exemplars of their art, if only for their prose style. In none of these reports is there a single mention of the Iraq-Kuwait frontier, although all the rest of Iraq's boundary problems and settlements get full attention.[32]

2. The political agent in Kuwait, Major More, and his successors (including Colonel Dickson from 1929 to 1936) submitted annual administrative reports to London on the affairs of Kuwait, with never a mention of the Cox-More Memorandum. It was apparently first published in 1933 in the Indian government's official *Collection of Treaties, Engagements and Sanads Relating to India and Neighbouring Countries,* where it is correctly described this way: "In April 1923 the Shaikh of Kuwait was informed . . . through the Political Agent that His Majesty's Government recognized the Iraq-Kuwait frontiers claimed by him."[33] By the time this *Collection* appeared, Iraq was legally a fully independent state, the mandate having terminated in 1932.

3. Britain's prestigious and authoritative Royal Institute of International Affairs, also known as Chatham House, published an annual *Survey of International Affairs,* edited and largely written in those days by Arnold J. Toynbee. In the *Survey* for 1925 there is an account of the Uqair Conference, followed by this: "Thereafter the Shaikh of Kuwait notified the competent British authorities the northern frontier which he claimed as towards Iraq, and his claims were accepted in April 1923. The Kuwait-Iraq frontier, which was settled in this manner, followed the Batin . . . "[34] Nine years later, the RIIA *Survey* for 1934 stated that all Iraq's boundaries "had been definitely settled . . . The Iraqi-Kuwaiti frontier by an agreement of April 1923."[35] A recent biography of Toynbee makes clear that the 1925 Chatham House *Survey* volume dealing with "The Islamic World" was written entirely by Toynbee himself. But "the surveys actually acquired a quasi-official status, since Toynbee adopted the practice of submitting his text to experts in the Foreign Office and other specially knowledgeable officials who were asked to comment."[36] By 1934 any of the scholars and researchers connected with Chatham House, any of the informed civil servants in Whitehall, could have taken the opportunity to suggest that the 1925 expression "settled" was an overstatement. In the intervening nine years, however, the Cox-More Memorandum had flowered into an "agreement," and what had originally been described as "settled" had somehow become "definitely settled." Did Toynbee mislead, or was he misled by, his contacts in Whitehall? The latter explanation seems the more likely. The question of the Iraq-Kuwait border would become a matter of intense concern when it came time to give up the mandate in 1932, and we shall examine the matter further in that context.[37]

Three weeks after writing the memorandum to Major More, Sir Percy Cox left Baghdad, covered with accolades and honors.[38] He was esteemed as few British civil servants have ever been. Yet this furtive final démarche was not his finest hour. It served Britain, Iraq, and Kuwait equally badly; and it even stalked the Gulf crisis of 1990. J. B. Kelly, the distinguished authority on Middle East diplomatic history, has written: "Britain, as the conqueror of the Ottoman Empire, as the mandatory power in Iraq and as the protecting power in Najd and Kuwait, had the inherent right as well as the legal authority to apportion frontiers to these states as she saw fit."[39] One must beg to differ. The central concept of the mandate idea as it took shape under the leadership of Jan Christiaan Smuts and Woodrow Wilson at the Versailles Peace Conference was that of the common-law trust. Article 22 of the Covenant of the League of Nations speaks (in admittedly somewhat lofty terms) of "a sacred trust of civilization."[40] Great Britain had no right, "legal" or otherwise, to play ducks and drakes with its obligations and responsibilities as a mandatory power under Article 22 of the Covenant.

Or did Winston Churchill have it right in July 1921 when he wrote that "all this obsolescent rigamarole [about 'Mandates'] is not worth telegraphing about"?

5. Invisible Lines at Geneva, 1932

Sir Percy Cox had achieved a great deal by bringing Abdul Aziz ibn Saud to the bargaining table at Uqair in 1922, but border incidents persisted between Saudi forces and Iraqi tribesmen for the rest of the decade. Wahhabi warriors from Najd raided and looted and slaughtered, evoking protests, warnings, threats, and military action from the British authorities in Iraq.

John Bagot Glubb (later known as Glubb Pasha) was a conscientious and ambitious British officer assigned to police Iraq's Saudi border (the area of Iraq occupied briefly by Coalition forces in early 1991 in the aftermath of Operation Desert Storm). Glubb was critical of the Iraqi-Saudi border agreed upon at Uqair, because he considered that it favored the Najdi tribes while ignoring the rights of those of Iraq.[1] "In Turkish times," he wrote, "the government had rarely attempted to extend its influence to a distance of more than two or three miles from the [Euphrates] river bank. If the Uqair protocols had not been negotiated . . . there would still have been a *de facto* frontier, but it would have been three or four miles from the Euphrates instead of one hundred and fifty . . . The existence of nomadism calls for freedom of movement across frontiers for the flocks of the nomads."[2]

Kuwait figures in Glubb's narrative partly because the shaikhdom came to be used from time to time as a refuge for outnumbered or beleaguered tribesmen and, even more, for their kinfolk and retainers. The British political agent in Kuwait was ever on the alert to protect the sanctity of the shaikhdom's frontiers; Glubb was sometimes vexed when his forces in hot pursuit of some miscreant were restrained by British directives from chasing them across the border into Kuwait: "R.A.F. aircraft and armoured cars were allowed to operate in Kuwait but the Iraq army and the

Desert Camel Corps were not," he related. "By a remarkable piece of diplomatic nicety, I was authorized to enter Kuwait territory by day, but not to sleep there." Later he got special permission to camp overnight in the territory with the desert camel police, but Iraq army detachments were never allowed to do so, or even to cross the border even temporarily.[3] Colonel Dickson, who arrived as political agent in 1929, persuaded British authorities in Iraq to agree to keep Iraqi police from crossing the border.[4]

When British troops landed in Kuwait in 1961 in response to Shaikh Abdullah's urgent call for assistance in meeting a threatened attack by Iraq's Abdul Karim Qasim, it was said that never before in all the years of Great Britain's stewardship had it been necessary to deploy British forces there. This was not quite true. Glubb relates that on February 17, 1928, "permission was granted for the R.A.F. to operate in Kuwait territory, and one flight of aircraft and one section of armored cars were based on Kuwait town. H.M.S. *Emerald* arrived in the bay of Kuwait."[5]

Eventually a sort of peace came to that contested corner of the desert. The rebellious Ikhwan were subdued by Ibn Saud himself. In February 1930 King Faisal of Iraq met with him aboard H.M.S. *Lupin* at the mouth of the Shatt al-Arab, where the two monarchs came to terms, bringing an end to the Saudi-Hashemite violence that had intermittently roiled the Arabian Peninsula for many years. After this latest British-brokered treaty Kuwait had less to fear from the Saudis and their clients. But had it not been for British support during the 1920s the shaikhdom might well have wound up as another province of Saudi Arabia rather than remaining an independent principality. The Saudi viewpoint was well expressed by H. St. John Philby, who had become a key adviser to Ibn Saud, in a personal letter to Harold Dickson some years later: "[Kuwait] is racially and geographically a part of this country [Saudi Arabia], though it is artificially separated from it by a political barrier which the British in their folly prefer to keep up. You might just as well make Hull and its district an independent principality under German protection—it would die, as all traffic would be diverted to Harwich (Jubail) or Dover (Ras Tanura)."[6]

Before the Uqair Conference, Colonel Dickson had been told that his contract for service in Iraq would not be renewed. Budget trimming at the Colonial Office had done away with his position as political advisor. He found an assignment in India and in 1928 was posted as secretary to the political resident in the Persian Gulf. In 1929 he finally found his lifetime niche when he was sent to Kuwait as political agent. He was to remain in this post until his mandatory retirement on his fifty-fifth birthday in 1936. Then, at the instigation of Shaikh Ahmad, he was immediately hired by the recently formed Kuwait Oil Company to be their chief local representative. It was a brilliant choice; no Westerner knew Kuwait as he did.

"The proper study of a boundary dispute," writes Ian Brownlie, "calls for the careful teasing out of the strands of history, politics, diplomacy, and law which go to make up the special universe of each boundary dispute."[7] To this formula one is tempted to add one more component: the human element. Violet Dickson has left a vivid and engaging picture of the Dicksons' life in Kuwait during her husband's seven-year assignment as political agent, beginning with their arrival on May 22, 1929, with their two small children.[8] The house that the Dicksons moved into belonged to Shaikh Ahmad and had been occupied by all the political agents since Capt. S. G. Knox opened the Agency in 1904. A new and grander Agency compound replaced it in 1935, but after Harold Dickson's death in 1959 Violet returned to live in their original residence, "by grace and favour," as she put it, for many more years.[9]

As there were no suitable schools, the Dickson children were tutored at home until they were deemed to be old enough to be sent off to England, the son at nine, the daughter at eleven. Zahra Dickson, returning from school in 1946, described the scene as she was driven home along the Zubair-Jahra road: "The oasis of Safwan rose above the horizon ahead of us . . . Here, marking the Iraq-Kuwait border, stands a cluster of gaunt palm trees, surrounding a group of wells. Beyond the trees the desert was black with hundreds of badawin tents."[10] Her description does not refer to the signboard erected in 1923 just south of Safwan to mark the boundary, for by then it was long gone.

The Missing Signboard

One day in June 1932, Political Agent Dickson learned from Shaikh Ahmad that the signboard marking the Kuwait-Iraq border on the Zubair-Jahra road just south of Safwan had mysteriously vanished. (This gravel road, opened in 1928, was then the only road in Kuwait worthy of the name.)[11] Ahmad knew exactly where the signboard was supposed to be, because he and Major More had personally supervised its installation just after Sir Percy Cox had recognized his frontier on behalf of His Majesty's Government in 1923. The sign, in Arabic and English, had been fashioned by an artisan in the Kuwait *suq*. It was embedded in the sand facing Iraq; in addition to pointing out where the border was, it cautioned drivers to switch from the lefthand to the righthand lane.[12]

Dickson traced the missing signboard to the Iraqi government's frontier post at Safwan, where, he was told, it had been taken to be repainted. It turned out, Dickson reported, that "the Iraqi authorities were unaware . . . that the board was put up by the Ruler of Kuwait and was his property." He raised the matter with the administrative inspector in Basra, a British officer named R. F. Jardine, who spoke to the mutasarrif (the Iraqi governor) of Basra, who agreed to arrange for its return. Dickson suggested through Jardine that Shaikh Ahmad would consider it a friendly gesture if the Iraqis were to repaint it before sending it back, but this was not to be. Jardine closed the incident with an apologetic letter to Colonel Dickson:

> Apparently the cost of transporting the board to Basra terrified the [Iraqi] police, though I must say I thought it rather boorish that they didn't complete the painting, having removed it for this purpose. But boorishness and the present Mutasarrif are not strangers . . . Please tell the Shaikh how sorry I am, but as you and I know, the Eastern nations when they first get what they call their independence, are apt to think, like certain horrid schoolboys, that it also means being freed from the boring restrictions of good manners.[13]

Preparing for Geneva

As it happened, the sign-removal incident took place just at the time the Colonial Office in London was preparing the necessary documentation to accompany Iraq's request for admission to the League of Nations, due in September 1932 in Geneva. Although the application was confidently expected to succeed, British officials were devoting unusual attention to the matter because in a 1930 revision to the Anglo-Iraqi treaty Britain had formally undertaken to expedite Iraq's membership. Any delay could reflect badly on their intentions. Iraqi political leaders also were anxious to get on with the application, for it meant that Iraq would at last emerge as a fully independent, internationally recognized state, the first of the former Ottoman-Arab territories to achieve such a status. On January 28, 1932, the Council of the League of Nations agreed in principle to entertain Iraq's application. The matter would be considered first by the League's Permanent Mandates Commission, an advisory body to the Council. A questionnaire to be answered by the applicant's sponsoring power (in this case Great Britain) sought confirmation among other things that the applicant had "a stable government and well-defined frontiers."

Now Iraq had boundaries, clockwise from the west, with Trans-Jordan, Syria, Turkey, Persia, Kuwait, and Saudi Arabia. In view of all the problems that had attended the establishment of the new Iraqi state, its boundaries were in surprisingly good order.[14] There was, however, the matter of its frontier with Kuwait. A Kuwait-Iraq boundary had first been described in the unratified Anglo-Ottoman Convention of 1913, and the same line had been accepted by Britain in the Cox-More Memorandum of 1923. But nothing had yet been said on the subject to the Iraqi government, nor had its views been solicited. The civil servants at the Foreign Office, the Colonial Office, and the India Office put their heads together to decide what would need to be done and how to go about it. At a meeting at the Colonial Office, it was first agreed that the line would be identical with that identified in 1913 and again in 1923.[15] The challenge was to draw up proper documentation that would not upset either Iraq or Kuwait but would also meet the requirements of the Permanent Mandates Commission.

A formal treaty between Iraq and Kuwait, perhaps along the lines of the Uqair Protocol of 1922, signed for Iraq in the name of King Faisal and for Najd in the name of Ibn Saud, was a possibility, but experience had shown that treaties could take time to negotiate, draft, execute, and ratify, and time was rushing on.[16] The first substantive discussion of what would be required appears in a memorandum of March 12, 1932, by J. Hathorn Hall, a

Colonial Office lawyer seconded to the Foreign Office to assist George Rendel, head of the Eastern Department, in working out the details of the termination of the mandate.[17] Hall reviewed the various boundaries that would have to be covered, at first curiously omitting any reference to the one with Kuwait. But he filled the gap with another memorandum on April 8:

> The Iraqi Prime Minister must be armed in September with full information regarding the various instruments affecting Iraq's frontiers, but there is no need to disclose the nature of those instruments now, which . . . is just as well, since as regards the Iraq-Kuwait frontier the position is far from clear. We cannot refer to the Anglo-Turkish Agreement of 1913 . . . because it is a secret unpublished document (which incidentally never entered into force) and the correspondence of 1923 between the High Commissioner and the Political Agent, Kuwait . . . is not a very suitable basis for a formal frontier settlement. It may be thought necessary to confirm the 1923 correspondence by a formal agreement between Iraq and Kuwait, but this is a point which might be discussed with the Foreign Office.[18]

A. F. Morley of the Political Department at the India Office perused Hall's memorandum and weighed in with his own on May 7, reflecting the particular concerns of that department:

> It has consistently been the policy of this Office not to interest the League of Nations in our position in the Gulf, and it may be thought unwise to attract attention to our relations with Kuwait, which are, apart from the Agreement of 1899, not based on a formal Treaty, but rest on our letter to the Shaikh of [November 3] 1914 . . . and our not very clearly defined undertaking in 1899, to support him and accord him our 'good offices' (that term being interpreted at the discretion of His Majesty's Government).

Mr. Morley frankly counseled against producing the existing documents publicly in connection with Iraq's application at Geneva.[19]

What was needed now was not a new agreement, but merely acceptance by Iraq of what had already pleased the ruler of Kuwait. The Foreign Office recommended a simple exchange of notes between the government of Iraq and Shaikd Ahmad agreeing upon the frontier. In the case of Kuwait, the agreement should bear the endorsement of His Majesty's Government, since "it is important to avoid what might constitute a precedent for independent action on the part of the Shaikh in the foreign affairs of his [!] country."

Then J. E. W. Flood of the Colonial Office suggested a procedure to cater to the Foreign Office caveat about appearing to concede too much autonomy to the shaikh:

1. The Iraqi prime minister would write to the ruler of Kuwait proposing reaffirmation of the existing frontier.
2. The ruler would write to the political agent at Kuwait requesting the approval of the British government.
3. The political agent would indicate approval in a reply to the ruler.
4. The ruler would respond to the Iraqi prime minister, accepting the proposal in (1).

Mr. Flood observed that the correspondence relating to steps (2) and (3) "would not be for publication except in case of necessity." He said that the Colonial Office did not anticipate any difficulty in obtaining the approval of the Iraqi government to the proposed arrangement.[20] The India Office added its concurrence.[21]

In the meantime, the proposed transaction had been referred for review and comment to the political resident in the Persian Gulf, Sir Hugh Biscoe; he immediately passed the matter along to Colonel Dickson in Kuwait. The latter telegraphed bluntly on June 2: "I personally think re-affirmation of existing frontier unnecessary and liable to be misunderstood."[22] Nevertheless, Dickson knew where his duty lay. He prepared to broach the matter with Shaikh Ahmad. But before he could make his way to the palace he was informed on June 5 of the ruler's alarm at having discovered that his frontier signboard near Safwan had disappeared. Sixty years later, it is clear that the bizarre intersection of these events was merely a lamentable coincidence. But it did not appear so to Shaikh Ahmad, and for a long time Dickson himself was incredulous. At all events, Dickson called upon the ruler on the following day, June 6. Shaikh Ahmad, he reported on June 7, was "surprised and somewhat startled" that the British government saw fit to raise a question that he thought had been settled. Ahmad feared that it "might easily encourage Iraq, with her pseudo-Persian mentality, to think the opportunities too good to be missed of attacking a frontier line fixed by His Majesty's Government."[23] Dickson followed this message with a coded telegram on June 10: "Shaikh, who fears that reaffirmation proposal may lead Iraq to attempting alteration of existing frontier line, favours leaving whole matter alone; he nevertheless will abide by His Majesty's Government's wishes if [given?] necessary assurances."[24] The secretary to the political resident sent Dickson a stinging response the following day:

> There is not the smallest basis for the Shaikh's apprehensions
> . . . There is no dispute about the frontier . . . which . . . is
> accepted by both parties, and the re-affirmation, so far from
> leading to any attempt at alteration, will definitely prevent any
> such attempt either now or in the future . . . Sir Hugh Biscoe
> considers that so far from this being any way detrimental to the
> Shaikh's interests the re-affirmation will definitely safeguard
> them.[25]

Events would override the soothing assurances of Sir Hugh Biscoe. As Shaikh Abdullah III was to find when confronted with Iraq's claims in 1961, his cousin Ahmad's reservations were well founded.

Biscoe reported the substance of this exchange to the India Office. He pointed out that "it is not customary [for] Iraq authorities [to] deal direct with Shaikh, and the latter is adverse from procedure proposed." Biscoe suggested instead that the government of India address the high commissioner in Baghdad, who would then forward the proposal to himself as political resident in the Persian Gulf; Biscoe would send it to the political agent in Kuwait for presentation to Shaikh Ahmad, "intimating it has approval of His Majesty's Government," and the ruler's acceptance would come back by the same route.[26]

"I Think Your Excellency Will Agree . . ."

In due course Biscoe's proposed procedure was agreed; drafts of all the correspondence were typed up in London to be bundled along to Baghdad, Bushire, and Kuwait, so that there would be no confusion as to what was expected. The minuet was about to commence. On July 14, 1932, the Colonial Office sent Telegram No. 180 to Sir Francis Humphrys, the high commissioner for Iraq, outlining the procedure that had been established in London. Two days later Humphrys wrote to the acting president of Iraq's Council of Ministers (that is, the acting prime minister), Jaafar Pasha al-Askari, enclosing a draft to be signed and returned to the high commissioner. "The frontier line described in the enclosed draft," Humphrys explained, "is that which was laid down by Sir Percy Cox in correspondence with the Shaikh in April, 1923, and which has subsequently been accepted as the de facto frontier between the two countries." Jaafar Pasha, a very astute politician who was presiding only in the temporary absence of Prime Minister Nuri Said, left the response for the latter to handle. Humphrys' draft was retyped on the prime minister's official letterhead, labeled "Secret," signed by Nuri Said as prime minister, and returned to the high commissioner on July 21. Here is the text of the letter:

> My dear Sir Francis,
> I think your Excellency will agree that the time has now come when it is desirable to reaffirm the existing frontier between Iraq and Koweit.
> I therefore request that the necessary action may be taken to obtain the agreement of the competent authority or authorities in Koweit to the following description of the existing frontier between the two countries:—
> From the intersection of the Wadi-el-Audja with the Batin and thence northwards along the Batin to a point just south of the latitude of Safwan; thence eastwards passing south of Safwan Wells, Jebel Sanam and Um Qasr leaving them to Iraq and so on to the junction of the Kohr Zobeir with the Khor Abdullah. The islands of Warbah, Bubiyan, Maskan (or Mashjan), Failakah, Auhah, Kubbar, Qaru and Umm-el-Maradin appertain to Koweit.[27]

Aside from immaterial wording changes and spelling variations, this is precisely the description contained in the Cox-More Memorandum. But now it is the prime minister of Iraq who suggests that the British high commissioner "will agree that the time has now come."

The full circumstances surrounding the signature of Nuri's letter of July 21, 1932, have never been disclosed by Iraq. But according to a statement released by Saddam Hussein's government on September 12, 1990, the "reaffirmation" matter was discussed at an Iraqi cabinet meeting on July 30, 1932, nine days after Nuri's letter was sent to the high commissioner. At that meeting, Defense Minister Jaafar al-Askari (who, as acting prime minister, had received the British draft in Nuri's absence) is said to have expressed strong reservations about confirming Kuwait's sovereignty over Warba and Bubiyan.[28]

The Conscience of Whitehall

The high commissioner sent Nuri's letter along to Biscoe's recently appointed replacement in Bushire, Trenchard C. Fowle, on July 25.[29] On the very next day, just by coincidence, Iraq formally applied for admission to the League of Nations.[30] There was no time to lose, for Iraq's application would be up for consideration in Geneva in barely eight weeks. Fowle, the new political resident, passed the papers to Dickson in Kuwait on July 30. Dickson wrote to the ruler on August 9; Shaikh Ahmad responded the following day, agreeing to the reaffirmation of the existing frontier. All the paper was then returned by Dickson to Fowle, and by Fowle to Humphrys in Baghdad; Humphrys sent Ahmad's letter to Prime Minister Nuri Said on August 22. Copies of the documents were dispatched from Baghdad to the Colonial Office, which sent them across the way to the Foreign Office on September 6.[31]

The first person in London to scan the documents was P. J. Dixin at the Foreign Office, who on September 13 noted on the correspondence: "The cycle is now complete." But there was more to be done. And some were not even quite satisfied with what had been achieved so far. Dixin's superior and head of the Eastern Department, Sir George Rendel, noted testily on September 14: "I do not altogether like the phrase 'the frontier proposal . . . is approved' but I think the next (and final) sentence makes the position safe."[32] Whatever document contained the offending words quoted by Rendel has been removed from the file at some point during the past sixty years, but one can surmise that it was the transmittal letter from the high commissioner's office in Baghdad. Rendel, having carefully orchestrated the entire correspondence, was apparently concerned that at the very end the game would be given away by an inadvertent admission that the "re-affirmation" formulation was a bit of bootstrapping. That was the "position" that had to be kept "safe."

Now it will be recalled that the underlying purpose of all this sanitized paper-shuffling through the channels of the British bureaucracy was in order to be ready to satisfy the Permanent Mandates Commission of the League of Nations that the boundaries of Iraq were not so insecure or unstable as to bar or delay her entry into the League, now projected for early October 1932 in Geneva. Yet none of these papers was ever delivered or shown to the League of Nations. Why?

The answer seems to be that Sir George Rendel and his colleagues had reservations about the whole transaction and were determined to keep it as quiet as possible, at least until after Iraq had actually become freed of the mandate and admitted to the League. Some of the papers were actually available in the brief-cases of the British delegates who formally presented Iraq's application in Geneva in September, but evidence about the Iraq-Kuwait frontier was never produced because it was never asked for. (Had not Professor Toynbee written in 1925 that the boundary had been "settled" in 1923?) All that was said in the written response to the item on the commission's questionnaire pertaining to frontiers was that "Iraq possesses well-defined frontiers with all limitrophe states."[33] Otherwise the League of Nations record is blank. The minutes of the Permanent Mandates Commission reflect serious discussion of other issues, notably concern over whether Iraq's various minorities (Kurds, Assyrians, Yezidis, and others) were going to be properly protected after Britain gave up the mandate, but not one word about boundaries in general or the Kuwait frontier in particular.[34]

Two German researchers in the early 1960s, Ulrich Gehrke and Gustav Kuhn, tracing all Iraq's borders for a pioneering monograph on the subject, were plainly baffled by this lack of documentation.[35] They ransacked the Geneva archives of the League of Nations and came away empty-handed. The British archives for 1932 were not available to Gehrke and Kuhn; their research, published in 1963, was done mainly in 1961 and 1962, and under the "fifty-year" rule for British archives, the 1932 records were still closed. (In 1966 the waiting period was reduced from fifty years to thirty.)[36] But on July 25, 1961, Gehrke noticed a letter in the *Times* of London from one C. J. Edmonds, a retired British official who had written to take issue with Iraq's claim to Kuwait, which had created such a stir earlier that summer (see Chapter 9). Edmonds wrote: "The boundary between Iraq and Kuwait defined in 1923 was reaffirmed, on the initiative of the Iraqi Government, in July, 1932, by an exchange of letters between the Prime Minister and the British High Commissioner in Baghdad. These letters were communicated to the League of Nations in support of Iraq's application for admission."[37] Gehrke sent a note to the seventy-one-year-old Edmonds, now retired and living in Tunbridge Wells, explaining that he had been unable to trace the papers in Geneva, and received this response:

> The exchange of letters referred to in my letter . . . was arranged for the specific purpose of . . . the Iraqi application for admission to the League of Nations. I can assure you from my firsthand personal experience that it did take place, and that it took place on the initiative of the Iraqi Government . . . It is indeed curious that there should be no record of this agreement by exchange of letters in either the British report to the League or the publications of the League.[38]

Cecil John Edmonds was a distinguished and conscientious British civil servant whose service in the Middle East, particularly in Iraq, spanned many years. When Edmonds wrote to the *Times* to challenge the claims of Abdul Karim Qasim to Kuwait, he spoke as one who had served for many years as an adviser to Iraq's Ministry of the Interior. But in the case of the boundary with Kuwait, he had his facts wrong. It was not simply an old man's lapse of memory. The British establishment had done everything it could to cover its tracks, even from the experts.[39] Whitehall sought to attract as little publicity as possible concerning Iraq's border with Kuwait. If a bureaucracy can be said to have a conscience, perhaps this frontier was on its conscience. And if it is true that conscience doth make cowards of us all, then it was not to be expected that Whitehall would be exempt.

In sum, it was recognized (though it could not be conceded publicly) that the Cox-More Memorandum of 1923 fell far short of providing an adequate basis for Iraq's application to the League of Nations. The Kuwait-Iraq border had not been "established" in any legal sense, because Iraq was not bound by it, indeed had not even been officially apprised of it. British officials knew what was required, but they had to work out a way to get there without risking the reopening of the whole frontier question, just as Shaikh Ahmad feared when he was first approached by Colonel Dickson in July.

The matter of documentation for the British delegation to Geneva was tied in closely with the question of publicity in general. The Foreign Office view was expressed by Rendel in a memorandum to W. E. Beckett, his staff lawyer, on July 4, 1932:

> I agree . . . it would be better to defer [publication] until Iraq has been admitted to the League. We want the frontier settlement to fall back on and produce *if necessary*. But it is not ideal, as it may lead to questions as to how, since it is only a "reaffirmation" of an "existing" frontier, that frontier was originally laid down. Do not let us therefore invite questions on this point by producing and publishing the settlement prematurely. Once Iraq is a member of the League it will matter much less if such questions are raised and if our case, in reply, is not quite as watertight as we would like.[40]

George Rendel had the responsibility of briefing the British delegation that was to go to Geneva to present the application. On September 23, 1932, he addressed a note to his superior at the Foreign Office, the permanent under secretary, A. M. G. Cadogan,[41] enclosing a briefing memorandum for Sir Francis Humphrys, the high commissioner in Iraq, who was to head the delegation. Rendel pointed out that the League's questionnaire asked (among other things): "Is the applicant a nation with a stable government and well-defined frontiers?" On this subject Rendel's briefing note says:

> In April 1923 the Shaikh of Kuwait was informed that His Majesty's Government recognized the frontier claimed by him as between Kuwait and Iraq. This was the frontier indicated by the green line of the Anglo-Turkish Agreement of 29 July 1913, and the description of this line (though without mention of the Anglo-Turkish Agreement) was set out in the communication to

the Shaikh. No more formal agreement in regard to this frontier seems to have been framed. The communication to the Shaikh was not referred to the League of Nations in any form. It was felt to be necessary, however, that the frontier should be re-affirmed in a formal manner which would be suitable for production if necessary at Geneva . . . It was therefore arranged in July last that letters regarding the re-affirmation of the 1923 frontier should be exchanged between the Iraqi and Kuwaiti authorities. This exchange of letters has now been completed, and copies . . . are attached as Appendix 5.[42]

The text of Rendel's "Appendix 5" is missing from the files, but it was referred to in a memo by Dixin of the Foreign Office on October 11, 1932, with the notation, "The portions omitted are merely 'transmitters' between the various posts concerned."[43] So it would appear that the delegation to Geneva had with them only Nuri Said's letter to Humphrys of July 21, 1932, and the letter from Shaikh Ahmad to Dickson of August 9, 1932. In the event, even these never had to be produced in Geneva.

Now up for discussion was the question of what part, if any, of this correspondence should be "printed." There was a distinction between "printing" for internal government use and "publishing" to the world. The Foreign Office had a long-established practice of printing important and confidential documents for purely internal distribution.[44] These days it is perhaps hard to realize that before the introduction of the photocopier it was not very easy to standardize working copies of important documents; with a reliable and secure printing operation the process was accurate, legible, and authoritative, and distribution of copies could be controlled by numbering them. George Rendel noted on September 14, 1932: "I think we ought now also to consider the question of printing the relevant correspondence about the frontier (in a single section) in our series (Eastern—Iraq)." Back from P. J. Dixin on October 11, a week after Iraq's admission: "We might print those parts of the correspondence which were selected for inclusion as Appendix 5 in the brief for the U.K. Delegate at the last Assembly at Geneva." A note from J. C. Sterndale Bennett of the Foreign Office on October 12: "I think that would be enough." Rendel on October 12: "I agree. Print accordingly. Eastern (Iraq)."[45]

And that is how the expurgated version of the 1932 letters came to be printed in a confidential compilation of documents known as "The Pink Volume."[46] The complete documentation has never been published, even for confidential British government use. The 1932 correspondence formed the very core of an agreement between Iraq and Kuwait in 1963 whereby Iraq renounced its Kuwaiti claims for all time. But the high officials who signed that 1963 agreement on behalf of their governments did not have the whole story.

6. Britain and Kuwait between the Wars

The "Status" Question

In the late 1920s, British officials began to worry about what was going to become of Kuwait after Iraq became a fully sovereign and independent state. They were already concerned about the threat to Kuwait from Abdul Aziz ibn Saud. In 1928 an official historical summary prepared for the British Cabinet pointed out "the desirability of securing that the Shaikh shall not escape absorption by Ibn Saud only to end by absorption by an Iraq no longer under British mandate."[1] It was perfectly apparent that Kuwait was vulnerable from both sides; the questions for Britain were whether Kuwait was worth preserving as an independent entity; and, if so, what Great Britain should do to achieve that end. Thus arose the perennial Whitehall agenda item with the title "Status of Kuwait," the subject of many a meeting and memorandum until World War II.

As early as 1919 the acting civil commissioner in Baghdad, Sir Arnold Wilson, had proposed the declaration of a formal British protectorate over Kuwait. The notion attracted no support from the government of India, and Wilson's suggestion was shelved. For the time being, Great Britain was content to rest its authority in the shaikhdom on the assurance given to Mubarak on November 3, 1914, that "Kuwait shall be recognised as an independent principality under British protection."[2]

In 1928 the political resident in the Persian Gulf, Sir Lionel Haworth, reported that "the bazaars were alive" with rumors that Kuwait would eventually be joined either to Britain, to Najd, or to Iraq; he cautioned against any loose statements out of mandated Iraq that might encourage such ideas. Even so, Haworth conceded, "it is, perhaps, the natural development that Kuwait should draw close to Iraq while we are there [that is, in Iraq], but we do not desire her to get so close that . . . she would be left there when we leave." Although Haworth's warning was taken seriously in London, a Cabinet subcommittee on Persian Gulf policy in 1929 once again rejected the idea of declaring a protectorate. On the other hand, Acting High Commissioner Hubert Young recommended from his vantage point in Baghdad in the summer of 1930 that Britain "should aim at the gradual absorption of Kuwait by Iraq"—stark heresy from the standpoint of Anglo-Indians who had worked so hard to establish and maintain the status of Kuwait.[3]

Since 1923 Ibn Saud had maintained and enforced a tight blockade against Kuwait, aimed at Kuwait's refusal to collect customs and transit duties for Ibn Saud's account, on traffic bound for the interior. Relations between Shaikh Ahmad and his British mentors suffered because of suspicions that the British were behind this ruinous blockade or at least could induce the Saudis to lift it if they tried. (The British finally succeeded in having the blockade removed in 1937.)

In August 1933 the British ambassador to Saudi Arabia, Sir Andrew Ryan, suggested that Ibn Saud might have in mind bringing Kuwait into his still expanding orbit, if only by way of a "political deal" that Shaikh Ahmad might find impossible to turn down. In a message to the Foreign Office, Ryan imagined Ibn Saud fashioning a proposal like this: "You are not really independent, my dear fellow. You are under the thumb of the English. They might annex you at any moment, or even present you to Iraq . . . I should not mop you up, of course. You would rule your state under an understanding with me."[4]

Sir George Rendel, head of the Eastern Department at the Foreign Office, found Ryan's speculative fancy so interesting— perhaps so alarming—that he convened a meeting in London in October 1933 for a full-scale review of the status of Kuwait. At the meeting the representative of the India Office took the view that Kuwait was now more important to the British government than ever before, citing the development of the air route to Asia and Australia, as well as the uncertain future of Iraq's relations with Britain following the expiration of the mandate the previous year. Rendel agreed, stressing Kuwait's economic and geographic vulnerability, cut off as it was from its desert hinterland by the Saudi blockade, and dependent on Iraq for water from the Shatt. Rendel proposed that Kuwait's weakness coupled with its increased strategic importance might make it advantageous to convert Britain's treaty relationship into a definite protectorate. This, he suggested, would "ensure Kuwait more effectively against absorption than the present attempt to maintain the shaikhdom as a kind of political vacuum." The India Office representative, J. G. Laithwaite, agreed that the present treaty arrangements were unsatisfactory, in that the Anglo-Kuwaiti relationship rested entirely upon three rather insubstantial documents: the 1899 "good offices" agreement; the promises in the 1907 Lease Agreement that the town of Kuwait and its boundaries belonged to Mubarak and his heirs; and the 1914 pledge that in the event of victory over the Turks Kuwait would be recognized as an independent principality under British protection. But Laithwaite cautioned against declaring a formal protectorate, which might cause apprehension elsewhere in the Gulf. Instead, he proposed "filling the gaps" in the existing arrangements by strengthening and adding to them. Ambassador Ryan supported Rendel in favor of a clear protectorate, observing that the British were not in a strong tactical position "to warn Ibn Saud to keep his hands off Kuwait, since they were committed to maintaining that Kuwait was technically an independent state."

The Foreign Office proposal for a formal protectorate was not adopted, and in fact the meeting ended without taking any significant decisions at all about the status of Kuwait. By way of catering to Ambassador Ryan's imaginative concerns, which had provoked the meeting in the first place, Ryan was instructed to emphasize to Ibn Saud the closeness of the British government's relations with Kuwait, and Shaikh Ahmad was to be told to stop corresponding with Ibn Saud on political subjects; further efforts would be made to get the Saudis to lift the blockade.[5]

Oil: The Beginnings

There was one significant omission from the record of the 1933 Foreign Office meeting: there was apparently no discussion about petroleum. The conventional wisdom holds that British policy in the Middle East was driven more by oil than by any other consideration, almost from the days of Nebuchadnezzar. Petroleum was discovered in Persia before World War I, in northern Iraq in 1927, and in Bahrain in 1932. At the time of the Foreign Office meeting Shaikh Ahmad himself was deeply involved in negotiations with American as well as British oil interests, which resulted in the award of an oil concession in 1934 for "the entire area of Kuwait" to the American-British jointly owned Kuwait Oil Company (KOC). But oil was certainly not on the minds of the officials who met in October 1933 to consider British policy toward Kuwait; in fact oil seems to have played no great part in British policy anywhere in the Gulf in the 1930s.[6]

Kuwait Oil Company struck oil at Burgan in April 1938. Because of World War II there were no exports until June 1946.[7] Before production began to soar in the early 1950s, the impact of oil in Kuwait was mainly on internal politics. From the start, Shaikh Ahmad regarded all revenues accruing from the oil concession as his own. What rationale beyond ordinary human avarice informed this view is difficult to discern; surely the concept that the entire area of the shaikhdom (including underground resources) was his personal property had little support in tribal custom, logic, or judicious statesmanship. At all events, Ahmad took care to stipulate in the concession agreement that revenues from KOC were to be paid to his personal account at the Ottoman Bank in Basra.[8]

The merchant community in Kuwait not unnaturally came to resent Ahmad's high-handedness, which departed significantly from the traditional consensus polity that had been an integral part of Kuwait's rise to prosperity since the beginnings of the community in the 1750s.[9] In 1938, when Shaikh Ahmad agreed to the request of his newly formed Legislative Council to share his oil revenues with the people, cynics took his sullen acquiescence as a sign that the council would soon be dissolved, and they were proved right.

Rendel on British Governance

In 1937, shortly before he left as head of the Foreign Office's Eastern Department, George Rendel visited Kuwait for the first time. "Our position," he wrote later, "seemed to me to be . . . anachronistic and ill-defined. The Shaikh was a more or less sovereign ruler, though he had agreed by treaty with us to refrain from piracy, gun-running and the slave trade, and to put his foreign relations in our hands." In Rendel's view the political agent/political resident/government of India/India Office chain of command "seemed . . . to be becoming more and more out of key with modern conditions."[10]

Until India achieved independence in 1947, all the political agents in Kuwait and elsewhere in the Persian Gulf were drawn from the Indian civil service or army. Appointed by the government of India, they were trained more as administrators than as diplomats. (Later on the political agents were supplied by the Foreign Office, which took over administration of Persian Gulf affairs in March 1948; at the same time, the Persian Gulf residency was moved from Bushire, in Iran, to Bahrain.)[11] Locally the agents enjoyed immense prestige, backed by the full power and panoply of the British government. An American missionary doctor, Paul Harrison, wrote in the 1920s: "The local political agent . . . conceals his hand carefully and interferes in local affairs only on the rarest of occasions. Nevertheless, if necessity arises, he is an absolute czar."[12] There was a saying that the political agent "left the Shaikh free to be good, but not to be bad."[13] Sir Ronald Storrs, who served in a somewhat similar role in mandated Palestine, put it rather suavely: "We deprecated the Imperative, preferring the Subjunctive, even the wistful Optative mood."[14] For the most part the incumbents in Kuwait seem to have got along well with the rulers, although few developed the sort of companionable relationship that was so fulfilling for Harold Dickson. One or two of them were conspicuously unsuccessful and left under a cloud.[15]

George Rendel may have hoped to use his 1937 inspection trip as the basis for reforming the British administrative structure in the Gulf, but he seems to have come away disillusioned. "It is one of the strongest instincts of the British character," he wrote ruefully in his memoirs, "to distrust definition, to prefer a purely empirical approach to any problem, and to allow an existing situation to continue with the minimum of alteration."[16] Perhaps the rejection of his 1933 proposal for a formal protectorate still rankled. Right after Rendel's visit the British promoted Shaikh Ahmad from "His Excellency" to "His Highness."[17]

Colonel Dickson and the Date Gardens

In his annual report for 1932, Political Agent Harold Dickson passed along Shaikh Ahmad's concern that Ibn Saud was maintaining the blockade in order to bring Kuwait under Saudi control. Iraq's tactics, on the other hand, were more subtle: "Iraq pins her faith on putting pressure on the Shaikh of Kuwait's private purse in the shape of attacks on his gardens, etc."[18]

It will be remembered that for many years Al Sabah had owned extensive properties inside Iraq, chiefly date plantations situated along the Shatt al-Arab. A family dispute over inherited rights to the properties had been settled in 1902 with a great deal of tension and acrimony, and considerable arm-twisting on the part of British officials in Basra and Kuwait. In November 1914, when the British obtained from Shaikh Mubarak his pledge to assist in the war against the Turks, the ruler got something in return: in addition to recognition as an independent state, the British promised that the "date gardens situate between Fao and Qurnah shall remain in your possession and in possession of your descendants without being subject to the payment of revenue or taxes." This pledge was no small matter for Mubarak after his earlier troubles. Before the oil era the principal source of revenue for Al Sabah was from these agricultural estates. In 1920 the tax exemption was worth about 60,000 rupees to the shaikh.[19] It was a measure of Mubarak's concern about the vulnerability of the property that more than once he had actually considered taking Ottoman citizenship, the better to protect it legally. (Such notions created consternation among British policymakers, who were determined for their own reasons that no cloud should shadow his "independence" under their aegis, and they talked him out of it.)[20]

Dickson reported that in 1931 the Iraqi authorities decided to impose taxes on produce from the Al Sabah estates, taxes to which the British in their wartime promise had told Mubarak he and his descendants would not be subjected. Until then, the pledge had been implemented through a special arrangement between the British authorities in Kuwait and in Baghdad, an arrangement facilitated by Britain's control as the mandatory power in Iraq. The 1931 tax, known as the *ushr* (one-tenth), was harder to deal with, since it took the form of a 10 percent charge on the value of agricultural products, payable by the purchaser. The tax was not precisely on the date gardens themselves, but it came to the same thing, because the buyer simply deducted the amount of the tax from the price paid for the produce. This tax was levied in 1932 for the first time. To add to Shaikh Ahmad's woes, customs duties were now demanded and taken on his own garden produce exported for his private use in Kuwait, overriding an exemption granted by the British authorities in Iraq in 1917.

Continuing his litany of the ruler's new vexations, Dickson mentioned the fact that Kuwait depended on its fleet of some forty-eight boats shuttling constantly back and forth to bring fresh water from the Shatt al-Arab. On May 15, 1932, Shaikh Ahmad had reported that these vessels were being detained by Iraqi customs authorities at Fao. Despite protests lodged by Dickson on Ahmad's behalf, these irksome restrictions were still in effect at the end of the year.

And finally, said Dickson's 1932 report, a lawsuit had been commenced in May in a Basra court in the name of "a certain Arab lady" against the shaikh, claiming title to his estate known as the "Faddaghiyeh," which had been purchased twenty-five years earlier by Ahmad's grandfather, Mubarak, for the equivalent of £160,000. "This," wrote Dickson, "even though the British revenue authorities (Sir Henry Dobbs) had early in the War confirmed the Shaikh in these properties and given him proper Tapu papers (title deeds)."[21] Dickson said that Ahmad had already called upon the British government to fulfill its 1914 pledges to him and protect his interests.

These events taken together, the political agent summed up, had "awakened a feeling of distrust in the mind of the Shaikh of Kuwait, who feels that his interests are no longer adequately guarded by his reliance on the word of His Majesty's Government alone . . . His personal anxiety regarding the security of his properties in Iraq has seriously curtailed the measure of financial relief he would under favourable circumstances have been able to afford."[22]

Dickson's report makes it clear that the properties in question were by no means trivial. They appear to have exceeded 20,000 acres, or more than thirty square miles of rich agricultural soil. British officials, especially staff lawyers at the Foreign Office, were deeply involved in the date garden problem for many years because they took seriously the 1914 pledge to Mubarak; any argument by Britain that it was no longer bound by that agreement would undermine the declaration in the same document of the status of Kuwait as a de facto protectorate, and this the British did not care to risk. As Britain was preparing to relinquish the mandate in 1932, someone in the Colonial Office suggested adding the shaikh's tax exemption to a list being drawn up of financial obligations and "acquired rights" to be assumed by Iraq upon its attaining independence; this ingenious idea was jettisoned when it was pointed out that since the pledge had been made by the British in 1914, it did not qualify as a British obligation undertaken during the period of the mandate.[23] In a 1935 review of outstanding matters affecting Kuwait, the Political Department of the Indian government highlighted the date garden issue with a delicate swipe at Whitehall mismanagement: "In the view of His Majesty's Government this [1914] promise has now devolved on the Iraqi Government, but unfortunately the former [British government] failed, during the currency of the Mandate, to obtain from the latter an undertaking to do so . . . The continued inability of His Majesty's Government to fulfill their pledge to the Shaikh has naturally had an unfortunate effect on our relations with the Shaikh."[24]

At one stage in the Basra court proceedings lawyers for Great Britain advanced the argument that the tax exemption granted to Mubarak by the 1914 pledge constituted a valid gift by Britain, and that all later treaties between Iraq and Great Britain bound Iraq to honor this and all other international commitments entered into by Britain. But counsel for the Foreign Office were hampered by their client's unwillingness to produce the entire 1914 document in court, because of its secret political provisions. In 1953 Shaikh Abdullah III was still pursuing the Al Sabah claim against Great Britain at the time he visited England for Queen Elizabeth's coronation. The ruler was eventually paid a handsome settlement in sterling for the release of his claims.[25] To Dickson and his successors at the Political Agency, looking through their particular prism in the direction of Iraq, the date garden issue was a pernicious attempt by Iraq to bring pressure on the Kuwaitis to make concessions on the unsettled border between the two states. For Dickson himself the gardens became a personal trial. He had to give up his home leave in 1933 to spend all summer in Baghdad working on the litigation, and in 1935 he was told by his superior, the political resident, that he could not accept an invitation from Shaikh Ahmad to accompany him on a trip to London "as interpreter and friend," for much the same reason.[26]

Shaikh Ahmad Feels the Pressure

Working against the British objective of keeping as much distance as possible between Kuwait and Iraq was the fact that there were many close—albeit informal—ties between their respective citizens. Colonel Dickson sounded an alarm as early as 1930, attributing a growing annexationist sentiment in Kuwait to some unidentified source in Iraq: "There is little doubt in my mind that important Basrawis [Basra residents] who come down here on visits, or who own property in Kuwait, are by order actively engaging themselves in anti-British propaganda as well as preaching the doctrine of the amalgamation of Kuwait and Iraq."[27]

The diverse forces arrayed against Shaikh Ahmad included not only the stern, conservative neo-Wahhabi regime in Saudi Arabia and annexationists in Iraq and perhaps under his very nose, but also Kuwaiti notables and townsmen who smarted under his increasingly autocratic rule. His responses to these challenges were fragmentary. In 1937 it was reported that he abandoned European tailoring, to which he had grown accustomed, reverting to customary Arab dress in a display of Muslim piety.[28] He likewise ordained certain restraints on women in society, in deference to Ibn Saud's austere pronouncements. But there was serious trouble early in 1938 over the flogging of an agitator on the orders of the shaikh. The Iraqi press and Baghdad radio stepped up their attacks on the shortcomings of Ahmad's regime; a growing number of Kuwaitis seemed ready to entertain the idea that Kuwait would be better off under Iraqi administration.

The merchant families of Kuwait had not forgotten that in 1921 they had joined together to condition their consent to Ahmad's accession upon his promise to set up an advisory council to participate in decision making. With the encouragement of Political Agent Gerald de Gaury (acting on his government's instructions), the merchant-notables reminded Ahmad of his earlier pledge and forced him to decree the establishment of a People's Legislative Council. Just as at Runnymede in 1215, this was no quantum leap to full parliamentary democracy, but it was a start. The Council consisted of fourteen members, and the electorate was confined to adult males from some 150 families. The decree signed by the shaikh on July 2, 1938, stated that the function of the People's Legislative Council was to be "the source of all treaties and internal and external concessions and agreements, and whatever is initiated in this respect will not be considered legal except with the agreement of the council and its supervision." (The Legislative Council sent a message to Captain de Gaury's superior, the political resident in the Persian Gulf, to assure the British government that the new law would not affect existing treaties, concessions, and agreements—including, of course, KOC's 1934 oil concession as well as the web of agreements with His Majesty's Government.)[29] In December 1938 there was open confrontation between Shaikh Ahmad and his new council, several of whom were advocating closer ties with Iraq. Some of the members barricaded themselves in the Palace of Nayif, an arsenal; they surrendered after they had been surrounded by tribal warriors summoned by the ruler. The Council was dissolved; there were riots and loss of life. Many nationalist dissidents fled to Iraq.

Early in 1939 another council was formed, this time with twenty members. It never met, however; it was dissolved in March by Shaikh Ahmad because its members would not agree that Ahmad should have power to veto its decisions. Shaikh Ahmad was to remain in almost sole control of Kuwait's internal affairs until his death in 1950.[30]

Britain in Kuwait: An Accounting

The approach of World War II provides an occasion to pause and examine what Great Britain had achieved in Kuwait since that day in January 1899 when Colonel Meade dropped in on Shaikh Mubarak and obtained from him the "bond" that was to link Kuwait and the British for the better part of a century.

First, in terms of Britain's own political and strategic objectives, the relationship had been for the most part an outstanding success. Unlike other areas of British dominance (such as Palestine, Egypt, India, and Ireland), Kuwait had been a showpiece of quiet and effective imperial administration. In Kuwait the British hold was as firm as it needed to be; the cash costs were reasonable; there was no drain on Britain's military strength. The system had worked.

Second, in terms of preserving the shaikhdom as a distinct and (nominally) independent entity free from outside interference, Britain had succeeded just as admirably. It is hard to avoid the conclusion that Kuwait and Al Sabah would at some point have fallen under the sway of the Ottomans, the Saudis, or the Iraqis had it not been for consistent British support.

But as far as Kuwait's own political and social evolution is concerned, the picture is more mixed, and indeed there is much room for disagreement. In the first place, Britain's unconditional support of Al Sabah, to the exclusion of other elements in the mercantile consensus, probably had much to do with the later rulers of Kuwait becoming more monarchical, more "royal," than their forebears. The stability for the shaikhdom provided by a firm supportive hand at the Political Agency was undermined by the damage done to the earlier political equilibrium.

The government of India/political resident/political agent chain of command was, after all, practically the antithesis of democratic government. There was no way for the shaikh to appeal over the head of the political agent, who was assigned to his post without the consent of the ruler and could not be removed (as an ambassador might be) as persona non grata. By the same token, there was no effective way (as the 1938 events showed) for citizens to appeal over the head of the shaikh.

Apart from its firm support of the legitimacy of the house of Sabah, the British took very little part in the internal affairs of Kuwait. Having proved themselves to be such able and conscientious administrators in varied circumstances all over the empire, one may ask why the British in Kuwait did not take more initiative in such fields as education, public health, government organization, and fiscal management. One reason, certainly, is that Great Britain never treated Kuwait as a full protectorate, much less a colony (one thinks of Barbados, Nigeria, Bermuda). The British were always leaning over backward to stress Kuwait's "independence." But there was another, rather special, reason why Britain was loath to press for even such modest steps forward as the abolition of slavery—the looming presence over the desert horizon of the new Kingdom of Saudi Arabia: powerful, acquisitive, and overwhelmingly opposed to Western modernizing influences.

A recent observer, Glen Balfour-Paul, suggests that Britain bequeathed to the Gulf Arabs a respect for law and law enforcement, some recognition of the value of social stability, and "an embryonic concept of structured administration in a Western and perhaps irrelevant sense." But he considers that as a consequence of British hands-off policies with respect to internal affairs, the Arabs of the Gulf were "ill prepared for the almost simultaneous arrival of oil wealth and independence." Said one of them: "Our great misfortune was that you people never colonised us. If you had, you would at least have spent some effort on our development and we would have had the pleasure of finally throwing you out."[31]

7. Iraq on Its Own

We have seen how, on the eve of Iraq's independence, its British sponsors patched together a secret frontier arrangement between Iraq and Kuwait so that Iraq's membership in the League of Nations would not be impeded or delayed. On October 3, 1932, the much-troubled British mandate came to an end, in the only case in the history of the League in which a mandatory power sought to divest itself of its rights and responsibilities. In September 1933 King Faisal died in Berne, Switzerland, of coronary thrombosis at the age of forty-eight.[1] He was much mourned and honored after his death for having given the new state at least some semblance of political focus and cohesion. He was succeeded on the throne, but not in prestige, by his only son, Ghazi.

Iraq's Hashemite monarchy was to survive for twenty-six more years, until it fell with a crash in the revolution of July 14, 1958. Britain had not disappeared from the scene, however; under the 1930 Anglo-Iraqi treaty that led to the end of the mandate, Britain was to retain very important privileges and rights, including Iraq's "full and frank consultation with Great Britain in all matters of foreign policy."[2] Britain's direct influence began to wane, if at first only imperceptibly. For a long time many a British hand could be found somewhere behind the scenes in the government, in the courts (where British judges sat on cases involving foreigners), and in the armed forces. Their continuing effectiveness owed a great deal to British ties with a handful of steady anglophile political leaders, most notably the seemingly imperishable Nuri Pasha al-Said, never far from the British embassy except during certain periods when he found it expedient to leave the country.[3]

As Iraq gradually but not entirely shook off British influence and progressed by uncertain steps toward true independence and nationhood, the question of the frontier with Kuwait continued to simmer. For many Iraqis it rankled that their country's access to the rest of the world by way of the Persian Gulf was closely circumscribed. True, there was the amply endowed Shatt al-Arab, the confluence of the mighty Tigris and Euphrates; during the 1930s the port of Basra was developed under expert British management into a substantial world-class facility.[4] But the Shatt lay between Iraq and Persia (in those days coming to be restyled as "Iran"), and relations between these rivals were hardly more cordial than they are today. And aside from the Shatt, prospects for developing Iraq's maritime resources were rather dim. The western bank of the Shatt al-Arab is less than five miles from the mouth of the Khor Abdullah estuary, and in between lie some of the most wretched and inhospitable mudflats in all the world. Pursuing the left (northern) bank of the Khor Abdullah one reaches after another thirty-five muddy miles a junction with the Khor Zubair, which wanders northward toward Umm Qasr, where a terminus for the Baghdad Railway was once projected. Those plans had not survived World War I, and the entire region remained undeveloped. The right (southern) bank of the Khor Abdullah was commanded by the islands of Warba and Bubiyan; and those islands belonged to Kuwait—so said the Nuri-Ahmad letters of July 21 and August 9, 1932, which "re-affirmed" the border originally described in the Anglo-Ottoman Convention of 1913 and echoed in Sir Percy Cox's memorandum of April 19, 1923.

The geographic situation at Umm Qasr and the Khor Abdullah preyed increasingly on the minds of Iraqi officials and politicians. Their frustration was not alleviated by the fact that as long as Great Britain remained as protector of the shaikhdom of Kuwait, Iraq's opportunities to improve its own position were limited.

British officials in Iraq were aware of Iraq's aspirations for improved access to the Gulf. In 1933 Iran was creating difficulties over the Shatt al-Arab, leading to an Iraqi complaint before the League of Nations; the matter was resolved favorably for Iraq, with quiet backing from the British, by an Iraqi-Persian border agreement in 1937, which set the international boundary along the eastern bank of the Shatt (except for a stretch at Abadan, where the frontier skipped out to midstream for five miles). The problems with the Persians focused attention in Baghdad upon the possibility of an alternative port somewhere along the Khor Abdullah or the Khor Zubair, perhaps near the dilapidated old Turkish fort at Umm Qasr. C. J. Edmonds, an experienced member of boundary commissions for the Iraq-Syria and Iraq-Turkey borders, had served as an adviser to Iraq's Ministry of the Interior since 1926. In early 1934 Edmonds went down to have a look on behalf of the Iraqi government. (Edmonds surmised that his investigation of the Umm Qasr site was the first ever, unless the Germans had looked it over in connection with plans for the railway before the war.)[5] He arrived in Basra on March 16 and arranged with Sir John Ward, head of the Basra Port Directorate, to take him by launch to the Khor Abdullah and the Khor Zubair. On the night of March 19 they anchored off Umm Qasr, returning to Basra the following day. Two days later Edmonds flew from Basra to Kuwait town to examine the terrain from the air. In Kuwait he conferred at length with the political agent, Colonel Dickson, but "I thought it better not to see the Shaikh of Kuwait himself." Edmonds concluded in his report (marked "secret") that "the Khor Abdullah and the Khor Zubair together constitute a broad waterway capable of being navigated by ships of deep draft. In view of the proximity of the Shatt al-Arab there is no reason for endeavouring to develop it. It is however conceivable that temporary use might be made of it if ever exceptional circumstances were to interfere with the navigation of the Shatt al-Arab."[6]

Iraq Makes Its First Move

On April 12, 1938, during a visit by British Ambassador Sir Maurice Peterson to the Iraqi minister of foreign affairs, Taufiq Suwaidi, the latter unexpectedly raised the question of the international status of Kuwait. Peterson reported to London:

> He had with him Volume XI of *Aitchison's Treaties,* and read out to me article 6 of the Anglo-Turkish Agreement (unratified) of July 1913, inviting my particular attention to the reference to the Shaikh of Koweit as an Ottoman Kaimakam which occurs therein. What, he said, does this mean? Surely it indicated that Koweit was not really an independent State, and was it not arguable that, since in 1913 Koweit had been technically a Kaza

of the Basra Vilayet and as the sovereignty of this Vilayet had since then passed from the old Ottoman Empire to the new Iraqi Kingdom, Koweit now stood in relation to Iraq in the same position as it had stood in relation to the Ottoman Empire . . .

Taufiq Suwaidi acknowledged that in 1932 Nuri Said had written a letter recognizing a certain line as being the frontier, but thought that "the reaffirmation of this frontier could not be held . . . to have brought any change to the status of Koweit." The foreign minister explained that the matter was of importance not only because of proposals for the control of Kuwaiti smuggling into Iraq (a major issue at the time), but also because the government of Iraq was thinking about "the extension of the Iraqi railway to Koweit Bay, in order to provide Iraq with a port on the Persian Gulf . . . [Suwaidi] thought that in view of the Anglo-Iraqi Alliance, His Majesty's Government should see no serious objection in principle to these projects and it had occurred to him that a re-examination of the status of Koweit on the basis of the Anglo-Turkish Agreement of 1913 might reveal a way to overcome any political difficulties of a technical character."

All this was news to Ambassador Peterson. He promised to look into the matter. In reporting the conversation to London, he said that it appeared to him that "from the point of view of international law Koweit's independence began from the date of the ratification of the Treaty of Lausanne (6th August, 1924). On this date also, Turkey renounced all rights over Koweit and these rights, whatever they may have been, thereupon terminated and were not transferred to any other State." He sought advice as to whether he could give oral explanations to the Iraqis on these lines, as well as any further arguments "with which to refute the suggestion that Iraq has acquired certain rights over the territory of Koweit. In particular it would, I feel, be an advantage to show that the Iraqi Government had in some way recognised both the independence of Koweit and the special relations between His Majesty's Government and the Ruler of Koweit."[7]

The smooth and rather innocent-sounding query of the Iraqi foreign minister caused a considerable stir at the British Foreign Office. It took almost two months for C. W. Baxter, Sir George Rendel's successor as head of the Eastern Department, to respond to the ambassador in Baghdad, and the response, sent from London on June 15, 1938, was not entirely comforting. (The Foreign Office did not include this reply among the documents selected for internal publication in 1938, but a carbon copy was sent over to the India Office, where it seems to have gone virtually unnoticed for the next fifty-odd years.) Baxter called his message an "interim reply":

> Although we have, we think, sufficient material to show that Iraq has no rights of any kind over territory beyond the actual frontier between Iraq and Koweit and that the Iraqi Government have accepted this position, we do not think that it is on the provisions of Article 16 of the Treaty of Lausanne alone that we should rely in refuting any suggestion that Iraq may have inherited any suzerain rights over Koweit from Turkey.
>
> I enclose a copy of a minute by Beckett [a Foreign Office lawyer] which sets out the position as we see it . . . The Library have however been looking to see whether they can trace any kind of document, e.g., some decision of the Supreme Council [of the Principal Allied Powers], which laid down what "Iraq" was to consist of, but without success . . . [I]nsofar as we have been able to determine, no actual communication was ever made to and acknowledged by the Iraqi Government at the time, setting out specifically the boundaries of their State.
>
> It might, nevertheless, be helpful to know what action, if any, was taken by the High Commission in Bagdad on the Colonial Office despatch No. 96 of the 2nd February, 1923 . . . Would you therefore be so good as to have the papers looked up, and let us know the result as soon as you conveniently can. This may enable us to produce a cast-iron argument in reply to the suggestions put to you by the Iraqi Minister for Foreign Affairs regarding the relationship of Koweit to Iraq.

Enclosed with Baxter's letter to Ambassador Peterson was a memorandum from C. H. Fone of the Foreign Office library, stating that no trace had been found of any definition of Iraq's frontiers in the wartime or immediately postwar Foreign Office papers, beyond an indication from the Civil Commissioner for Iraq on December 8, 1918, that the Iraq-Kuwait frontier would have to be delimited "in cooperation with the Shaikh of Koweit." The unratified Treaty of Sèvres of August 10, 1920 (the first, unsuccessful attempt to settle a peace with Turkey), was equally vague.

The library researcher had also found a Foreign Office note to the Cabinet Offices dated November 3, 1920, stating that draft mandates for Mesopotamia (as well as Palestine and Syria) were almost ready to be presented to the Council of the League of Nations. The note cautioned that the draft mandates would make no mention of frontiers, "as . . . Lord Curzon [the foreign secretary] wishes to postpone for the present the definition of . . . the southern boundary of Mesopotamia." The reason for Curzon's hesitancy is not given.

Then the librarian referred to the post-Uqair correspondence leading up to the Cox-More Memorandum, beginning with the dispatch from Baghdad on December 20, 1922, suggesting that with the two Saudi boundaries settled, it would be "convenient" to fix the Iraq-Kuwait border as well. In that dispatch Sir Percy Cox had mentioned that "the question of the Iraqi-Koweiti frontier had not hitherto been raised by King Faisal or his government and that they would presumably accept the decision of His Majesty's Government in regard thereto." The library note added: "The High Commissioner's proposals were approved but we have nothing to suggest that the matter was ever mentioned to the Iraqi Government." Following the Cox-More Memorandum, no further reference to the Kuwait-Iraq frontier could be found until the exchange of correspondence of July–August 1932.

Here was a classic case of the proverbial failure of institutional memory. Baxter did not specify what he meant by "sufficient material to show that Iraq has no rights of any kind over territory beyond the actual frontier between Iraq and Koweit." After sixteen years Whitehall had lost all trace of what Sir Percy Cox did after receiving the February 2, 1923, Dispatch No. 96 from the Colonial Office. That document had in fact simply approved the boundary description proposed by Cox, without prescribing any specific action. As we saw earlier, Cox relied on the dispatch as his authority for the Cox-More Memorandum, but he never shared either document with the Iraqi government. Cox might well have remembered this chain of events, but he had died the previous year while hunting. So Peterson was instructed to rummage around in the embassy files in Iraq. The public records do not tell us what he came up with, but we can infer that the cupboard was just as bare in Baghdad as it was in London. The hoped-for "cast-iron argument" would have to be forged from something else.

The Foreign Office Legal Memorandum of May 30, 1938

Also enclosed with Baxter's letter to Peterson was a memorandum prepared by W. E. Beckett, a staff lawyer at the Foreign Office, setting out his views as to why it would be helpful from the legal standpoint to have further documentation beyond the Lausanne Treaty. In view of the widespread opinion among present-day lawyers that Article 16 of the Lausanne Treaty disposed of any Iraqi claim to Kuwait based on its status as successor to the Ottoman Empire,[8] it is worth examining why Beckett had serious doubts about it in 1938.

First, the Treaty of Lausanne fixed the future boundaries of Turkey and provided that Turkey renounced all rights outside those boundaries. For Iraq, therefore, the Lausanne Treaty was relevant only with respect to its frontier with Turkey. "The other boundaries of Iraq depend on the settlements made by the 'parties concerned.'"

Second, "In order to ascertain what the frontiers of Iraq are on any other boundary, we have to look entirely at what the Allied Powers decided." What they decided, said Beckett, was that there should be a mandated territory in Mesopotamia, with Britain as the mandatory power. The mandate took the form of the 1922 treaty, which was amended by two subsequent treaties. "None of these Treaties in any way defined the boundaries of Iraq, but all proceeded on the basis that its area was something which was already defined."

After discussing Iraq's boundaries with Persia, Syria, Trans-Jordan, and Najd, Beckett proceeded to Kuwait, recalling the 1899 Covenant and the draft Anglo-Ottoman Convention of 1913. Without noting that the latter was never ratified, Beckett asserted that in the Convention "the boundaries of Koweit are fixed, dividing this Koweit territory from the Basra Vilayet of the Ottoman Empire, of which Koweit is to form an autonomous kaza."

From Article 16 of the Lausanne Treaty; Article 94 of the Sèvres

Treaty; the November 3, 1914, assurance to the ruler of Kuwait; the December 4, 1918, message from the Civil Commissioner; and the other material cited in the Library memorandum, Beckett concluded: "It is plain that, from the beginning, there was no intention on the part of the 'Powers [*sic*] concerned' (Article 16 of the Lausanne Treaty) or of the principal Allied Powers (Article 94 of the same [*sic*] Treaty) to include Koweit in any shape or form within the boundaries of Iraq nor is there any decision that Iraq shall include the Basra Vilayet as such."

There are two material errors in Beckett's analysis: (1) There is no Article 94 in the Lausanne Treaty; the correct reference is to Article 94 of the rejected and unratified (and therefore legally inoperative) Treaty of Sèvres. (2) More important, because it exposes the major flaw in Beckett's analysis, is that there is no reference in Article 16 of the Lausanne Treaty to "*powers* concerned." Article 16 states: "Turkey hereby renounces all rights . . . respecting the territories situated outside the frontiers laid down in the present Treaty . . . the future of these territories being settled or to be settled by the *parties* concerned" (emphasis added).

Now the Treaty of Lausanne does not specify what is meant by the expression "parties concerned," but a commonsense interpretation would surely include the new government of Iraq. It would also, arguably, include the government of Great Britain, but only in its role as mandatory for Iraq, entrusted by its mandate with jurisdiction over Iraq's foreign affairs, but constrained by the same mandate not to alienate any Iraqi territory. In the initial postwar period the victorious European nations designated themselves as "Principal Allied Powers," and they justifiably claimed the victor's right under international law to make important decisions unilaterally. (A familiar example is the Allied control of Berlin after World War II, which lasted technically from 1945 to 1990.) But by the time of Lausanne, Britain's role in former Mesopotamia was no longer that of a victorious military power. It was that of a custodian of a new country under a mandate from the League of Nations.[9] What to Beckett was "plain" gradually becomes a little less plain.

Whether intentional or simply careless, Beckett's misrepresentation of Britain's role after 1922 provided the basis for his conclusion that Britain as a "power" was entitled to act unilaterally with regard to Iraq's boundaries. This semiarticulate major premise guided the rest of his exegesis:

> In December 1922 . . . it was decided, by His Majesty's Government at any rate, that the frontier . . . should be the same frontier as that fixed in the Convention with Turkey of 1913 . . . [I]t is clear enough that this frontier of Koweit was adopted as the frontier of Iraq at that time, and, in fact, has formed the frontier ever since. It is clear that the Treaty of Alliance of 1922, when it refers to Iraq, must be Iraq with boundaries at that time in force. When the Council of the League accepted this Treaty in lieu of the mandate, it clearly accepted the boundaries of the mandated territory as being those that had been fixed and were then operating.

Beckett then drew an analogy to the frontier between Iraq and Trans-Jordan, another British mandate, which "had only been fixed administratively" and had later been fixed definitely by an "international instrument" in order to facilitate Iraq's entry into the League of Nations in 1932. The case of Kuwait was similar: "Where the territory on the other side was under British protection, there was no formal international instrument." Later, when the need for such an instrument was recognized, and for the same reasons, "this was done by an exchange of notes which fixes the frontier between Iraq and Koweit. There can be no doubt that this exchange of notes was a formal confirmation of the line previously existing and that this line was the frontier of Iraq leaving Iraq no rights beyond it."

This leg of Beckett's argument contains yet another inconsistency. Whatever Kuwait's international status was in 1922, it had not changed in any way between then and 1932. Yet Beckett explained Britain's having acted "administratively" (that is, unilaterally) in 1922 on the basis that Kuwait was "under British protection," whereas the carefully orchestrated letters of 1932 created an "international instrument" to which Iraq and Kuwait were made to appear as the principal parties.

In his concluding paragraph, Beckett summarized his analysis:

> Iraq, in order to establish any claim to Koweit, whether in respect of suzerainty or otherwise, has to show some decision of the

Allied Powers and the Powers concerned giving her these rights over Koweit, for all her claims must rest upon what these Powers allotted to her. There is nothing to indicate that these Powers ever allotted Iraq any rights over Koweit, or even issued any decision allotting her the Basra Vilayet as such. From the moment when Iraq began to have an independent existence, which cannot be placed earlier than 1922, there was a frontier drawn with Koweit in the same sort of way as there was a frontier drawn with Trans-Jordan. The responsibilities of Iraq and His Majesty's Government under the Treaty of Alliance towards the Council of the League must, when they referred to Iraq, have referred to Iraq with these two frontiers then in operation. In 1932 when Iraq became a member of the League, the frontier with Trans-Jordan and the frontier with Koweit were confirmed by an exchange of notes in exactly the same way.[10]

The letter from C. W. Baxter and its enclosures were sent off to the embassy in Baghdad for Sir Maurice Peterson to make of them what he could. His reply, and there must have been one, is not in the India Office file that contains the Baxter letter itself. In any case, it could not have been much use to Baxter, Beckett, and others in the Foreign Office seeking documentation with which to "produce a cast-iron argument" (Baxter's phrase) to use with the Iraqi foreign minister, for the embassy files in Baghdad can have contained no evidence that Iraq had ever been consulted or informed about its frontier with Kuwait prior to the note from Sir Francis Humphrys to the Acting Prime Minister dated July 16, 1932.

Ghazi Lays Claim to Kuwait

Faisal I had been, all things considered, a satisfactory king; even many Iraqis who had reviled him when alive shared in the genuine regret at the passing of perhaps the only person who could have done as much as he did, under very difficult circumstances, to bring Iraq along the road toward genuine nationhood. His son and successor, King Ghazi, was another matter. Raised as a spoiled palace brat, he evolved without much adjustment into an irresponsible playboy. His immaturity, his dubious companions, and his flagrantly unsettling life style were to vex and roil the Iraqi political scene almost without respite until his untimely death in 1939 at the age of twenty-seven.

The real political power in Iraq after the death of Faisal in 1933 came increasingly into the hands of Nuri al-Said. It was well known in informed Baghdad circles that Ghazi feared Nuri and Nuri detested the king. One of Ghazi's pranks, involving his passion for aircraft, undoubtedly fueled Nuri's hatred. In 1935 a palace retainer, having displayed his terror of flying, was nonetheless ordered into the air along with Nuri's son Sabah, a trained pilot. The servant panicked, grabbed wildly at controls, and sent the plane crashing to earth. The servant was killed, and Nuri's son spent months in an English hospital recovering from a cracked skull and broken bones.[11]

In 1936 Iraq was rocked by the news that Ghazi's sister, Princess Azza, had run off with a Greek hotel employee she had met in Rhodes, and had converted to Christianity before marrying him. Her apostasy and elopement created a major crisis for the Sunni Muslim monarchy. Prime Minister Yasin al-Hashemi told British Ambassador Clark Kerr that Nuri (then serving as a cabinet minister), who had been nervous and distraught since the maiming of his son, "seemed to have lost his sense of proportion." Nuri, it appeared, was determined to remove Ghazi from the throne and to replace him either by a regency until Ghazi's only son, the infant Faisal II, should come of age, or perhaps even by the introduction of a substitute dynasty—meaning the House of Saud. Yasin pleaded with Kerr to talk to Nuri and try to make him see reason. At a private embassy dinner the following evening Kerr brought the two leaders together and urged them to try to "purge the Royal household of the equivocal people with whom King Ghazi had chosen to surround himself, to establish strict control over His Majesty's actions and movements, to keep him for a time in the background, and to hope that, with care and hard work, his reputation and authority would be restored in time and the unhappy story of his sister forgotten." Both Nuri and Yasin expressed doubts about their ability to implement such a difficult policy in the face of pressure from the political opposition, Nuri saying that it would not be possible without continued support from the British government. Kerr promised to speak to Ghazi and plead with him to mend his ways. His conversation next day with the king "was not as painful as I had expected. I like to think that I was gentle with him." The ambassador advised Ghazi to "put himself for some time into the hands of his Ministers and closely follow their guidance, for they had his welfare at heart."[12]

Ghazi retained his throne, but his conduct continued to cause consternation. In 1938 the new British ambassador, Sir Maurice Peterson, had yet more bad news to report:

> The tarnished personal reputation of King Ghazi has, I regret to say, been besmirched further in the course of the last few days. On or about the 18th June a negro youth, employed as a personal servant to His Majesty, was found shot within the palace precincts. According to the official story, death was due to the accidental discharge of the young man's revolver . . . [I]t seems far more likely that the young man was murdered, either because he had become a source of embarrassment to the King or by some adherent of the Queen [Aliya, Ghazi's estranged wife, also his first cousin], who . . . regarded the youth with deep aversion as the King's boon companion in debauchery.

Peterson was inclined toward some drastic measure such as establishing a council of state to control the King, but felt that political circumstances precluded forceful action by the embassy. He concluded his dispatch with a prescient warning: "The risk, whatever it may be, that the King may fall a victim to some Palace plot originating in an incident, such as that described in this despatch, must also continue to be run."[13]

In addition to Great Britain's formal duties and prerogatives as set out in the 1930 Anglo-Iraqi treaty, the British felt other, more subtle responsibilities in Iraq. This had been explained to the young King Ghazi early in 1935 by the first British ambassador (and before that, high commissioner), Sir Francis Humphrys, in a suave but very frank letter just before the end of his tour in Baghdad:

> Your Majesty,
>   Shortly after the entry of Iraq into the League of Nations, His Majesty the late King Faisal expressed to me his desire that the closest touch should continue to be maintained between His

Majesty's Embassy and the advisers to the various departments of the Iraqi Government.

His Majesty, with the full approval of the then Prime Minister, asked me to arrange that the advisers should keep me *privately* informed of developments affecting the mutual interests of our two Governments, although the *official* relations which formerly subsisted between the advisers and myself as High Commissioner had been definitely terminated . . .

I shall be glad to learn that I may inform my successor that Your Majesty approves that the Iraqi Government will extend to him the same facilities and courtesies as those given to me.[14]

The ambassador handed this letter to the king at an audience on March 6, asking for a reply before he left Iraq.[15] Ghazi's response, remarkably polished in view of his rather rudimentary knowledge of English (he had spent a few unhappy months at Harrow), came the following week; although it avoided any specific reference to a back-channel between the embassy and the departmental British advisers, its general tone could not have disappointed the Foreign Office:

My dear Sir Francis,

I have received your Excellency's letter dated the 28th February, 1935, and greatly regret to learn that you will soon be leaving this country.

The close intercourse which I have had with your Excellency in these latter times, so full of eventful happenings, has provided ample confirmation of the truth of the accounts which I so often heard from my father of your wise guidance and constant help in all that was conducive to the welfare of this country, its future prosperity and the strengthening of the foundations on which it has been established . . .

You may be assured that my Government will not hesitate to afford your successor all the facilities which may be necessary to enable him to carry out the duties which will devolve upon him regarding our mutual interests.

Your sincere friend,

Ghazi[16]

But this letter perhaps represents the apogee of King Ghazi's relations with the British. Deeply committed as they were to the monarchy not only as an institution but also as an instrument to channel their increasingly exiguous influence, they were loath to criticize the monarch in public. (Ambassador Peterson has been singled out as "perhaps the only English writer with official connections who, when dealing with Iraqi politics under the monarchy, did not choose to disguise and palliate.")[17] As war clouds gathered over Europe in the late 1930s, British anxieties increased. For one thing, Ghazi appeared to be susceptible to Axis propaganda. He openly admired Mussolini's Italy. He was suspected by some to have come under the baneful influence of German ambassador Fritz Grobba. Ghazi had acquired a radio transmitter, some said given to him by the Nazis, installed at his residence in the Qasr al-Zuhur (Rose Palace).

Suddenly Ghazi was no longer simply a profound royal nuisance; he was out of control, a loose cannon on the slippery deck of British imperial security. In an age when broadcast propaganda was of untested political consequence in the Middle East, the young king began in 1938 to beam the message that Kuwait was part of Iraq.[18] The broadcasts coincided with, and fanned the flames of, nationalist pressures in Kuwait that were threatening the Al Sabah dynasty from within. Whether or not it was instigated by Axis agents, Ghazi's propaganda played upon the theme that the ruler of Kuwait was a feudal despot whose backward rule contrasted poorly with the progressive government in Iraq.

On March 7, 1939, for example, this news item was aired on Ghazi's radio: "The Kuwaitis, and especially the youth, do not recognize the [British] protection. The history of Kuwait is a great testimony. No one represents Kuwait except its free-born deputies. We are Iraqis by flesh and blood. Our history supports the annexation of Kuwait to Iraq. We live and die under the Hashemite flag."[19] Ambassador Peterson undertook to have another word with the king the very next day. He reported to London by telegram:

> As I anticipated, King Ghazi this morning entirely collapsed as soon as I mentioned Koweit. His Majesty's rather incoherent explanations were to the effect that he had no intention of attacking Koweit, but wished only to egg on its ruler to concede liberal institutions. I asked whether His Majesty really imagined that Iraq could offer herself as an example at present time; I

had repeatedly warned him of impropriety of using his private transmitter set for propaganda . . .

King Ghazi said that . . . he and his Government were seriously concerned over influx of Persians into Koweit, which they regarded as endangering Iraq's communications with us in the event of war. I replied that we could be trusted to look after that ourselves . . .

King expressed great regret and made fullest promises of amendment. Needless to say, none of these is of any value whatsoever.[20]

Time and again Ghazi was cautioned, not only by the ambassador but also by Nuri and other senior Iraqi political figures; they tried to reason with him, pointing out that in 1932 the Iraq-Kuwait frontier had been confirmed by Prime Minister Nuri al-Said himself.[21] In London, in reply to a question in the House of Commons, a government spokesman stated that "urgent representations had been made . . . to secure the cessation of the propaganda against the Ruler [of Kuwait]."[22] The steaming kettle was on Great Britain's front burner. But now Ghazi went beyond mere propaganda; he moved to take charge: "One evening, shortly before his death, when the prime minister [Nuri] was abroad, Ghazi summoned the chief of the general staff and ordered him to arrange for the army immediately to occupy Kuwait. The order threw his entourage into a panic and they summoned the acting prime minister who persuaded the king to abandon the scheme."[23]

Peterson's tour of duty as Ambassador to Iraq was drawing to a close. His protests and admonitions had had no apparent effect on the reckless young monarch. "That King Ghazi must either be controlled or deposed had become obvious," he wrote in his memoirs, "and I hinted as much in a farewell visit which I paid to the Emir Abdul Illah, the present Regent. The solution, had I but known it, lay only a short month ahead. I was sitting in the Condestable Hotel at Burgos [Spain] when an English journalist told me that King Ghazi, driving as usual his own sports car, had dashed himself to death against a telegraph pole . . . German propaganda tried to saddle us with responsibility for his death."[24]

Actually, the circumstances surrounding the death of King

Ghazi have never been fully clarified. In 1939 Capt. Gerald de Gaury was posted to Iraq where, to judge by his revelatory book, *Three Kings in Baghdad,* he developed an intimate familiarity with Iraq's royal family. (De Gaury had been serving as political agent in Kuwait; his career, however, had been in British intelligence.) De Gaury wrote of Ghazi's anti-Kuwait propaganda: "Sir Maurice Peterson was the right man to deal with such bizarre irregularities of behavior, and he succeeded in achieving better results than could have been expected."[25] De Gaury's account does not say what Peterson did to achieve "better results," and Peterson's own memoirs indicate that he had been able to accomplish little or nothing by the time he bade farewell to Prince Abdul Ilah. Peterson writes that he was on holiday in Spain at the time of Ghazi's death, and he seems to have regarded it simply as a providential accident. The local authorities issued a statement that "it has been proved that the crash was purely accidental."[26]

Hanna Batatu, a thoughtful and thorough present-day Arab historian, is not so sure. In his enormously rewarding study, *The Old Social Classes and the Revolutionary Movements of Iraq,* Batatu takes up the story at the end of 1938, when Nuri returned as prime minister after a period out of the country: "Once in the saddle [on December 24, 1938], Nuri turned his attention to the Palace. He had never approved of Ghazi. From the first he thought he was unfitted for the Crown. In 1933 he had talked to the British about changing the law of succession to keep Ghazi away from the throne . . . [Nuri] found himself unable to bring any influence to bear on the young king."[27] Nuri, now prime minister, engaged unsuccessfully in various intrigues to force Ghazi into the background. On March 1, 1939, he told Ambassador Peterson about a plot to depose the king and enthrone Prince Abdul Ilah, and a few days later he made the "plot" public. But Nuri had a well-founded reputation as a schemer, and his discovery of a "plot" was regarded in some quarters as a devious way of enhancing his own position and that of his close political ally, Prince Abdul Ilah. Batatu writes: "The atmosphere created by this episode should help to explain the suspicion of foul play aroused in the minds of Iraqis by the sudden announcement scarcely a month later—on April 4—of the death the night before of Ghazi from injuries sustained in a collision by the car personally driven by him with an electric light pole near a canal culvert close to his palace."[28]

As we have seen, the previous summer Ambassador Peterson had been expressing fears for the king's longevity, but it seems that neither he nor the Foreign Office favored replacing him; on December 31, 1938, Peterson warned London that "the dethronement of Ghazi might split the country in a way which would be inconvenient and dangerous." Nevertheless, Batatu does not entirely rule out the possibility that the British had a "change of heart" in light of the crescendo of anti-Kuwait propaganda in early 1939. They appear to have been speculating once again about a successor shortly before the king's death. Batatu checks off some of the circumstantial evidence suggesting foul play: that two of Ghazi's companions said to have been riding with him had mysteriously vanished after the accident; that the car itself was only very lightly damaged. Batatu offers no judgment. These particulars, he writes cautiously, "do not add up to anything conclusive, but neither do they dissipate the doubts that still surround the incident . . . The lurking suspicion of having masterminded or played roles as accessories to outside influences in the king's death pursued Nuri, Abdul Ilah and Queen Aliyah to the end of their lives."[29]

There is one more odd circumstance not mentioned by Batatu: the index to Colonial Office records in Britain's Public Record Office at Kew lists a file numbered CO 732/85/8 and designated "1939. Death of King Ghazi of Iraq," with the annotation "Wanting," meaning that it cannot be found. A researcher may perhaps be pardoned for wondering what has become of that file.[30]

By all accounts, in any case, it was Ghazi's obsessional posturing over Kuwait that played the most crucial part in his failure to cope with his royal responsibilities. His extravagances make at least one thing clear: an Iraqi does not have to be a radical republican or a Baathist to have designs on Kuwait; Iraq's aspirations with respect to the Gulf have always far transcended domestic politics.[31]

8. The Undemarcated Boundary, 1938–1958

Britain's diligent search in London and in Baghdad for evidence to persuade the Iraqis that Iraq had no legitimate claim to Kuwait had been touched off in April 1938 by an inquiry to British Ambassador Peterson from the Iraqi minister of foreign affairs. In the course of their discussion, Foreign Minister Taufiq Suwaidi had indicated that Iraq was raising the question because it had in mind "extension of the Iraqi railway to Kuwait Bay, in order to provide Iraq with a port on the Persian Gulf."[1]

Suwaidi's demarche proved to have been only an opening shot. Later that year the foreign minister, in a speech before the Iraqi parliament, referred to Kuwait as an inseparable part of Iraq and as Iraq's natural outlet to the sea.[2] In Geneva on September 28, 1938, he handed to R. A. Butler, the British parliamentary under secretary for foreign affairs, an aide-mémoire stating firmly: "The Iraqi Government, as the successor to the Ottoman Government in the Wilayets of Mosul, Baghdad and Basra, considers that Kuwait should properly be incorporated in Iraq. If incorporation should take place, Iraq would agree to maintain the local autonomy of Kuwait."[3]

Foreign Minister Suwaidi's note provided the basis for a vigorous discussion a week later when he called by appointment at the Foreign Office in London. The arguments in C. W. Baxter's letter of June 15, 1938, to the ambassador in Baghdad were trotted out. Shortly after the meeting the British embassy in Iraq presented Iraq with its own *note verbale:* "The Shaikhdom of Kuwait was for a considerable period in an anomalous state of semi-dependence on the Ottoman Empire; His Majesty's Government have nevertheless been in treaty relations with the Shaikhs since 1841, and Kuwait finally became completely independent of Turkey and

114

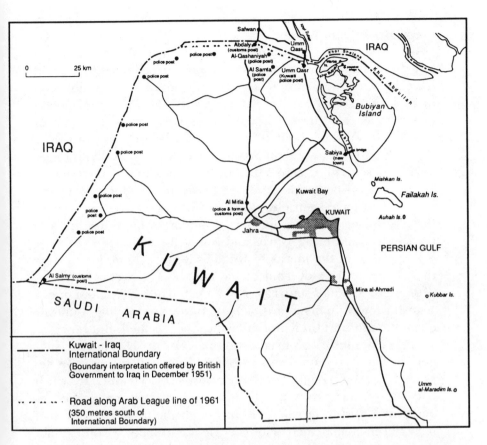

Map 2. Kuwait's boundaries as generally accepted today. Iraq's route to the Gulf from its major port at Umm Qasr is guarded by Warba and Bubiyan islands, which belong to Kuwait. Note the "Arab League" line of 1961; the police post at al-Samita (here "Al Samta"), scene of a 1973 border clash; and the 1982 bridge from the new town of Sabiya to Bubiyan Island.

Kuwaiti nationality finally came into existence on the same date as Iraq and Iraqi nationality."[4]

As the official *Persian Gulf Historical Summary* points out, the "date" referred to was purposely left vague, presumably because specifying any particular date would have been likely to raise more questions than it answered. (The reference to "treaty relations . . . since 1841" also involved a stretch: the 1841 maritime truce agreement between Britain and Shaikh Jabir I lasted only a year; from

1842 to 1899 there were no agreements whatever in effect between Britain and Kuwait.)

Just how serious the Iraqis were at this time about their claim to Kuwait is open to question, but it seems unlikely that they could have expected the British to act upon it. Indeed, the Suwaidi aide-mémoire suggested a somewhat less drastic alternative: the northern frontier of Kuwait should be redrawn along the line of 29°35'N (instead of about 30°N as in the 1932 delimitation). This slight alteration, Suwaidi's note suggested, would make it far easier to control smuggling across the border—an acknowledged matter of concern on both sides.[5] The note did not mention, however, what would have been obvious to anyone who looked at a map: that redrawing Kuwait's northern boundary some thirty miles to the south would bring Warba and Bubiyan into Iraq.

Regardless of the merits of Britain's legal position, it was clear that His Majesty's Government was not about to permit any compromise of Kuwait's status as an "independent" shaikhdom under British protection. The possibility of Iraq's constructing a railway terminus and port on Kuwait Bay must be scotched. But how? Sir John Ward, the British head of the Basrah Port Directorate, suggested that Iraq's ambitions involving Kuwait Bay might be derailed by encouragement of a similar project at Umm Qasr, which had the distinct advantage that it was generally recognized as being inside Iraqi territory, even though the boundary line had never been demarcated. However, it was equally beyond doubt that the islands of Warba and Bubiyan, which guarded the seaward channel from Umm Qasr, belonged to Kuwait. If Britain were to promote the idea of developing Umm Qasr, the question of the frontier line and the islands would have to be faced, because no one was going to be able to convince Iraq to invest in port and rail facilities at Umm Qasr without good assurances that they could be used without interference from any other government. Iraq had already seen enough of that kind of trouble in the Shatt al-Arab.

In October 1938 the British government suggested to Iraq the possibility of building a port near Umm Qasr; it pointed out that the water was deeper there than at Kuwait Bay and dredging costs would be correspondingly lower. Moreover, the proposed site would be closer to the existing Iraqi rail system.[6] Nothing was heard in response from the Iraqi Foreign Ministry for more than a year—a year punctuated by the distractions of King Ghazi's propaganda and demise, civil commotion in Kuwait leading to the creation of the short-lived Legislative Council, several incursions into Kuwaiti territory by Iraqi police, and the resumption of efforts by the authorities in Basra to dispossess Shaikh Ahmad of some of his date garden real estate.

As the British embassy continued to press Prime Minister Nuri al-Said to put a stop to the press and radio campaign being carried out in Iraq against Kuwait, Nuri confided that he had a plan to set matters straight: the government of Iraq would send a messenger to the ruler of Kuwait to smooth things over. To the British this seemed a singularly bad idea. William Houstoun-Boswall, the chargé d'affaires, reported:

> I used all the obvious arguments. I said that it seemed to be quite uncertain what message the messenger was to take. The first idea had been that it would consist of apologies for the palace broadcasts. Later it had been suggested that the messenger would advise the Ruler on the administration of his State, and even offer the services of Iraqi police to keep order for him. Now it seemed that the message would also embrace an appeal from His Majesty [Ghazi] for clemency for those who were responsible for the recent attempt to organise a revolt in Koweit against the ruling family. I enlarged on the absurdity of sending an apology to the sheikh while the King's wireless was still abusing him . . . The second idea, I said, paid no heed to the special treaty relations of Koweit with Great Britain, and was, moreover, quite gratuitously impertinent . . .

Nuri did not pursue the matter, although Houstoun-Boswall expected that he might raise it again, even after Ghazi's death in April.[7]

In November 1939 the new British ambassador, Sir Basil Newton, was summoned to the Foreign Ministry, where he was told that if the Iraqis were to consider building a port and railhead on the Khor Abdullah, they would find it necessary to secure sovereignty over both banks along the route to the open waters of the Gulf. For that purpose it would be necessary to acquire Warba and Bubiyan. Both islands, Newton was informed, "were barren sand and mud banks and were quite valueless to Koweit . . . I reminded him that the reaffirmation of the frontier contained in the [1932] notes exchanged between the Iraqi and Koweiti governments . . . specified quite clearly that the islands . . . belonged to Koweit, and I warned His Excellency that the Iraqi Government could hope for no advantage from any attempt to dispute the validity of the frontier contained in those documents."[8]

This self-described "warning" from the newly appointed British envoy seems to indicate that British diplomats were unwilling to base their position on W. E. Beckett's tortuous analysis of the postwar treaties in his legal memorandum of the previous year. Lacking the "cast-iron" case the Foreign Office had sought, they relied merely on the 1932 letters, plus a thinly concealed threat of trouble.

But it was apparent that the Iraqis were becoming more insistent, and the Foreign Office had a plan to ease the situation. On December 16, 1939, a memorandum was sent over to the India Office suggesting that Kuwait be urged to cede rights in the Khor Abdullah to Iraq in exchange for a payment of money. "It is understandable," wrote the Foreign Office, "that the State which controls the Mesopotamian plain should desire to have undivided control of at least one good means of access to the sea, and Lord Halifax [the foreign secretary] thinks that on a long view it is likely that, if Iraq were given this access, it would make for steadier conditions in that part of the world in years to come."[9] But when the sensible and prophetic thoughts of Lord Halifax reached the Gulf, the political resident, Lt. Col. Charles Geoffrey Prior, objected strenuously on political and strategic grounds. He was backed up by the government of India, the India Office, and eventually even by Ambassador Sir Basil Newton in Baghdad. Shaikh Ahmad himself refused to consider any concession of territory, telling Prior that he would give the Iraqis "nothing at all"; what he wanted from them was to "keep out of Kuwait." In the face of all this opposition the Foreign Office proposal was quietly shelved.[10]

The Need for Demarcation

Demarcation of the frontier between Iraq and Kuwait was long overdue, and not just to control smuggling.[11] In 1934 Shaikh

Ahmad had awarded an oil concession to the Kuwait Oil Company, owned jointly by Anglo-Iranian Oil Company and Gulf Oil Corporation. The concession granted KOC exclusive rights "within the State of Kuwait including all islands and territorial waters appertaining to Kuwait as shown generally on the map annexed hereto," without further description of the area.[12] Oil was discovered at Burgan on February 23, 1938, just a few weeks before the Iraqi foreign minister first officially raised the question about Kuwait's being part of Iraq. As for Iraq itself, in July 1938 the government awarded a concession covering an area corresponding to the old Ottoman vilayet of Basra to Basrah Petroleum Company, another joint enterprise of major oil companies.[13] (Anglo-Iranian, a majority of whose shares were owned by His Majesty's Government, had an interest on both sides.) Accordingly, the location of the boundary was of potential concern not only to the governments directly involved, but also to important and divergent commercial interests backed by their home governments, notably the United States.[14] The time had come for the British to lay the frontier question to rest for good and all, if they could.

Although the boundary between Iraq and Kuwait had been *delimited* (that is, described in words) in 1913, 1923, and 1932, it had never been *demarcated* (that is, laid down on the ground and marked with pillars, monuments, or other permanent structures), and there was nothing in the way of an agreement about how that should be done.[15] Demarcation of international boundaries is a specialized art with a vocabulary all its own. For example, *thalweg* is an old German word meaning "valley path"; as it applies to international waterways it designates the line of maximum depth of the channel used by shipping along the length of the waterway. But how does one measure depth in a turbulent, muddy estuary? For practical reasons the thalweg is often construed to mean the median line between the opposite shores, or alternatively between the opposing sides of the main channel. But from where does one measure, when the shores consist of muddy tidal flats whose contours can fluctuate greatly with tides, the phases of the moon, or even a brisk gale? And who is to determine the ground rules, the procedures, the means of reaching agreement and settling disputes?

The Demarcation Drive Begins

On March 30, 1939 (during its long wait for an Iraqi reply to the suggestion that a port be built near Umm Qasr), the Foreign Office instructed the British chargé d'affaires in Baghdad to see the foreign minister and "urge him strongly to agree to Iraqi cooperation in the early demarcation of the frontier."[16] Houstoun-Boswall reported back:

> I have strongly advised the Prime Minister to consider the possibility of making early arrangements for the demarcation of the Kuwaiti-Iraqi frontier. He received the suggestion without enthusiasm, saying it would not stop smuggling. I observed, however, that a line of beacons would, in my opinion, serve as a useful reminder of a pact, both to the Iraqi police and to intending smugglers. I propose to discuss this matter with him again and more fully.[17]

So far the discussion had centered on smuggling and border incidents, but just beneath the surface was the British determination to deal with the larger Iraqi threat to Kuwait's status as a sovereign state under British protection. The real challenge was to find a way to keep the Iraqis away from Kuwait Bay. For this, the British were willing to offer a little bait.

In May 1940 the Foreign Office advanced a proposal that in return for a commitment by Iraq to agree to demarcation, Britain would agree that the line to be demarcated would be shifted just slightly, "interpreted" in Iraq's favor in the region of Umm Qasr, so as to make it clear that the entire length of the Khor Zubair, including the southernmost section between Umm Qasr creek and Warba Island, would fall on the Iraqi side. Such an adjustment, relatively minor for Kuwait, was considered to be a price worth paying in return for agreement on demarcation. The India Office sent the suggestion to the political resident, who forwarded it to the political agent, who spoke to Shaikh Ahmad.[18] This time word came back that all were agreed that the proposal should be tried on the Iraqis. On October 7, 1940, Ambassador Newton, writing on behalf of the ruler, addressed the prime minister (the perdurable Nuri al-Said) in those terms.

But the ploy did not work. On November 21 the Iraq Foreign

Ministry responded negatively, suggesting that, "due to the inter-connection between the Iraqi-Saudi Arabia boundaries and the Iraq-Kuwait border problems," the demarcation should not be rushed. The British tried again in February 1941, with no better success. They recognized that the Iraqi excuse about the Saudi border was a smokescreen. Iraq was apparently holding out for a bigger prize: the entire islands of Warba and Bubiyan.[19] Nevertheless, Iraq's unwillingness even to negotiate is puzzling. It may simply have reflected the fact that at the time Iraq lacked the resources and determination to build a port at Umm Qasr in any case. Ironically, during World War II the British themselves con-structed a military port facility just south of the Umm Qasr creek and then largely dismantled it once the war was over, at Shaikh Ahmad's request. The abandoned wooden jetty would provide fuel and building material for bedouin tribesmen in the area for years to come.[20]

In early 1945, as the war was drawing to a close, the subject of demarcation resurfaced briefly with a new Iraqi foreign minister, Sayed Arshad al-Umari. C. J. Edmonds, who had been involved with the area on and off ever since his original investigation in 1934, wrote to Umari on March 9, 1945, on the letterhead of the Ministry of the Interior (to which he was still an adviser), pointing out that the Iraq-Kuwait boundary had never been formally de-marcated. For a description of the appropriate line he referred to the letter from the British Ambassador, Sir Basil Newton, to the foreign minister dated October 7, 1940, with its attached "interpretation." He also pointed out that the "authoritative and legal" description of the line was incorporated in the notes ex-changed between the Iraqi prime minister and the British high commissioner in July 1932.

Edmonds told the foreign minister that the text of the 1932 letters "was then communicated to the League of Nations in con-nexion with the entry of Iraq into the said League." This state-ment, as we now know, was simply not true. Was Edmonds com-pounding the Whitehall deception of 1932, or was he himself one of the deceived? We shall never know (Edmonds died in 1979), although the puzzlement portrayed in his 1961 letters to Ulrich Gehrke bespeaks sincerity.

Edmonds' letter to the Iraqi foreign minister continued with a number of specific and detailed suggestions that the demarcation commission, once it was formed, should take into account. In particular, he dwelt at length upon the paragraph of the note attached to Ambassador Newton's letter of October 7, 1940, offering to fix the line so as to allocate the entire Khor Zubair to Iraq, even though that appeared to be an expansive reading of the classic 1913–1923 line that had been "re-affirmed" in 1932. After thus stressing that the generous British offer of 1940 was still on the table, Edmonds then had to restate the hard part:

> It appears from the file that at the time [1940] the Iraqi Government did not consider the proposals on their merits but made excuses for postponing the matter because the Ministry of Defence wished to incorporate the islands of Warba and Bubiyan in Iraq. This was not a valid reason for postponing the demarcation since the original definition of the boundary specifically left these islands in Kuwait and the demarcation of the boundary, or neglect to demarcate, could make no difference to the legal position.[21]

Edmonds stated in closing that he was not suggesting that the demarcation matter should be reopened; he was writing "only to place the relevant facts on record." And in fact the matter lay dormant for another several years. Early in 1950, Shaikh Ahmad was succeeded by his cousin, Abdullah III. On December 18, 1951, having obtained the consent of the new ruler, the British once again invited Iraq to make arrangements for demarcation; Iraq replied six months later, stating with refreshing candor that since Iraq planned to build a port at Umm Qasr, "she wishes to have possession of the island of Warba, before agreeing to the demarcation."[22]

In 1954 the Iraqis themselves came up with a proposal: in return for the transfer of "Warba island and a coastal area of 4 kilometers, south of the present boundary, to Iraq so that the latter could have enough territory to develop Umm Qasr port," Iraq would provide Kuwait with piped fresh water from the Shatt al-Arab. For the next couple of years variations on this theme were developed, including the possibility of a lease of Warba to Iraq, but without concrete result.[23]

In October 1960 Shaikh Abdullah unexpectedly asked the British to raise the boundary question with the Iraqis once again. The Foreign Office welcomed the initiative and prepared to send this message to Ambassador Humphrey Trevelyan in Baghdad: "We should like to give the Ruler all the help and encouragement we can in his new-found enthusiasm for settling Kuwait's frontiers— a welcome change from his dodging on the issue in recent years." But before the cable could be sent, word was received from Kuwait that "the Ruler would prefer Her Majesty's Ambassador to Baghdad to suspend action on his request."[24]

Britain would bow out of Kuwait the following summer, with the termination of all the agreements by which Kuwait and Al Sabah had been protected since 1899. From then on its border problems with Iraq would be Kuwait's very own.

The Last Years of the Iraqi Monarchy

In the years that remained to the Hashemite dynasty in Baghdad, Nuri al-Said assumed more and more the role of absolute dictator. He was deeply committed to maintaining strong links with the Western powers, as much for the sake of his own political survival against internal radical insurgency as for the sake of the anticommunist cause upon which the United States (under Eisenhower and Dulles) and Great Britain (under Eden and Macmillan) were embarked in those early years of the Cold War. In the Middle East the principal manifestation of the "pact-itis" policy of containment of the Soviet Union that will forever be identified with Secretary of State John Foster Dulles was the Baghdad Pact, cobbled together in 1955 with Iraq a willing, nay fervent, charter member. Its membership also included Turkey, Iran, and Pakistan. Nuri had the happy thought of bringing in Kuwait as another member, not only to lend an air of greater Arab involvement in the enterprise, but chiefly with a view to leavening the financial burden imposed on Iraq by its new treaty obligations. By this time Kuwait, having begun to export oil in 1946, was becoming one of the world's leading producers, with revenues to match. Nuri may well have had no more sinister motive than the financial one for seeking to embrace Kuwait in this military alliance. But the wary Shaikh Abdullah rejected the idea out of hand. According to Waldemar J. Gallman, the American ambassador in Baghdad from 1954 to 1958, "The Kuwaitis feared that the Iraqis had ambitions to 'reabsorb' them, and the Iraqis did nothing to dispel these suspicions."[25]

In February 1958, as the end approached for the monarchy, Nuri launched his own miniversion of pact-itis, the so-called Arab Federation. The charter members, and indeed the only members, were the regimes of the Hashemite cousins in Baghdad and Amman. Shaikh Abdullah was invited ceremonially to the Iraqi capital, where he took dinner with King Hussein and King Faisal and was urged to have Kuwait become the third member. Abdullah "not unnaturally fought shy of a formal tie-up," wrote Nuri's biographer.[26] Again the Iraqis' chief interest may have been financial, inasmuch as Iraq was committed to meet 80 percent of the operating expenses of the federation. The British reaction was frosty; they pointed out that Kuwait could hardly be considered eligible for membership in such an alliance so long as it was not fully independent. Nuri flew to London to engage Prime Minister Macmillan and Foreign Secretary Selwyn Lloyd on the matter and returned home to talk to U.S. Ambassador Gallman about enlisting American influence to persuade Britain to relent.[27] Gallman now perceived that Nuri was desperate, willing to concede almost anything to win Kuwait's adherence, including demarcation of the frontier and a guarantee of the shaikh's sovereignty.[28] Nuri's initiative was in vain. The Arab Federation sank without a trace on the morning of July 14, 1958, when Nuri and King Faisal II lost their kingdom and their lives. From now on Kuwait and its rulers were going to have to live with an entirely different kind of regime in Baghdad.

A Look Back

In retrospect it seems very likely that sooner or later Kuwait's independence would have fallen victim to Iraq's aspirations in the Gulf, had it not been for the restraining hand of the British on both sides of the frontier. Independent Iraq had been dealt rather inferior geographic cards. But nothing in the British archives indicates that the 1913/1923/1932 boundary was some clever plot to deprive Iraq of meaningful access to the waters of the Gulf. That boundary had been negotiated at arm's length between Britain and the Ottoman Turks before World War I, albeit as a quid pro quo for Kuwait's status as an Ottoman *qaza*. When Kuwait's ruler asked the British for confirmation of that line in 1923, he got it; and when Iraq was preparing for independence in 1932 it was "re-affirmed" above the signature of Iraq's own prime minister. If during the mandate period and later Britain firmly thwarted any Iraqi move in the direction of Kuwait, it was out of concern to protect and preserve the quasi-independent shaikhdom under its control, not for the purpose of hobbling or penalizing Iraq.

The line the British tried to follow, fairly consistently while their influence remained (that is, until 1958 in Iraq and until 1961 in Kuwait), was to accept what they saw as Iraq's legitimate aspirations as long as those did not unduly impinge on the separate status of Kuwait. They were unable to gratify Iraq's aspirations for better access to the Persian Gulf. The British could never find a formula (and perhaps there was none to be found) that would provide enough maritime flexibility to convince Iraq to agree to demarcation while at the same time coaxing Kuwaiti rulers into a recognition that some concession over the islands was not too great a price to pay for a definitive frontier. In the end British influence was swept away by the "winds of change" detected by Harold Macmillan and by severe financial stringency at home, which combined at long last to precipitate the end of British colonialism in the Persian Gulf. The tensions between Iraq and Kuwait which the British had been able to contain found release after they gave up their protective role in Kuwait in 1961, and then withdrew entirely from the Gulf ten years later.

9. Dress Rehearsal for Desert Storm, 1961

A group of nationalistic Iraqi army officers overthrew the monarchy in a bloody coup on July 14, 1958. Although the new regime promised a "people's republic," a sole leader soon emerged: Abdul Karim Qasim. But when Qasim announced on June 25, 1961, that Kuwait was part of Iraq, he was expressing a view that many Iraqis had held for much of the twentieth century; it had been taught in the schools since independence in 1932.[1] As the veteran British diplomat Sir Anthony Parsons recently put it, "In the Iraqi subconscious, Kuwait is part of Basra province, and the bloody British took it away from them."[2] The British had been prepared to acknowledge in 1913 that Kuwait could be designated as an "autonomous qaza" of the Ottoman Empire in return for Turkish recognition of Britain's role as Kuwait's protector. When World War I came along the 1913 formula fell by the wayside, but once the unratified Anglo-Ottoman Convention was published it gave Iraq an opportunity to claim that it was entitled to what the British had been prepared to offer to its Ottoman predecessors. True (an informed Iraqi nationalist might say), in 1932 the Iraqi prime minister had signed a letter accepting a frontier line that allocated the islands of Warba and Bubiyan to Kuwait; but just look at the circumstances:

1. In 1932 Iraq was still governed by the treaty mandate under the League of Nations, whereby Great Britain had authority to manage Iraq's foreign affairs.
2. Prime Minister Nuri al-Said had been presented by the British with a virtual *fait accompli*, under intense pressure not to

delay or impede Iraq's admission to the League of Nations and its juridical independence.

3. The British, while entrusted with the Iraq mandate, and posing as Iraq's patron and guide through the League's admission process, actually were dealing themselves high cards from a stacked deck, inasmuch as any Iraqi concession on the frontier was of benefit to Britain itself, still in full control of Kuwait as a quasi-colony.

4. Britain had done its level best to keep its maneuverings secret by withholding from the League of Nations the problematical process whereby the boundary had been "established."

5. Britain had encouraged successive Iraqi governments to explore the possibilities of developing Iraq's access to the Persian Gulf, but had never exerted enough pressure on its client, the shaikh of Kuwait, to let realistic planning go forward.

6. Poor King Ghazi, the only Iraqi leader bold enough to stand up to the British and assert Iraq's just rights in Kuwait, had been removed from the scene under suspicious circumstances just when it looked as though his patriotic efforts might begin to pay off.

A litany of grievances such as this might have struck a chord with the volatile Iraqi populace. But there were two important obstacles in the way of any aspiring nationalist who might have chosen to develop and orchestrate this theme: (1) Britain's continuing lock on Kuwait, which was by now a strategic asset not only because of its pivotal location, but also because of its increasing financial importance and its rocketing oil production; and (2) Nuri al-Said, a life-long friend of Great Britain, who knew which side his bread was buttered on. Any serious threat to Kuwait would have been unthinkable from Nuri, and impossible from any other Iraqi while Nuri remained in power.

And then, with almost startling suddenness, both impediments had vanished. Nuri had lost his life on July 14, 1958. And Great Britain, it turned out, was not destined to remain in charge of Kuwait forever.

The Twilight of British Power in the Gulf

In an official cabinet paper back in 1928, Kuwait had been rated after Bahrain and Muscat in importance to British interests in the Persian Gulf. After World War II the rankings shifted radically. By midcentury, 80 percent of United Kingdom petroleum imports were coming from the Gulf area. When exports from Iran were cut off following the nationalization of Anglo-Iranian in 1951, much of the gap was filled from Kuwait. Moreover, Kuwait invested a large part of its oil revenues in Britain, providing important support for the pound sterling. Beyond these purely economic and financial considerations, Britain's commanding position in Gulf affairs was important to its prestige in world politics; it became, as one analyst has observed, Britain's "ticket of admission to the White House."[3] During the final ministry of Sir Winston Churchill (1951–1955), with Anthony Eden at the Foreign Office, this ringing statement of policy was circulated within the government (July 24, 1953):

> During the last three years Kuwait has become of prime importance to the United Kingdom and to the sterling area as a whole. It is now a major source of oil supplies and an important element in our balance of payments. The expenditure of its large sterling revenue unless properly directed is capable of inflicting the most serious damage on the sterling area. Her Majesty's Government can no longer afford to confine themselves to the role authorised by the treaties and agreements in force and sanctioned by usage but must also interest themselves in all matters which affect the interests of the United Kingdom in the widest sense.[4]

These forceful words were followed by action. The post of political agent in Kuwait was upgraded. Instructions went out that on matters of major importance (especially those involving administration, finance, development, and security) the political agent would henceforth report to the Foreign Office, not to the Persian Gulf political resident, as all political agents had done since 1904. "It is of the highest importance," said the Foreign Office directive, "that the policy of the ruler both in internal and external matters should at all times be in harmony with the interests of Her Majesty's Government."[5]

But Great Britain's debacle at Suez in late 1956 put paid to her "moment in the Middle East."[6] After Nasser nationalized the Canal he rode high throughout the Arab world. In the Gulf a heady nationalism began to spread. Before long, internal pressures on Shaikh Abdullah III of Kuwait would force him to loosen the bonds that had tied Al Sabah to the British since the days of his grandfather, Shaikh Mubarak the Great. British officials began to recognize that a major shift in Britain's role would be required. They encouraged the Kuwaitis to get more involved with their neighbors, including Iraq—"to let Kuwait do more of its own dirty work," in the words of the political resident in 1957.[7] And Kuwait's self-confidence surged. Following the coup in Iraq in July 1958, Great Britain offered to station 700 British troops in Kuwait for its own protection; Shaikh Abdullah declined, saying that in all the years since 1899 no Kuwaiti leader had ever permitted a single British soldier to land on Kuwait soil for the purpose of defending the shaikhdom.[8]

But there were still British interests in Kuwait to be protected. In January 1960 Richard Beaumont, head of the Arabian Department at the Foreign Office, sent this message to Political Resident George Middleton: "The irreducible interest of the United Kingdom in Kuwait is that 'Kuwait shall remain an independent state having an oil policy conducted by a government independent of other Middle East producers.'" (At this time the formation of the Organization of Petroleum Exporting Countries (OPEC) was only a few months down the road; Kuwait would become a charter member and would voluntarily reduce its oil "independence" to the extent that it agreed to abide by OPEC production and pricing policies.) Beaumont added: "A corollary of this is that Kuwaiti independence will not be preserved unless any government, which might wish to subvert or overthrow it, is convinced of Her Majesty's Government's willingness and ability to defend Kuwait by force of arms if necessary."[9]

But during 1960 Shaikh Abdullah came to believe that British protection would no longer be required, and negotiations for full independence began. In January 1961 Great Britain formally relinquished control of Kuwait's foreign affairs.[10] On June 19, 1961, Great Britain and Kuwait announced that they were canceling the 1899 Agreement. The announcement stressed that Kuwait had moved a long way toward nationhood; it did not mention that after sixty years the British were wearying of their role as protector. But the new exchange of letters, in a controversial paragraph (d), affirmed "the readiness of Her Majesty's Government to assist the Government of Kuwait if the latter request such assistance."[11] And in fact Her Majesty's Government had not long to wait. Six days later, on June 25, Abdul Karim Qasim declared that Kuwait was part of Iraq. On July 1 the British announced that the ruler had asked for assistance, and a detachment of British troops arrived by air from Kenya the very same day.

A great deal has been written on the question of whether Iraq's 1961 threat to Kuwait was "real." The British government certainly appeared to take it seriously.[12] On June 30 Prime Minister Harold Macmillan cabled Commonwealth leaders: "There are indications that Kassem is preparing to send a substantial force from Baghdad to Basra. From there he could of course, should he decide to do so, invade and seize Kuwait territory in a very few hours . . . It is more than likely that the Ruler will make an appeal to us for help . . . In the nature of the case we may have to act at very short notice."[13] Sure enough, on the very same day, June 30, Abdullah III dispatched a note to John Richmond, the British consul general in Kuwait (his title having changed from political agent on June 19): "In view of the military movements which have been undertaken by the Iraqi Government on the borders of Kuwait and which are such as to threaten the security of Kuwait, I have decided to submit a request to Her Majesty's Government in accordance with the notes which I exchanged with Sir William Luce [the political resident] on June 19, 1961."[14]

Contemporary observers were divided as to whether Qasim intended to back up his claim with force. Iraqi spokesmen denied any such intention and protested vigorously that no Iraqi troop movements had taken place in the vicinity of the Kuwaiti frontier.[15] Sir Humphrey Trevelyan, the British ambassador in Baghdad, made every effort to find out what, if any, military movements were under way; in the end he was unable to dismiss the reports entirely, although he recommended deferring the introduction of British forces until after Iraq had taken the first step.[16] John Daniels, an Arabic-speaking British resident of Kuwait, wrote later: "Some commentators claim that the threat was exaggerated. Nevertheless, I can confirm from personal experience that the situation was viewed seriously by the Kuwaitis themselves."[17]

But there have been skeptics.[18] According to John Bulloch, a veteran British journalist, "There was little doubt that his [Shaikh Abdullah's] 'request' was a formality, and that Britain had pushed him into making it." Moreover, "the pressure came from the War Office, not the Foreign Office . . . There had been no advice from Britain's own representative, John Richmond, saying that military support was needed . . . What appeared to have happened was that the War Office saw a good opportunity to test a new defence concept—fast-moving mobile forces to deal with 'brush-fire wars.'" Bulloch's conclusion is that Britain's Kuwaiti expedition was "contrived."[19]

According to Mustafa M. Alani, the idea of continuing to be able to ask for British assistance was controversial among members of the Kuwait Supreme Council, composed of members of the Al Sabah ruling family. Unable to decide the matter, the Council sent a delegation to call upon Abdullah III, who was at the time summering in the mountains of Lebanon. Having heard both sides of the argument, the shaikh decided that paragraph (d) should be included in the June 19 declaration. Alani makes other useful points:

1. Qasim's claim was not meant as a prelude to a takeover of Kuwait; his main object was "disruption of the new Anglo-Kuwait alliance . . . Qasim's move was directed against the [June 19] agreement, not against the notion of Kuwait's independence."
2. Kuwait's only source of information about the alleged Iraqi military threat was the political agent, John Richmond, whose only information was coming from Ambassador Trevelyan and the embassy staff in Baghdad.
3. "According to a source in the British Political Agency in Kuwait . . . the Foreign Office in London issued instructions to the Agency to work to secure from the Ruler a formal request for British military assistance, and an invitation for British forces to defend Kuwait." Richmond protested; he opposed British military intervention out of conviction, and

he saw no evidence of a direct Iraqi threat. Richmond was not against Britain's assisting if requested, but he objected to procuring the request.

4. Shaikh Abdullah hated asking the British for assistance but in the end decided he had no choice. Afterward he became very depressed and morose, and his son Jabir found him weeping.[20]

Qasim States the Iraqi Case

Qasim's speech on June 25, 1961, had been foreshadowed earlier that year. Rumors were circulating that Great Britain was thinking of bringing Kuwait into the Commonwealth, and Qasim denounced the idea in a statement on April 30.[21] Majid Khadduri relates that Qasim's adviser on Gulf affairs told Khadduri later that Qasim began at that time to ask for information about Iraq's historical connections with Kuwait.[22] By the time the new Anglo-Kuwaiti agreement was announced, he was ready for it. His address to a gathering of journalists in Baghdad made the following points:[23]

1. The 1899 agreement was "forged," "treacherous," and "internationally unrecognized." Qasim wondered how a mere *qaimmaqam* of an Ottoman province could conclude a treaty without the knowledge of the proper authorities. Agha Muhammad Rahim, who had added his signature to the 1899 agreement beside that of Shaikh Mubarak, was "the imperialists' lackey in the Gulf."
2. Observing that Mubarak had been paid 15,000 rupees by the British Residency for signing the forged agreement, Qasim asked, "is there anything other than factors of treason against the legitimate government in Iraq . . . that have bound the esteemed Shaikh of Kuwait to this commitment?"
3. The 1899 agreement was fabricated. The British and the shaikh "hid [it] away from the legitimate authority in Iraq as well as from the Ottoman authority, which, however, soon discovered its falsity." Qasim's distinction here between the "Iraq" authority and the "Ottoman" authority was perhaps meant to suggest that Iraq itself was already a poli-

tical entity during the Ottoman period. (The term *Iraq*, however, was not in general use before World War I except in reference to the ancient civilizations of Mesopotamia.)

4. After the secret 1899 agreement became public, the Ottoman authorities demanded that Shaikh Mubarak reverse his attitude. As a result the shaikh, accompanied by various Ottoman officials, "declared before the crowds in Fao his association with the Governorate of Basra. He said that he was the *qaimmaqam* of Kuwait and pledged loyalty to the Sultan."[24]

5. Qasim related a story of a caravan belonging to the shaikh of Bahrain that was attacked by the Marra tribe near al-Qatif (in present-day Saudi Arabia). Many of the Bahrainis were killed, and their shaikh protested to the British political resident in the Gulf. The resident and the government of India replied that the attack had occurred in Ottoman territory, which fell under the *qaimmaqam* of Kuwait, who was subject to the Basra governorate. "This incident," declared Qasim, "proves that even after the conclusion of the forged and illegitimate agreement the British Government had recognized that the area belonged to the Basra Governorate."

6. In 1897, said Qasim, the British ambassador in Constantinople asked the Foreign Office about the extent of Great Britain's relationships with Kuwait and the Gulf area, and was told on July 1, 1897: "The existence of Kuwait under the rule of the Ottoman Sultan was a fact which could not escape recognition."[25]

7. "Iraq and Kuwait remained one indivisible whole until 1913. Since then the people have been fighting imperialism to get rid of it. But the stooges of imperialism were too many . . . The leaders of the defunct [Hashemite] regime sold out their homeland and country to the British imperialists, and therefore were unable to demand the establishment of one administration to rule both countries."

8. Friendly efforts by Iraq to pipe fresh water to Kuwait had been blocked by the imperialists because they wanted to sell water desalinization equipment to Kuwait.

9. "There exist absolutely no boundaries between Iraq and

Kuwait. If anyone claims that there are boundaries then let
him prove it."

10. As for the recent agreement with Great Britain: "It is the
Iraqi Republic and no one else which signs agreements for
Kuwait."

11. "We will issue a Republican decree appointing the present
esteemed Shaikh of Kuwait as *qaimmaqam* of the district of
Kuwait, who shall come under the authority of the Basra
Province . . . If this Shaikh misbehaves, then he will be
severely punished and regarded as an insurgent."

That was what Prime Minister Abdul Karim Qasim told the
assembled journalists in Baghdad on June 25, 1961. He did not
tell them that an earlier prime minister of Iraq had, on July 21,
1932, signed a letter reaffirming in detail just where the boundary
was, and confirming Kuwait's title to Warba and Bubiyan.

In the Security Council

The Security Council of the United Nations convened in New
York at the request of the United Kingdom at 11:30 A.M. on
Sunday, July 2, 1961, and it met three more times during the
week that followed, to consider the threat to peace and security
posed by Iraq. (Iraq countered with a complaint that the presence
of British troops in Kuwait constituted a threat to Iraq.) Sir Patrick
Dean opened by outlining the new agreement of June 19 between
Britain and Kuwait, the threat to Kuwait contained in Qasim's
address of June 25, and Britain's military response to reported
Iraqi troop movements. He declared that the June 19 exchange
of letters merely recognized a state of affairs that had been in
effect "for some time past" (in fact the shaikh and the political
resident had exchanged letters to that effect just six months earlier)—that Kuwait "possessed entire responsibility for the conduct
of its own international relations." He pointed out that, with the
support of Great Britain, Kuwait had already joined a number of
international organizations as an independent state.[26]

Iraq was represented by Adnan Pachachi, who spoke in English:
"Kuwait is not more than a small coastal town on the Gulf. There
is not and never has been a country or a national entity called

Kuwait, never in history." When the present shaikh's family migrated to Kuwait in the eighteenth century, "their first act was to send their chief to Basra where he paid homage to the Ottoman governor of the province, which included the coastal area in which the town of Kuwait is situated." He compared the 1899 agreement to the situation in the United States if one of its states were to make a secret treaty with a foreign power without reference to Washington. "The secret treaty of 1899," he declared, "has no legal validity whatever." Moreover, in the draft Anglo-Ottoman Convention of 1913 the British had recognized Ottoman sovereignty over Kuwait. In 1922, said Pachachi, Sir Percy Cox tried "to impose on Iraq an arbitrary frontier with Kuwait. He was unsuccessful."[27]

When the debate resumed the following Wednesday, July 5, it was apparent that Pachachi had done some research over the long holiday weekend. He referred to *The Arabian Peninsula,* a book published in 1954 by a U.S. State Department public affairs officer, Richard Sanger, for the stormy proceedings of Kuwait's Legislative Council in 1938, where one faction favored "annexation of the shaikhdom to Iraq," an idea that was summarily vetoed by the ruler with some loss of life and the dissolution of the Legislative Council.[28] Pachachi reiterated that Qasim's recent remarks had constituted no threat; Iraq had made it clear from the very outset that it would use only peaceful means to attain its legitimate national rights. He asserted that the British government had "persisted in fabricating false rumors about alleged Iraqi troop concentrations" and had "ordered the Shaikh of Kuwait to ask for assistance."[29]

Kuwait, since it was not yet a member of the United Nations, needed special permission to attend, which was granted over the objections of Iraq. Its spokesman, Abdul Aziz Hussein, declared that "Kuwait was never under Turkish rule. Furthermore, the Ottoman Government never appointed a representative to Kuwait as it did to other Arab countries." He quoted a 1958 letter from Qasim himself to Shaikh Abdullah, referring to Iraq and Kuwait as "two countries," and he recalled that in 1958 Iraq had requested an exchange of consular representatives. As recently as June 5, 1961, just a month before, the two governments had joined in a statement regarding a trade mission, and he reeled off a list of international organizations of which Iraq and Kuwait were fellow members.[30]

The next day Pachachi pressed Iraq's historical argument further. Bypassing the detailed provisions of the 1913 Anglo-Ottoman Convention whereby the Turks had accepted the status of Kuwait under Britain's influence, he stressed once more that the Convention recognized Kuwait as an "autonomous qaza." But in any case, said Pachachi, the Ottoman Empire at that time "had just come from a disastrous defeat in the Balkan wars and it was under duress that the Sublime Porte was forced to conclude that Treaty," which at all events had never been ratified.[31] With regard to a point made earlier by Sir Patrick Dean, that under Article 16 of the Treaty of Lausanne (1923) Turkey had renounced any claims to former Arab provinces of the empire, Pachachi advanced an interesting lawyer's argument: he compared Article 16 to Article 15, under which Turkey renounced certain territories "in favor of Italy"; in other words, Article 15 called for a transfer of sovereignty from Turkey to another state. As for Article 16, he said, "There is no mention in the Treaty of Lausanne about the transfer of sovereignty over Kuwait, as indeed there could not have been, because Kuwait was part of one of the [Ottoman] sub-districts. That was surrendered by the Ottoman Empire to the Allies of the First World War, and the sub-district of Basra, together with the two sub-districts of Mosul and Baghdad, subsequently became the State of Iraq, and was placed under the mandate of the League of Nations, but the British persisted in separating Kuwait from the sub-district of Basra."[32] (Pachachi had picked up the very point referred to by C. W. Baxter of the Foreign Office in 1938, when he cautioned that "it is [not] on the provisions of Article 16 of the Treaty of Lausanne alone that we should rely" to refute an assertion that Iraq had succeeded to Ottoman suzerainty over Kuwait.)

The British delegate declined to be drawn into Iraq's historical argument. He did point out that only a few weeks earlier, on June 13, the Iraqi delegate to a conference of the International Labor Organization had welcomed Kuwait as a full member of the ILO with "pride" and "warm affection."[33]

The Security Council met once more that week to vote on two resolutions. The first, introduced by Great Britain, called for all states to recognize the independence and territorial integrity of Kuwait; it was vetoed by the Soviet Union on the ground that it did not also call for the withdrawal of British forces from Kuwait. The other, introduced by the United Arab Republic (a short-lived union of Gamal Abdul Nasser's Egypt with the Republic of Syria as a junior partner), called simply for the withdrawal of British troops. Egypt's resolution, supported only by the Soviet Union and Cuba, also failed.[34]

Thus ended for the time being the United Nations' consideration of the Kuwait question. Toward the end of the year the Security Council would meet to consider the application of Kuwait to become a member of the United Nations.[35] In the meantime Arab diplomacy was at work.

The Arab Solution

Even as the Security Council debate was under way, Egypt (technically, the United Arab Republic) took the initiative, its prime objective to bring about the early departure of British troops from Kuwait. The Arab League, with its headquarters in Cairo, was a well-established and internationally recognized regional organization, most of whose energies were perennially directed toward Israel and the Palestine question. But it had inter-Arab purposes as well: "strengthening of the relations between the member states; the coordination of their policies in order to achieve cooperation between them and to safeguard their independence and sovereignty . . ." (Charter of the Arab League, Art. 2). Article 1 of the charter provided that "Any independent Arab State has the right to become a member of the League." So it was hardly surprising that on June 20, 1961, the day after the abrogation of its long-term exclusive agreement with Great Britain, Kuwait submitted to the secretary general of the League its request to become a member.[36] Abdul Khalik Hassouna, a senior Egyptian foreign service officer who served with distinction for many years as the League's secretary general, announced that the Council of the League would meet shortly to consider the application. He said that Kuwait's membership was already supported by Saudi Arabia and Jordan, and that the Council would "undoubtedly" welcome Kuwait as a full member. That was on June 23. Two days later

Qasim announced Iraq's claim to Kuwait. The Arab League Council met on July 4 to consider Kuwait's request and immediately adjourned until July 12. By this time Hassouna had had a chance to do some shuttle diplomacy, and he offered a proposal that he indicated had the support of the Kuwaitis: either Iraq would drop its claim to Kuwait, recognize Kuwait's independence, and register that recognition with the Arab League and the United Nations; or the Arab League would form an Arab force to replace the British forces then in Kuwait. It was clear to all that if Iraq would not agree to the first alternative, Egypt would press for Arab League action on the second one. No decision was taken at that meeting, but on July 20 the Council met again, this time to consider Kuwait's application for membership. Iraq, as was no doubt expected, opposed the application on the ground that Kuwait was not truly an "independent Arab State." During the debate the Iraqi delegation walked out in protest, and the remaining members of the Council voted unanimously to admit Kuwait as a member.[37]

The resolution adopted on July 20, embodying the "Arab Solution," reads as follows:

First: (a) The Government of Kuwait undertakes to request the withdrawal of British forces from Kuwaiti territory as soon as possible.

(b) The Government of the Republic of Iraq undertakes not to use force in the annexation of Kuwait to Iraq.

(c) The Council undertakes to support every wish Kuwait may express for a union or a federation with other countries of the Arab League in accordance with the League's Pact.

Secondly: The Council decides: (a) To welcome the State of Kuwait as a member of the Arab League.

(b) To assist the State of Kuwait in joining the United Nations.

Thirdly: The Arab states undertake to provide effective assistance for the preservation of Kuwait's independence, upon its request, and the Council confers upon the Secretary-General the power to take the necessary measures for the urgent implementation of this resolution.[38]

As soon as the resolution was adopted, Secretary General Abdul Khalik Hassouna set to work. On July 22 he canvassed the membership to find out which countries would participate in the Arab forces to be sent to Kuwait to replace those of the British. Saudi Arabia became the main contributor to the force, with smaller contingents from Egypt, Sudan, and Jordan. On August 12 Shaikh Abdullah of Kuwait and the secretary general signed a status-of-forces agreement. Kuwait, now a member of the League, joined its Joint Defense and Economic Cooperation Treaty, the legal basis for the Arab League Force. At the same time, the ruler formally asked the British to withdraw their troops. The British Foreign Office promptly announced that British troops would be withdrawn as soon as they could be replaced. A Saudi Arabian officer was named head of the Arab League Force. Other documents were signed, including an important agreement establishing a "Financing Fund" whereby Kuwait undertook to pick up the costs of the operation. The Arab troops began to arrive on September 10; they were all in place by October 3. On October 11 the ruler reported to Secretary General Hassouna that the British withdrawal was complete. Over the ensuing year almost all the Arab contingents were withdrawn, leaving only a "military observation corps" of Sudanese troops to keep an eye on the Kuwait-Iraq border.[39]

While they were in Kuwait, representatives of the Arab League forces laid out a temporary boundary line, intended to serve until final demarcation should take place. They built a gravel road about 350 meters (400 yards) along the Kuwait side of the boundary that had been agreed to by Shaikh Abdullah and offered on his behalf by the British to Iraq in December 1951. This is still known as the "Arab League line."[40] It would be interesting to know if the British, while their troops were there from July to October 1961, played a part in fixing the "Arab League line."

The Arab Solution evolved into a very workable compromise. British troops were promptly removed from Kuwait (this having been the major aim of Egypt) and replaced by Arab forces; Kuwait gained recognition and prestige in the Arab world as a full-fledged member of the League; the Arab League itself was strengthened not only as an institution but also through the accession of an eminently solvent new member; the British basked in a flag-showing exercise to restore their Suez-dented pride, and not so incidentally gained practical experience in desert warfare. Qasim himself emerged as the main loser: "The Kuwait affair isolated Qasim from all his Arab neighbors and gained nothing," wrote the historian Phebe Marr. "It was apparent to all that a change must be made. It was merely a question of who would undertake it, and when."[41]

Some observers have been inclined to disparage the role of the Arab League in addressing the 1961 Kuwait crisis.[42] But in fact the Arab League under the leadership of an experienced and professional secretary general played a constructive part in solving what could have developed into a very messy regional conflict. It was in part the 1961 experience that raised hopes in some quarters for an Arab Solution in 1990.

Aside from absorbing the costs of the military operations, Kuwait continued to pay handsomely for the Arab League's assistance in removing the 1961 Iraqi threat. The midsummer crisis had hardly subsided when the Kuwaiti government announced the formation of the Kuwait Fund for Arab Economic Development (KFAED). The "linkage" was only tacitly acknowledged: Kuwait was seen by its Arab neighbors, especially the Egyptians, to be swimming in oil revenues. Kuwait began to get used to the idea of paying cash for its independence. From 1962 to 1989, KFAED laid out more than $5 billion for development projects in other Arab countries; and expenditures out of the State Reserve Fund for more directly political purposes were probably even higher.[43]

Kuwait States Its Own Case

Although the immediate threat to Kuwait had eased, Iraq's claims on the shaikhdom were by no means dead. Both sides set out to restate and elaborate their positions before the world. Kuwait's case was set out in a pamphlet titled *The Kuwaiti-Iraqi Crisis*, issued by its Printing and Publishing Department on August 23, 1961. It contained these main points:

1. Kuwait is geographically a part of the Arabian Peninsula, not of Iraq; it has strong bonds of kinship, character, and customs with the peninsula. Throughout its history Kuwait has been an independent entity.
2. In fact, Kuwait was independent before Iraq was. In 1871

Midhat Pasha, the *wali* (governor) of Baghdad, led an expedition into the Arabian Peninsula to subdue the area, to establish Ottoman garrisons, and to combat European penetration. He sought the assistance of Shaikh Abdullah II (1866–1892) and rewarded him by naming him *qaimmaqam,* which is no more than "an honorific title similar to Effendi, Bey or Pasha, which Ottoman authorities often bestowed on Ottoman subjects and close friends. This title . . . was used only by the Turks. It was never used in Kuwait."

3. Historically, Kuwait was frequently a haven for political dissidents from Ottoman rule. This could not have happened if Kuwait had itself been part of the Ottoman Empire.

4. "In 1899 [Kuwait] concluded a treaty with the British, a fact which in itself is evidence that Kuwait constituted, then, an independent legal entity."

5. "The Ottomans were conquerors, and like all conquerors often changed the frontiers in our countries . . . Do such arbitrary changes constitute a justification to attack a country, subdue it, and destroy its independence?" (Of course Qasim had not actually done any of these things, despite his fierce rhetoric.)

6. In support of his claim, Qasim has argued that Iraq rendered postal services to Kuwait from 1921 to 1941. It is only usual for small countries to receive such services from neighboring countries. Kuwait postal services were handled by India from 1879 until World War I. During that war Iraq came under British military administration, which was replaced by civil administration in 1921. "Iraq postal stamps were never used in Kuwait. The ordinary stamps of the Government of India with 'Kuwait' superprinted on them were in use." India had resumed responsibility for Kuwait's postal services in 1941, on the recommendation of the International Office of the World Postal Union. Kuwait had been running its own postal services since February 1, 1959.[44]

An appendix to the Kuwaiti government's pamphlet presented documents to show that the Iraqi regime then in power had recognized Kuwait as an independent country and a separate political entity. The dossier was impressive:

a letter from Qasim himself to Shaikh Abdullah on October 5, 1958, referring to him as "Amir" and "Your Highness"

a letter from the Iraqi Foreign Ministry on December 29, 1958, proposing that Iraq open a consulate in Kuwait to "serve as a liaison between the two sister countries"

a speech on behalf of the Iraqi delegation to a conference of Arab Chambers of Commerce held in Kuwait on October 14, 1959, conveying a message in Qasim's name which refers to Kuwait as a "sister country" and a "genuine Arab country"

a letter from Iraqi Minister of Foreign Affairs Hashim Jawad to the head of Kuwait's Department of Finance, referring to "cooperation between our two countries"

a follow-up letter from the Iraqi Foreign Ministry on October 19, 1960, referring to "the Governments of Iraq and Kuwait"

a letter from Iraq's minister of oil, on the stationery of the recently formed Organization of Petroleum Exporting Countries, October 16, 1960, addressed to Kuwait along with Iran, Saudi Arabia, and Venezuela as "the Governments concerned" in establishing OPEC

a note from the Legal Division of Iraq's Foreign Ministry, February 25, 1961, informing Kuwait that Iraq will recognize judicial documents of Kuwait's Department of Justice

a letter from Foreign Minister Jawad to Shaikh Abdullah on March 5, 1961, referring to Kuwait repeatedly as a "sister country" or "sister state"

Also included were a photograph of a site plan displayed on a signboard erected for the inauguration on March 26, 1961, of Iraq's Umm Qasr port development project, showing a line just south of the site labeled "Iraqi-Kuwaiti Frontier";[45] and a map of Kuwait prepared for use in Iraqi schools, taken from an atlas published with the cooperation of several prominent Iraqi educators, showing Kuwait's "international frontier" corresponding to the 1913/1923/1932 line.

The Kuwaiti pamphlet then listed the various international organizations of which Kuwait and Iraq were fellow members, including the World Health Organization, Food and Agriculture Organization, UNESCO, and so on, together with Kuwait's dates of admission from 1959 to 1961. "Kuwait had already, even before the official termination of the protectorate, entered the field of international activities . . . The Government of Iraq, through its delegates, supported Kuwaiti requests to join international organizations."

Finally, in a section headed "Accusations," the pamphlet rejected specific allegations by Qasim:

> Qasim had accused Shaikh Mubarak of having been a British agent during World War I, on the basis of a "message . . . written by the British Counsul [*sic*] to the Shaikh of Kuwait." (The reference is perhaps to the letter to Shaikh Mubarak from Political Resident Sir Percy Cox on November 3, 1914.)
>
> Qasim had described the new agreement between Kuwait and Britain as "one of the intrigues of imperialism," which made Kuwait "a bridgehead of imperialism." The Kuwaiti pamphlet countered by stating that during the Suez campaign (1956) Kuwait had warned Britain that no part of Kuwait could be used for military operations; and that at the time of the Iraq revolution (July 14, 1958), when American troops were landed in Lebanon and British troops in Jordan, "not one single British soldier landed on Kuwait soil because the Government of Kuwait would not permit it."

Kuwait Tries to Join the United Nations

On June 30, 1961, the same day Shaikh Abdullah asked for British assistance to head off the Iraqi threat, Kuwait sent a message to the secretary general of the United Nations asking to be considered for membership.[46] For some reason, perhaps not unrelated to the evolution of Arab diplomacy and the establishment of KFAED over the summer, nothing was done about the application for more than four months. Then, on November 19, Egypt requested a meeting of the Security Council to consider it.[47] When the Security Council convened on November 30, Iraq was still opposed. Once more its spokesman was Adnan Pachachi, this time armed with the most comprehensive brief so far to argue that Kuwait was not entitled to membership. The outcome of the debate was never in doubt, because the Soviet delegate made clear from the outset that the USSR would oppose the application, and would kill it by veto if necessary. Nevertheless, the proceedings are enlightening because they reflect the full extent of the Iraqi historic claim to Kuwait up to that point.

First it was up to the Egyptian delegate, Umar Lutfi, to make the case for membership. He rattled off statistics to show that Kuwait was one of the world's leading oil-producing states, and elaborated on the commendable way oil revenues were being applied to economic and social development. He pointed out that an electoral law had recently been promulgated for the establishment of a constituent assembly, which would be elected in December 1961 to draft a constitution. British troops had already been withdrawn. After recalling the abrogation of the 1899 treaty with Britain earlier that year, Lutfi stated that sixty-two members of the United Nations, a majority, had recognized Kuwait as independent and sovereign. Kuwait was already a member of the Arab League and a wide array of other international organizations.[48]

Lutfi was warmly supported by Sir Patrick Dean of the United Kingdom, who declared that Kuwait's "blessings of nature have been matched by the wisdom and statesmanship of successive rulers and their governments, so much so that Kuwait today is an example of enlightened rule and social progress."[49] Now it was Iraq's turn.

Pachachi's submission had three parts: first, that Kuwait possessed none of the prerequisites of statehood; second, Kuwait had always been considered as an integral part of Iraq; and third, Kuwait was still for all practical purposes a British colony.

On the first count, he described the territory controlled by Al Sabah as "rather featureless and barren country, a desert surrounding a small coastal town . . . which is the only center of population controlled by the Shaikh." Kuwait, he declared, "is a small town outside the confines of which there exists no settled population but only roaming nomads, and yet we are asked to admit this overgrown village to membership of the United Nations."[50] It was almost as though Pachachi and Dean were describing two entirely different countries—and perhaps, after all, from their divergent standpoints they were.

Turning to the second point, the Iraqi delegate stated that "from time immemorial the territory . . . has been a part of the southernmost area of Mesopotamia . . . Under the early Arab

Islamic Caliphate it formed the southern part of the province which the Arabs called Al-Iraq." The center of that province was the ancient city of Basra. Kuwait's inhabitants "naturally looked towards Basra, barely seventy miles to the north." The Sabah family, he said, originally came from Umm Qasr in Iraq, thirty-five miles west of Basra.[51]

When the British first appeared in the Persian Gulf, the city of Basra and the areas around it, including Kuwait, formed the Ottoman province or vilayet of Basra. The British government never questioned Ottoman sovereignty over the vilayet. Until quite recently, Pachachi continued, Britain's policy in the Gulf had been dictated by protection of its communications with India. Since the decaying Ottoman Empire itself had presented no serious threat, British policy during most of the nineteenth century had been to shore up its territorial integrity against encroachment by other European powers. Later, with the evolution of Germany as a world power, Britain's policy had changed; it had begun to work through the government of India to undermine Ottoman authority in the Persian Gulf area. In Kuwait, an opportunity had been presented in 1896 when Shaikh Mubarak, having usurped power by murdering his two elder brothers, feared vengeance and appealed to Great Britain for protection.[52]

Pachachi then dealt at length with the 1899 agreement, explaining that "the entire British case is based upon it . . . It is in accordance with this treaty that Britain claimed for itself the rights and privileges of a protecting Power. It was by virtue of this treaty that Britain made the claim that Kuwait was a distinct entity in order to justify its separation from Iraq." The shaikh of Kuwait had had no right to enter into any commitment with a foreign government. He was an administrative official of the Ottoman Empire, a *qaimmaqam,* "and he himself acknowledged at all times that he was a subject of the Ottoman Sultan and an official in his service."[53] Moreover, this had not been a valid protectorate treaty, because Kuwait was not a State, and "protection is a relationship between two States." There had been an Ottoman garrison in Kuwait (Pachachi neglected to mention that the outpost had been on Bubiyan Island, not in Kuwait town, as he implied). The Ottoman flag had flown over the town until the British took it down after the start of World War I. Mubarak had tried to conceal the treaty and had continued to acknowledge that he was under the jurisdiction of the governor of Basra; he had visited the governor many times and each time declared his allegiance.[54]

Pachachi read out (not entirely accurately) the first part of the March 21, 1902, memorandum from Foreign Secretary Lord Lansdowne to the British ambassador in Constantinople. Pachachi said, "I have rarely seen a more cynical and sordid communication by a Government which prides itself on being one of the most civilized in the world." He quoted Article 1 of the draft 1913 Convention, whereby Britain recognized Kuwait as an autonomous *qaza* of the Ottoman Empire. He ignored all the rest of the 1913 Convention, including the parts that constituted the quid pro quo for that recognition.[55]

As for the postwar period:

At the Paris Peace Conference in 1919 where the Covenant of the League of Nations was drafted, it was decided, in accordance with article 22 of the Covenant, to place under mandate the territories in the Near East which formerly belonged to the Ottoman Empire. Thus, it was decided to place under British Mandate the former Ottoman provinces of Baghdad, Mosul and Basra which were unified into one State, the State of Iraq. However, the final disposition of the former Turkish territories was made by the treaty of peace with Turkey, signed at Lausanne on 24 July 1923, in which Turkey ceded all the territories which were outside the frontiers fixed for what is now the Turkish Republic . . .

[I]t would be naturally assumed that Kuwait, like other parts of the Basra province, would be placed under the mandatory regime . . . However, Britain exploited its military occupation of the country and its control of its destiny to detach Kuwait unilaterally and illegally . . .

By a memorandum dated 19 April 1923, the British High Commissioner for Iraq informed the Shaikh of Kuwait that his territory, the territory of Kuwait, was being detached from the rest of the Basra province and that its frontiers were delimited in accordance with the delimitation agreed upon in the Anglo-Turkish Convention of 1913. [Pachachi's characterization of the Cox-More Memorandum differs in important respects from the memorandum itself; for one thing, Cox had made no mention whatever of Basra.]

In acting in this way, the British High Commissioner violated in a most flagrant and outrageous manner the mandate which his government had accepted as a sacred trust of civilization. The terms of the mandate expressly prohibited the ceding of any territory which was placed under mandate.

Pachachi concluded this admittedly "somewhat lengthy juridical analysis" by stating that "the Iraqi people . . . never recognized the frontiers illegally delimited by the British High Commissioner in 1923." But he made no reference to the 1932 letter, in which the Iraqi prime minister's signature was affixed to a proposal that precisely those frontiers should be adopted.[56]

The third leg of Pachachi's argument was that Kuwait was ineligible because it was still "for all practical purposes . . . a British colony," despite the exchange of notes between the shaikh and the British political resident on June 19, 1961.[57] "The exchange of notes is not resorted to in international relations except for agreements on matters of secondary importance . . . [T]he true aim of the agreement . . . is to continue British control for the purpose of protecting British interests in Kuwait." This was shown in particular by paragraph (d). "Can there be any doubt that the British assistance pledged under this paragraph will be given only in return for considerations directly concerning existing British interests in Kuwait?" he demanded rhetorically. "The British created an artificial crisis [in July] and then ordered the Shaikh to ask for their military intervention. They falsely alleged that the Iraqi troops were massed to invade Kuwait . . . [but] at no time was there the slightest military threat from Iraq." Pachachi ended his address by saying that the real motive behind Britain's policy in Kuwait and the Gulf was "oil and nothing but oil" and asking whether the world could "tolerate the continuance of such an unholy alliance between feudalism and colonialism." Nowhere did he mention the speech by his leader, Abdul Karim Qasim, to the journalists assembled in Baghdad on June 25, which had ignited the whole crisis.[58]

But Adnan Pachachi, thorough and eloquent as he was, was speaking for the most part only for the record. The Soviet delegate expounded at some length on the subject of oil imperialism and capitalist colonialism, and suggested that it was time for lunch. At the afternoon session Britain again chose not to challenge

Pachachi's historical brief. The resolution calling for Kuwait's admission was vetoed by the Soviet Union. Kuwait had failed in its first attempt to become a member of the United Nations.[59]

In December 1961 Abdul Karim Qasim asserted his claims once again, prompting another British military alert in the Gulf and a formal protest by Kuwait to the secretary general of the UN.[60] Iraq thereupon announced that it would have to reexamine its attitude about maintaining diplomatic relations with countries that had recognized Kuwait's independence. Iraqi ambassadors were withdrawn from relevant capitals all over the world.[61]

The crisis of 1961 was followed by major steps toward representative government in Kuwait. Stung by Qasim's threats to the shaikhdom's integrity, Shaikh Abdullah sought to add legitimacy to Kuwait's status as an independent sovereign state. In December 1961 a Constituent Assembly was formed to draft a constitution, and the new constitution was signed by the ruler in November 1962. In January 1963 a National Assembly was elected, the first body of that kind in Kuwait since the short-lived Legislative Council of 1938.[62]

10. Reconciliation, Encroachment, and the First Gulf War, 1963–1988

Qasim's government was overthrown in another coup on February 8, 1963. The new Baathist regime under President Abd al-Salam Aref was recognized immediately by the ruler of Kuwait, who sent his hearty congratulations to the new Iraqi leader.[1] Even so, it took the new regime a little while to sort out its policy toward Kuwait. Aref's first public statement on the subject, in response to a reporter's question, was a bit Delphic: "The Kuwait affair is a purely Arab question. It concerns only the Arabs. Besides, there is only one Arab nation, not several."[2] Nevertheless, Kuwait apparently felt secure enough after the removal of Qasim that on February 12 it requested the Arab League to remove the remaining forces that had replaced the British in the summer of 1961. The last contingent of Sudanese border observers departed on February 19. Iraq, which had been refusing to participate in Arab League affairs, indicated that it was now prepared to resume active membership. When the Arab League Council met on March 23, 1963, all its members were represented for the first time in almost two years.[3]

Kuwait became the 111th member of the United Nations by acclamation of the General Assembly on May 14, 1963, its application having been endorsed by the Security Council a week earlier after only a brief debate. Iraq tried halfheartedly to delay action by the Security Council, Adnan Pachachi stating that Iraq's claims to Kuwait had not been abandoned. This time there was no Soviet veto.[4] Even before the UN action, there were signs that relations between Iraq and Kuwait were on the mend. On April 9 the government of Kuwait announced to its parliament that its June 19, 1961, agreement with Great Britain (which had provided the basis for British military intervention) was under review; the

149

statement referred to Arab unity as an "historical eventuality."[5] On June 2 a British newspaper reported (reliably, as it turned out) that a deal was in the works: Iraq would recognize Kuwait's independence in return for revocation of the 1961 agreement between Kuwait and Britain, along with a financial contribution by Kuwait to Iraq's economic development.[6]

And indeed relations between Iraq and Kuwait warmed during the summer of 1963. In September the Kuwait National Assembly approved a 30 million dinar loan for Iraq.[7] Negotiations ensued in Beirut and elsewhere, culminating in a formal delegation from Kuwait to Baghdad in October, headed by Shaikh Sabah al-Salim al-Sabah, heir apparent and prime minister. On October 4, 1963, in the Iraqi capital, he and the prime minister of Iraq, Maj. Gen. Ahmad Hassan al-Bakr, put their names to a formal document which, on its face, seemed to put an end forever to Iraq's claims. It would have been difficult to draft an agreement of greater apparent sincerity. The "Agreed Minutes between the State of Kuwait and the Republic of Iraq Regarding the Restoration of Friendly Relations, Recognition and Related Matters" commences by reciting "the desire felt by both parties to eliminate all that blemishes the relations between both countries"; it speaks glowingly of "an atmosphere rich in fraternal amity, tenacity to the Arab bond and consciousness of the close ties of neighborliness and mutual interests"; it rejects "the attitude of the past Qasim regime towards Kuwait before the dawn of the blessed revolution of the 14th of Ramadan [February 8, 1963]." Then come the operative provisions, starting with a covert but very specific reference to a thirty-one-year-old transaction:

> The Republic of Iraq recognizes the independence and complete sovereignty of the State of Kuwait with its boundaries as specified in the letter of the Prime Minister of Iraq dated 21.7.1932 and which was accepted by the ruler of Kuwait in his letter dated 10.8.1932.[8]

If that sentence means anything, it means that on October 4, 1963, Iraq's prime minister renounced Iraq's historic claims to Warba and Bubiyan. On the face of the agreement itself, Kuwait promised very little of substance in return for this extraordinary concession: nothing more than a rather weasel-worded reference to the statement delivered earlier that year by the government of Kuwait to the National Assembly, "embodying the desire of Kuwait to work for the termination, in due time, of the Agreement concluded with the United Kingdom." The document does not specify *which* agreement with the United Kingdom, although from the context it can mean only the letter exchange of June 19, 1961, the one that had stirred Qasim to assert his claims.

The Baghdad Agreed Minutes of October 4, 1963, raise important points.

First, the Kuwaiti delegation, if it had done its homework, should have been thoroughly familiar with the difficulties suffered by Kuwait over many years because of the consistent refusal of successive Iraqi governments to agree to the demarcation of the frontier. This was Kuwait's Achilles' heel, and, as we shall see, it was to remain so, even to the present day. How did the Kuwaitis miss the opportunity to insert a provision calling for binding demarcation?[9]

Second, why is there is no provision for ratification of the Agreed Minutes by the two governments? We will come back to this question later.

Third, the most obvious omission from the Agreed Minutes, although this was probably to be expected, is the price Kuwait paid for Iraq's concessions. Within a week of the signing, Iraqi Prime Minister Ahmad Hassan al-Bakr paid a return visit to Kuwait. On October 12 Kuwait announced that it was extending to Iraq an interest-free loan of 30 million Kuwaiti dinars, repayable over twenty-five years, in return for unrestricted access to fresh water from Iraqi territory.[10] At the going rate of exchange, this came to about $85 million, a significant sum in 1963.[11] The link between the October 4 agreement and the October 12 loan to the Iraqi government has never been acknowledged officially by either side, but all the circumstantial evidence, as well as accounts by contemporary observers, attest that this substantial purse was indeed a meaningful consideration for what Kuwait thought it received from Iraq. The common-law concept of "consideration" does not, it is true, have application to international law doctrines relating to the validity of treaties;[12] even so, Kuwait might have been entitled to hope that the payment had sealed a bargain that the Iraqis would honor.

The Agreed Minutes Go to the United Nations

Kuwait, at all events, took its new agreement seriously. Its state radio proclaimed: "Yesterday's agreement . . . will immortalize the date 4th October in the history of the two fraternal countries."[13] On January 10, 1964, the Arabic-language text of the Agreed Minutes, with English and French translations, was deposited by the government of Kuwait with the Treaty Section of the United Nations in New York.[14]

Notice of the registration duly appeared on page 11 of the UN's monthly publication, *Statement of Treaties and International Agreements Registered or Filed and Recorded with the Secretariat* for January 1964, with the notation: "Came into force on 4 October 1963 on signature." Had the parties agreed that no formal ratification would be required?

According to officials at the United Nations Secretariat, the UN's authority for including this annotation was a "Statement" furnished by Kuwait, dated December 4, 1963, in which the Kuwaiti minister of foreign affairs certified that "the agreement contained in the 'Agreed Minutes' signed between the State of Kuwait and the Republic of Iraq on 4th October, 1963, has come into force on the date of its signature and by signature only; no other subsequent measures being needed." Under UN practices, such statements can be introduced unilaterally by the registering party (in this case Kuwait); the UN assumes no responsibility for checking them with the other party or parties to the document being registered. It would be interesting to know whether Kuwait conferred with the Iraqis before submitting its foreign minister's statement, or whether the statement came as news to them after the fact. But in either case Iraq was very shortly on notice of it, because the monthly *Statement of Treaties* is forwarded to all governments concerned. Even if, through a misunderstanding or otherwise, Iraq had not agreed that the agreement was to come into effect on signature, there was plenty of time to take corrective action before the publication in 1965 of the permanently bound Volume 485 of the *United Nations Treaty Series*, where the same annotation appears with the full text of the Agreed Minutes in English and French translation (but not with the original Arabic).

Nothing along these lines has ever been received at the United Nations Secretariat.[15] Even after Saddam Hussein's war of 1990–91, however, Iraq would continue to insist that the 1963 Agreed Minutes do not bind Iraq because Iraq never ratified them.

Implementing the Agreed Minutes

In the 1963 Agreed Minutes Iraq recognized two separate things. The first of these was Kuwait's "independence and complete sovereignty." This part of Iraq's declaration was duly implemented. Diplomatic relations were established; ambassadors were exchanged in short order. Over the next few years the two governments entered into an array of different agreements; water to Kuwait from the Shatt al-Arab (February 11, 1964); KFAED loan for a paper mill at Basra (1966); another loan, this one for the Samarra barrage (a flood-control project, 1967); establishment of an industrial cooperation committee to consider iron and steel, sulfur, and petrochemicals (1968); and so on. Perhaps the most comprehensive of these arrangements was the Iraq-Kuwait Agreement on Economic Cooperation and Protocol on Investment, signed on October 25, 1964. Aside from its substantive content (among other things, elimination of most customs duties), this agreement provides an early example of Iraq's unequivocal recognition of Kuwait as a sovereign state, the parties being referred to as "the Republic of Iraq" and "the State of Kuwait."[16]

Iraq also agreed to steps implementing the other part of the Iraqi commitment, recognition of the 1913/1923/1932 boundary. In June 1966 an agreement to set up a joint boundary demarcation commission was announced, although the commission did not actually get down to work until October 1967. The commission met for four days and issued a joint statement that technical teams from both sides would have freedom of movement throughout the border area to gather information.[17] The work was again suspended, then resumed in February 1970. No further progress was made after that, and it became increasingly clear as time went on that Iraq was in no hurry to fix the line on the basis their prime minister had agreed to in October 1963.

What was going on? It is fortunate that Majid Khadduri was

able to interview many of the principal actors on both sides while memories were still fresh. In *Socialist Iraq* (1978) he writes:

> Iraq's recognition of Kuwait as an independent state in 1963, though originally intended to disclaim Qasim's territorial demands, was later construed not to imply acceptance of existing borders . . . From 1964 to 1967, when a joint commission composed of Iraqi and Kuwaiti delegates met to discuss ways and means of delimitation, it often found itself engaged not in a discussion on delimitation but on the legality of the frontier agreements. When the Iraqi delegates were reminded that they met to discuss the implementation and not the validity of the agreements, the Iraqi delegates replied that they were not empowered to accept the validity of the agreements.[18]

Once again, demarcation of the Iraq-Kuwait frontier was going to have to wait.

The Vulnerable Boundary

In April 1969 Iraq asked Kuwait to permit the stationing of Iraqi troops on Kuwaiti territory to protect the newly built port of Umm Qasr from possible Iranian attack. Under great pressure from two visiting Iraqi cabinet members, Kuwaiti Minister of Defense Shaikh Sa'd al-Sabah consented, entering into what came to be called the "unwritten agreement," whereby Iraq was allowed to station troops within a specified area of about two square kilometers adjoining the border south of Umm Qasr. In fact Iraqi troops had begun to cross the border even before the cabinet-level discussion. Shaikh Sa'd told Majid Khadduri later that his "tacit approval was considered as an agreement by the Iraqi Ministers."[19]

The Iraqi military forces remained. In December 1972 an Iraqi construction crew under armed escort began to build a road in Kuwait territory.[20] In March 1973 Iraq presented Kuwait with a draft treaty that would give Iraq extensive rights, including oil export facilities. Kuwait rejected it "virtually on sight."[21] The Iraqis reacted by reinforcing their garrison; they erected an installation at al-Samita, where a contingent of Kuwaiti soldiers was already stationed. When, on March 20, 1973, the Kuwaitis attempted to stop the work, they were warned by the Iraqi commander to withdraw; the Kuwaitis balked, and Iraqi troops opened fire. Two Kuwaitis and one Iraqi soldier were killed in the affray.

Two days later Kuwait lodged a protest with the Iraqi government, demanding that its forces withdraw behind the frontier. Iraq retorted that the boundary had never been formally fixed. Kuwait promptly referred the matter to other Arab League states for mediation. In April 1973 the secretary general of the Arab League, accompanied by representatives of Saudi Arabia and Syria, visited Baghdad and Kuwait, procuring Iraq's agreement to withdraw its troops from al-Samita. At the same time, though, Iraq declared that the frontier dispute was a matter to be settled between the two states and was of no concern to others.[22]

The al-Samita border incident of March 1973 has attracted less attention than the Qasim affair in 1961, partly because it came and went so quickly, and also because it involved no troop movements by third parties. Nevertheless, it was a significant episode for a number of reasons.

First of all, this was an important test of Kuwait's ability to resist Iraqi encroachment without British assistance. When the 1899 treaty was canceled in 1961, the British had nevertheless indicated their "readiness . . . to assist the Government of Kuwait if the latter request such assistance." This commitment was to "continue in force until either party gives the other at least three years' notice of their intention to terminate it." Seven years later, on May 13, 1968, Kuwait gave notice. (Kuwait's intention to "work for the termination, in due time" of the 1961 agreement had already been expressed in the Agreed Minutes signed by Iraq and Kuwait on October 4, 1963.) In another exchange of letters between the Kuwaiti minister of foreign affairs and the British ambassador to Kuwait, Kuwait declared that "since Kuwait has achieved success in her international relationships, the obligations arising from the [1961] Agreement . . . were no longer appropriate." Accordingly, Kuwait requested that, subject to the three-year minimum notice, the 1961 agreement cease to have effect. On May 13, 1971, therefore, Great Britain finally ended its historic role as Kuwait's protector.[23] It was truly the end of an era. Iraq's assertiveness at al-Samita less than two years later confirmed that

Britain's withdrawal had not escaped the attention of the Iraqi government.

Second, the 1973 border incident brought to light the "unwritten agreement" whereby Iraqi troops had actually been stationed inside Kuwait since 1969 with the reluctant and passive consent of the government of Kuwait. The "unwritten agreement" was the first successful attempt by Iraq to whittle away at the 1913/1923/1932 boundary created by the British and preserved by them through two world wars and almost sixty years of turbulence in the Middle East.

Third, as in 1961, and no doubt with that earlier crisis in mind, the 1973 border episode ended with an "Arab solution," solidifying the earlier precedent and perhaps lending plausibility to the idea of another "Arab solution" when Saddam Hussein made his move in August 1990.

The Aftermath of Samita

In response to the mediation of the secretary general of the Arab League and his team, the Iraqi troops withdrew from Kuwait—nineteen trucks of them—late on April 5, 1973. But in announcing its withdrawal, Iraq made it clear that the border issue was not dead. The Iraqi foreign minister, Murtada Said Abdul Baki, was quoted in the press as saying that the condition for withdrawal was the cession to Iraq of Warba and Bubiyan. "We could have occupied the area and then told the Kuwaitis to negotiate," he declared, "but we do not contemplate such measures against Kuwait."[24] On April 28 Iraq addressed a formal note to Kuwait, proposing discussion of the frontier dispute on the basis of previous correspondence between the two governments. Perhaps ominously, Iraq referred to this correspondence as "indications," not as "agreements." In its reply on May 5, Kuwait agreed to negotiate but emphasized that it was talking about binding international agreements, and not just "indications."

Kuwait's note drew a brusque rejoinder on May 17: Iraq rejected the validity of the documents that the Kuwaitis called "agreements" on the ground that they had never been ratified in accordance with Iraq's constitutional requirements. Moreover, according to Majid Khadduri, the Iraqi note stated that "Kuwait should bear in mind the radical change of circumstances—Iraq's rise to full international status and the elimination of foreign influence—and the Arab national goals to which the Ba'th and the Iraqi people have committed themselves." Since Kuwait persisted in regarding the frontier agreements as binding, the note went on, Iraq proposed to postpone further negotiations until circumstances were more auspicious.[25]

This Iraqi note of May 17, 1973, seems to have been the first formal notice to Kuwait of Iraq's position that previous frontier agreements were invalid because they had not been properly ratified. The documents to which the Iraqis referred obviously included the 1963 Agreed Minutes, which had been signed by their prime minister with full ceremony and under the glare of international publicity; this very document had been published by the United Nations with the annotation "Came into force by signature," and Iraq had been on notice of that fact for almost a decade.

But in denying the validity of the 1963 Agreed Minutes, Iraq was being rather selective. In signing that document Iraq had recognized two separate things: the sovereignty and independence of the State of Kuwait, and the boundaries as set forth in 1932. With regard to the former, Iraq had accepted, repeatedly and in many different contexts, the fact that Kuwait was a separate, independent, sovereign state. Qasim's 1961 claim that Kuwait was part of Iraq had been repudiated and condemned. Saddam Hussein himself, just then emerging as Iraq's strongman leader, told a group of Arab and foreign journalists on April 8, 1974, a year after al-Samita: "The sons of the people of Kuwait are our brothers . . . There was a problem related to the demarcation of borders. Iraq had not given an opinion on this question of accepting the demarcation of the borders for many reasons. We later informed our Kuwaiti brothers of our agreement to demarcate the borders . . . We are earnestly working towards resolving this issue in accordance with the interests of Iraq and Kuwait *as two states* [emphasis added]."[26]

It would seem that all that Iraq regretted—and in this at least they have been very consistent—was that Iraq's prime minister had put his name to a public document that unmistakably, if only indirectly, described the border as leaving the islands of Warba and Bubiyan to Kuwait. From now on it would become clearer than ever that Iraq would not willingly concede that it had released its claims to the islands; nor would it agree to any demarcation in the absence of some satisfaction of those claims.

But now Iraq moved into a period of relative stability. In 1975 a war in the north against the Kurds ground to a sullen halt; in the Algiers Agreement of March 6, 1975, Iran and Iraq reached a settlement at long last on the Shatt al-Arab, removing at least for the time being any military threat to Iraq from that quarter. Was this the time to try to reach a border settlement between Kuwait and Iraq? Crown Prince Fahd of Saudi Arabia visited Baghdad in June 1975, seeking to mediate between them; the Iraqis were not interested.[27] Some Iraqi troops remained on the Kuwait side of the frontier, but now the port of Umm Qasr no longer faced any immediate threat from Iran; perhaps, the Kuwaitis suggested, it was time for the Iraqis to leave—to cancel, in effect, the imposed "unwritten agreement" of 1969. Iraq was unmoved. In Baghdad in January 1976 Iraqi Foreign Minister Sa'dun Hamadi told an interviewer that Iraq was willing to accept the defined border if Kuwait would permit Iraq to use Warba and the northern half of Bubiyan for defense purposes under a long-term lease. Hamadi pointed out that the islands were uninhabited and of virtually no use to Kuwait in any case. "Such an arrangement," he said, "is a reasonable demand in view of Iraq's security needs and is not unprecedented in the relationship between two neighbors."[28] But the Kuwaitis did not see it that way, even though it could have meant not only reaffirmation of Kuwait's independence and sovereignty, but also the final and definitive boundary demarcation that it had sought for so long.

In fact the Kuwaitis began to be more assertive. Some rather ostentatious outposts and buildings began to appear on the islands, evidently meant as symbols of Kuwait's authority and jurisdiction. Officials pointed out that the islands are not small; they make up almost a quarter of Kuwait's total territory. Their control by a foreign power (Iraq) could not only compromise Kuwait's sovereignty but might also draw Kuwait into Iraq's conflicts with other states (meaning Iran). In July 1975 the Kuwaiti National Assembly adopted a resolution asserting "Kuwait's sovereignty over all the islands within her borders as specified in international agreements." Various officials expressed willingness to afford "all possible facilities" to Iraq, including economic assistance to develop the area on both sides of the frontier, but they could not agree to yield the islands for military purposes that might compromise Kuwait's neutrality.[29] These sturdy principles were not so easy to maintain once Iraq and Iran had gone to war.

Kuwait and the First Gulf War, 1980–1988

Kuwait's efforts to fend off Iraq's claims and demands were deeply affected by the outbreak of hostilities between Iran and Iraq in September 1980. Among the many factors that led to the conflict, the most significant from Kuwait's standpoint was the continuing conflict over the Shatt al-Arab. In 1969 Iran had denounced the 1937 Iraq-Iran agreement governing the Shatt, which had allocated to Iraq almost the entire course of the waterway up to the Iranian shore. For the next six years, says one observer, "use of the Shatt was on the terms laid down by Iran." These were not easy years for Iraq, deeply involved in a seemingly interminable war in the north to suppress dissident and rebellious Kurds, who received considerable support from Iran. But in 1975 a deal was struck: Iran would stop supporting the Kurds, and Iraq would agree to a thalweg (midchannel) line along the entire length of the Shatt.[30]

From the standpoint of Kuwait, the Algiers Agreement of 1975 was not necessarily good news, for any retreat by Iraq along the Shatt could mean a further squeeze on Kuwait to accommodate Iraq's long-standing desire for maritime access elsewhere. "Elsewhere," as always, could embrace only two possibilities: the channels and estuaries leading to Umm Qasr, or Kuwait Bay itself. And indeed from 1975 on there was a resumption of Iraqi diplomatic pressures on Kuwait, border incidents, and troop movements.[31] There were also intermittent boundary discussions. In mid-1978 it was reported that both sides had agreed to a two-kilometer-wide strip as a buffer zone along the frontier.[32] An idea was floated to divert Shatt waters through a new ship channel across the desert to Umm Qasr, bypassing the Shatt altogether.[33] In 1979 an agreement was reported to allow Iraq access to deep-water facilities at Mina Shuwaikh, west of the capital on Kuwait Bay.[34] Demarcation talks resumed in July 1980. Despite all this activity, nothing was settled by the time war between Iraq and Iran erupted in September.

One of the first war casualties was the Shatt al-Arab itself, which soon became a cluttered graveyard of scores of merchant vessels. As a result, "Kuwait became in effect an Iraqi port as soon as Iraq was denied access to the Shatt al-Arab."[35] With early Iranian military successes, Kuwaitis sensed the war coming closer: "They knew that Iraq was their only shield, though even then there were those in Kuwait who . . . would have been happy to have found some alternative protector."[36] Throughout the war, Kuwaiti officials declared their country's support for Iraq in countless statements, speeches, and resolutions. Some of them justified this support as being called for under the Defense Pact of the Arab League.[37]

And yet Kuwait's attitudes reflected a continuing duality. On the one hand, official policy consistently supported Iraq's side in the war, and this support was expressed in various substantive ways. Kuwait was first among Iraq's Arab neighbors to announce financial assistance, beginning with a $2 billion interest-free loan authorized by the National Assembly in April 1981. (Saudi Arabia, the United Arab Emirates, and Qatar shortly followed suit.) By 1987 Kuwait and Saudi Arabia together had advanced some $50 billion.[38] Iraqi shipping was given free access to Kuwaiti ports, and trucks by the hundreds rumbled northward across the desert from Shuaiba and Shuwaikh.[39] And on a local but nonetheless material level, when Basra's oil refinery came under Iranian air attack, Kuwaiti fire-fighting equipment sped up the road to fight the blaze.[40] Iraqi military aircraft routinely overflew Kuwaiti airspace on their way to attack Iranian shipping in the Gulf.

There was no doubt whose side the Kuwaitis were on in Iraq's war against Iran. Even so, when it came to its own sovereignty and territorial integrity, Kuwait continued to resist Iraqi encroachment, even under the onus of failing to cooperate fully in an Arab war effort. Kuwait could hardly claim to be "neutral" in the international-law sense, in view of its overt financial, logistical, and tactical support of Iraq. But when it came to Warba and Bubiyan, Kuwait remained as adamant as ever. In late 1981 and early 1982 Iraq tried once more to get a long-term lease over the islands, offering final demarcation in exchange. Iran threatened to bring

Kuwait into the war if Kuwait were to agree. At the very least, said one Iranian paper, Iran would be entitled to seize Failaka Island, which guarded Kuwait Bay from the sea.[41] A bit later Saddam Hussein scaled back the leasehold proposal to cover only part of Bubiyan, where he said he planned to construct a naval base for the protection of Kuwait as well as Iraq; and he offered to reduce the lease term from ninety-nine years to twenty.[42]

In August 1990, after Shaikh Jabir III and most of the ruling family had fled the shaikhdom before the lightning advance of the Iraqi army, the exiled ruler explained to Arab leaders in Cairo why he had not taken advantage of Iraq's involvement in the Iran war to press Saddam Hussein for final settlement of the border issue. Shaikh Jabir said that he had been urged by his ministers to do so, "but I said no, not while my Iraqi brothers were at war." Then he burst into tears and added, "It was a time when we were supporting the brothers against the cousins, and put all our facilities at their disposal; it wouldn't have been very gallant to press our claim during their plight."[43] Gallantry aside, there were certain pragmatic considerations for supporting Iraq's war effort: for one thing, Saddam Hussein was widely quoted as having said that Gulf shaikhs who were not with him could expect to be reached by terrorists "in their bedchambers." (In fact Shaikh Jabir narrowly escaped assassination by unknown assailants in 1985). Then again, with Iranian troops threatening to overrun southern Iraq in 1986, Saddam hinted that if they broke through at Basra, he would withdraw his forces to the north, leaving the Basra-Jahra highway wide open for them to swarm south into Kuwait.[44]

But as the pressures grew, Kuwait appeared to stiffen. Construction by Kuwait of new frontier posts and oil facilities along its northern border was taken by Iraq as a unilateral attempt to force the boundary issue.[45] In October 1982 Kuwait started building a bridge from the mainland to Bubiyan Island, a move judged to be politically motivated "by the fact that neither of the connected points has any population or installations, nor connecting roads; and by the exceptional speed of the construction, made possible by opting for a turn-key project (unusual for Kuwait), a revolutionary design and the use of Chinese workers."[46] In November 1984 Kuwait was reported to have installed antiaircraft artillery on Bubiyan, at the same time denying that any Iraqi artillery was in place there. The following March Kuwait declared Bubiyan an out-of-bounds military zone, a signal to Iraq as well as to Iran. Early in 1986 Iran warned Kuwait against letting Iraqi forces use the island for attacks on Iran.[47]

In 1988, after something like a million lives had been lost, and enormous treasure expended, the Iran-Iraq war ended. Neither side had accomplished much, except that Iraq had blooded itself for an even more devastating and equally incomprehensible war to follow.

11. Saddam Hussein and the UN: Clear Lines in the Sand?

"We have no opinion on the Arab-Arab conflicts like your border disagreement with Kuwait," said American Ambassador April Glaspie to Saddam Hussein on July 25, 1990, a week before Iraq's invasion.[1] If that was ever an accurate expression of American policy, it is no longer. For on April 3, 1991, in the aftermath of the Gulf War, the United States joined in the adoption of United Nations Security Council Resolution 687, which set a very firm position indeed. This, the celebrated "cease-fire" resolution, demanded among other things that Iraq and Kuwait each respect the inviolability of the boundary between them (including the allocation of islands) in accordance with a document called "Agreed Minutes between the State of Kuwait and the Republic of Iraq Regarding the Restoration of Friendly Relations, Recognition and Related Matters, Signed at Baghdad, on 4 October, 1963"—that is, the 1963 Agreed Minutes. Resolution 687 called upon Secretary General Javier Pérez de Cuéllar to "assist" Iraq and Kuwait in demarcating that boundary.[2]

In May 1991 a United Nations observer unit known as UNI-KOM (United Nations Iraq-Kuwait Observation Mission) was deployed along the border. A zone along the boundary, extending ten kilometers into Iraq and five kilometers into Kuwait, was to be demilitarized and patrolled by several hundred UN military observers with an armed guard of about 700 blue-helmeted infantry. Iraq and Kuwait retain civil authority on their respective sides of the border.[3]

The day after the adoption of Resolution 687, Kuwait responded that it would comply scrupulously and would cooperate fully with the secretary general. Iraq's reply, two days later, was rather less forthcoming. "The provisions of the Council's resolu-

163

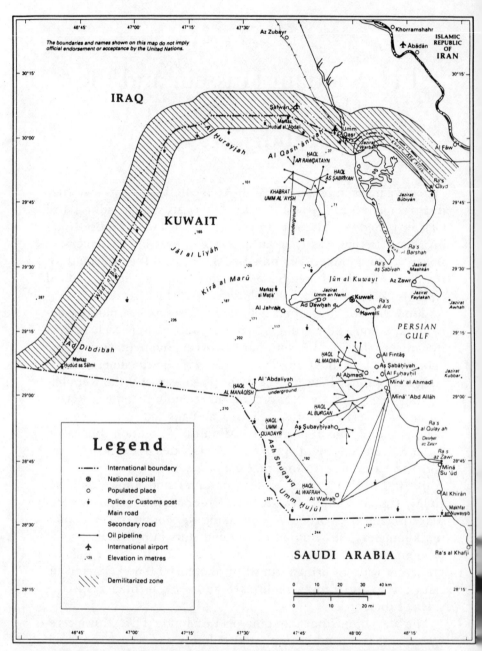

Map 3. *Following the Gulf War in early 1991, the United Nations Security Council established a demilitarized zone along the boundary (shaded area). This map was circulated by Secretary General Pérez de Cuéllar to show the location of the zone, which is to be monitored by the United Nations Iraq-Kuwait Observation Mission (UNIKOM).*

tion regarding the border issue are unfair," wrote Foreign Minister Ahmad Hussein, "and set a serious precedent in the history of this international body, a precedent which derogates the sovereignty of states." Nevertheless, he said, since Iraq found itself with no other alternative, it would accept the resolution.[4]

A month later, as called for by the resolution, the secretary general submitted his proposals for demarcating the frontier. He announced the formation of a Boundary Demarcation Commission to consist of five members (one representative each from Iraq and Kuwait, and three independent experts appointed by himself), which would take final decisions by majority vote. The commission's task is to establish the geographic coordinates of the 120-mile boundary and arrange for its physical representation by erecting an appropriate number of pillars or monuments. Although the commission is authorized to draw upon "appropriate material" (including a map furnished to the United Nations by the British government), it is required by Resolution 687 to fix the boundary in accordance with the 1963 Agreed Minutes; the secretary general's instructions confirm this requirement.[5]

In a further letter on April 23, Iraqi Foreign Minister Ahmad Hussein told the secretary general: "The Security Council has imposed a specific position with regard to the Iraqi-Kuwaiti boundary, whereas the custom in law and in practice in international relations is that boundary questions are left to an agreement between States, because this is the sole basis that can guarantee the principle of the stability of boundaries." Furthermore, said the foreign minister, the 1963 Agreed Minutes "have not yet been subjected to the constitutional procedures required for their ratification by the legislative authority and the President of Iraq, thus leaving the question of the boundary pending and unresolved." He added that Iraq was not a party to the map furnished to the UN by the United Kingdom, and does not recognize it; to use this map in the demarcation process is "an iniquitous and unilateral imposition against the will of Iraq . . . and a prejudgement of the course of the land boundary." Iraq would, nevertheless, cooperate and participate in the work of the boundary commission.[6]

Apparently at the heart of Iraq's objection to the boundary provisions of Resolution 687 is the mandatory application of the 1963 Agreed Minutes, which stipulate: "The Government of Iraq recognizes the independence and complete sovereignty of the

State of Kuwait with its boundaries as specified in the letter of the Prime Minister of Iraq dated 21.7.32 and which was accepted by the ruler of Kuwait in his letter dated 10.8.32."[7]

If Iraq holds to its position that the 1963 Agreed Minutes never went into effect because they were not ratified, it surely will encounter skepticism. As we have seen, Iraq shortly established diplomatic relations, exchanged ambassadors, and joined in the work of a boundary commission, all in implementation of the agreement signed by its prime minister. But even if the Iraqis can overcome the legal and common-sense consequences of their own actions after the signing of the Agreed Minutes and their long inattention to Kuwait's public affirmation that the Agreed Minutes had taken effect upon signature, they must face yet another hurdle, one that arises out of Iraq's own constitutional posture at the time. International law does not insist that *all* international agreements must be ratified; one must look to the intentions of the parties and also to the provisions of their own national laws.[8]

For a relatively young country, Iraq has had a checkered constitutional history. Under its first constitution, promulgated under the monarchy in 1925, "The King concludes treaties, provided that he shall not ratify them without the approval of Parliament."[9] But with the 1958 revolution Iraq became a republic: no longer was there a king to make and ratify treaties. The new regime promptly enacted a provisional constitution, whose first operative clause annulled the 1925 constitution as from the date of the revolution. Thirty articles follow, but in none of them is there any reference to treaties: how they are to be made, or whether and how they are to be ratified.[10] So if Iraq is to make headway with its argument that the 1963 Agreed Minutes "have not yet been subjected to the constitutional procedures required for their ratification by the legislative authority and the President of Iraq," it will have to summon up some legal requirement not contained in the constitution that was in effect at the time.[11] The 1958 provisional constitution was superseded and explicitly repealed by another interim constitution on April 19, 1964 (more than six months after the date of the Agreed Minutes), which provides that "the President of the Republic shall approve and ratify international treaties and agreements."[12] Does the insertion of the word "yet" in Iraq's letter of April 23, 1991, to the secretary general contain the hint that Iraq will in due course pursue its "no-ratification" strategy by reference to some ex-post-facto application of the 1964 constitution? We shall have to wait and see.

Iraq's Allegations and Claims

Iraq has two "historic" claims with respect to Kuwait, and they are related. The first is that Kuwait is actually a part of Iraq. The other (which appears to presuppose a negative answer to the first) is that Iraq has never agreed to any boundary between itself and Kuwait.

With regard to the first claim, one can grant the Iraqis the benefit of many a doubt and still conclude that their case is insubstantial. For the sake of argument one might concede that:

Shaikh Mubarak had no business making a deal with Great Britain in 1899 while he was nominally a subject and an appointed official of the Ottoman Sultan and professed loyalty to him.

The Anglo-Ottoman Convention of 1913, whereby Britain acknowledged that Kuwait was a *qaza* of the Ottoman Empire, underlined and confirmed Ottoman sovereignty over Kuwait. (Conceding this point entails disregarding all the other provisions of the Convention that pointed to Kuwait's autonomy and Britain's special role there).

The renunciation provisions of the 1920 Treaty of Sèvres had no application because that treaty was never accepted by the postwar Turkish government.

The 1923 Treaty of Lausanne had no application because it purported only to separate the new Iraqi state from Turkey; it did not deal with the question of what constituted the state of Iraq itself.

Although the Iraqi prime minister's 1932 letter to the British high commissioner implicitly recognized the existence of Kuwait as a separate state (by requesting the "re-affirmation" of the boundary between them), that letter was signed while Great Britain still controlled Iraq, and especially its foreign

relations, under the League of Nations mandate; it does not
bind Iraq as an independent state.

Evidence such as that produced by Kuwait in the summer of
1961 to refute Abdul Karim Qasim's claim is fragmentary
and insubstantial; to the extent that such evidence carried any
weight at all, it was countermanded by the pronouncements
of Qasim, the chief of state.

But even if one concedes hypothetically all of these points supporting Iraq's first claim (that Kuwait is part of Iraq), the whole
argument disintegrates because of the Baghdad Agreed Minutes
of 1963. In that document Iraq abandoned its first claim forever.
This was no empty piece of paper signed in a careless moment by
Iraq's prime minister in return for a financial subvention. It was
amply confirmed and implemented by Iraq's own conduct: acceptance of Kuwait as a fellow member of the Arab League and the
United Nations (even before the Agreed Minutes were signed),
establishing diplomatic relations, exchanging ambassadors, and
entering into a whole series of bilateral agreements. Since 1963
Iraq has had no viable basis for a claim that Kuwait is part of
Iraq.

A few days after the invasion of Kuwait in August 1990, Iraq
declared a "comprehensive and eternal merger" of Kuwait into
Iraq. Security Council Resolution 662, adopted on August 9, required Iraq to rescind its actions purporting to annex Kuwait.
Iraq paid no attention, and in fact a few weeks later issued a map
showing Kuwait sliced into two parts, divided by a line running
from the Iraq-Kuwait-Saudi junction (in the Batin) northeasterly
to skirt the northern rim of Kuwait Bay, reaching the Gulf near
the southern tip of Bubiyan Island. The area north and west of
that line was shown as having been integrated into Basra province,
whereas the remainder of Kuwait, including Kuwait City, was
labeled as a new province, "Kadhima," Iraq's nineteenth.[13] Then
on March 5, 1991, just after the end of the 100-hour battle ter-
minating the occupation, Baghdad radio announced that the Iraqi
government had "annulled the annexation"; that all applicable
decrees, laws, and regulations were now null and void.[14]

And yet it seems that the claim might still be made. Iraq's new
prime minister, Sa'dun Hamadi, interviewed in Baghdad on April

25, 1991, was asked if Iraq had abandoned its territorial claim to Kuwait. His reply was vague and not especially reassuring. "We are looking to the future and want to forget the past," he said. "Therefore, I don't like to raise issues that may disrupt the situation now."[15] In August 1991, according to press reports, Iraqi officials were still referring to Kuwait as Iraqi territory; Iraq's state-run television, which provides addresses of pharmacies that are staying open late, was including those in Kuwait City, the capital of the "nineteenth province."[16]

Iraq's second claim, that the boundary between the two states has never been determined, can be analyzed in much the same way. For argument's sake one might go along with Iraq on many of its points:

The boundary definition in the 1913 Anglo-Ottoman Convention was never operative because the Convention was never ratified.

The Cox-More Memorandum of 1923, confirming the 1913 line, did not bind Iraq and did not even purport to do so.

The Iraqi prime minister's letter of July 21, 1932, "re-affirming" the 1913–1923 line, signed in the closing days of the mandate under British pressure, does not bind Iraq.

But again, Iraq's argument must somehow overcome the formidably clear and unequivocal terms of the 1963 Agreed Minutes, whereby Iraq's prime minister recognized not only Kuwait's sovereign independence but also the 1913/1923/1932 boundary. Moreover, this boundary is now firmly embedded in Security Council Resolution 687, which Iraq says it has accepted.

UNIKOM set up seventeen posts along the border, but its patrols (as of August 1991) were operating only during daylight. Trucks were spotted removing military supplies by night from Kuwait's side of the demilitarized zone, crossing the border at will. At the end of August 1991, Kuwait complained to the United Nations that a party of Iraqis had tried to infiltrate Bubiyan; forty-seven had been captured, and forty more were believed to be in hiding on the island (although where they could find a hiding place on the barren mudflat was not explained.) Secretary General Pérez de Cuéllar pronounced the situation "serious," but it seems to have blown over quickly.[17] Will Iraq come to respect the line

mandated by the Security Council while it is being patrolled by
UNIKOM and after it has been demarcated by the UN Boundary
Commission? Probably it would be unrealistic to expect that border incidents will not occasionally occur, as they have ever since
the signboard was first planted by Shaikh Ahmad and Major More
in the desert sand beside the road, just south of the palms of
Safwan, in 1923. On the other hand, demilitarization of the channel approaches to Umm Qasr could be a significant consolation
prize for Iraq, affording the unimpeded access it has sought so
long.

The Oil Factor

Although the uneasy relationship between Iraq and Kuwait long
antedates the discovery and exploitation of oil in the area around
the head of the Persian Gulf, oil has probably made things worse.

In the first place, Iraq's aspirations for a coastline on the Gulf
intensified in the 1950s, when it began to appear that there might
be petroleum beneath the waters of the Gulf itself. Questions as
to how to carve up the subsurface of the Gulf among the various
adjacent states opened up a whole new field of international jurisprudence. One useful principle, with venerable historic roots,
is the common-sense notion of extending an existing land boundary into the sea on a line perpendicular to the shore; and this
principle can be applied not only to land boundaries but also to
waterways like the Shatt al-Arab, which themselves constitute a
frontier between two countries. But in a region like the Persian
Gulf, whose contours are essentially concave, there can be a bit of
a squeeze as the various perpendiculars converge and intersect.
Another sensible rubric, in a case in which two ambitious oil-
producing countries face each other across a body of water, is to
extend the offshore oil and mineral jurisdiction of each to a line
midway between them; this principle has been applied, for example, in the case of Saudi Arabia and Iran. Over the past forty
years most of the offshore waters of the Persian Gulf have thus
fallen into place, accompanied by much bargaining and compromise among the oil ministries of the states involved, assisted by
their geologists and lawyers. But Iraq has not been a party to any
of these arrangements, and the reason is apparent from a glance

at the map. It is not only that Iraq was disfavored by being endowed with a comparatively insignificant coastline (19 kilometers, in contrast to 250 for Kuwait, 1,833 for Iran).[18] When perpendiculars are plotted into the Gulf from the Shatt al-Arab and the Khor Abdullah, Iraq winds up with a little triangular wedge extending hardly beyond the horizon. Obviously, Iraq's situation would be very different if it owned Bubiyan Island, not to mention the "nineteenth province." In the 1960s Kuwait, Iran, and Saudi Arabia reached agreement on the extent of their offshore territories. Iraq's protests went almost unnoticed. In August 1960 Iraq offered oil exploration rights over its own exiguous offshore waters but attracted no bids.[19]

The Rumaila Dispute

In the last days before Saddam's invasion of Kuwait, and afterward in justification for it, Iraq asserted that Kuwait had been improperly siphoning off oil from Iraq's Rumaila field, to the tune of about $2.4 billion worth over the years 1980–1990. This, the Iraqis seemed to be saying, was not only grand larceny, but also amounted to trespass of a magnitude sufficient to offset any position the Kuwaitis might wish to take with regard to their boundary with Iraq.

The Rumaila field, west and south of Basra, was discovered in 1954 by Basrah Petroleum Company (BPC), a British corporation owned mostly by major European and American oil companies, which had held an oil concession in the area since 1938. BPC developed the field relatively quickly; by 1957 exports from Rumaila already exceeded those from the Zubair field, hitherto BPC's workhorse. By 1965 Rumaila was producing almost 300,000 barrels per day. (By 1990 production had leveled off at about 400,000 barrels per day.)[20] As further exploration drilling gradually confirmed the full extent of the field, its contours crept ever southward in the direction of Kuwait; geologists began to wonder if the southern part of the field actually underlay Kuwaiti territory. Accurate information about such matters is always "tight" (hard to come by) in the industry, but speculation along these lines would certainly not have escaped the attention of geologists and managers of Kuwait Oil Company (KOC), whose concession covered the area near Rumaila on Kuwait's side of the border, and indeed (at that time) the entire area of Kuwait. And the probabilities of such questions being discussed in one or another oil company mess were surely enhanced by the fact that British Petroleum, majority-owned by the British government, was an active participant on both sides, as a 23.75 percent shareholder in BPC and a 50 percent owner of KOC.

In 1951 KOC was told by His Majesty's Government that the company was free to operate up to 3.5 kilometers (about 2 miles) from the Iraq-Kuwait frontier.[21] (It seems more than likely that BPC, on the Iraqi side of the boundary, was requested to observe similar restraint.) KOC used this permission in 1964 to drill a test well in the area opposite Rumaila, although drilling was suspended at 4,336 feet "pending settlement of the border."[22]

The concessionary picture altered radically in the 1970s, when almost all the operations of privately owned oil producers in the Middle East were taken over by their host governments. The concessions of both KOC and BPC were nationalized, the former owners becoming mere purchasers of crude oil for export, with no further responsibility for exploration or oil production. In the late 1970s, Kuwait's nationalized operation began producing up to about 10,000 barrels per day from a new area called Ratqa, near the border opposite Rumaila. The question then became whether Ratqa is actually an extension of the Rumaila reservoir, and the consensus of industry opinion is that it is.[23] Even so, under the well-established common-law "rule of capture," which has found its way into international jurisprudence, a surface landowner has the right to exploit underground resources lying beneath the surface that belongs to him. This rule applies even to substances that can migrate because of changing reservoir pressures. There is ample precedent in international law and practice for coordination between producing operations in a common reservoir straddling an international boundary, if only for the purpose of optimizing the efficient exploitation of the field.[24] This sort of cooperation has never taken place between Iraq and Kuwait as far as the disputed Rumaila area is concerned.

Although Iraq's allegations about the Rumaila reservoir apparently date back to the time of the Iran-Iraq war, they received little public attention until just before Saddam Hussein's invasion of Kuwait.[25] On July 15, 1990, Iraqi Foreign Minister Tariq Aziz addressed an extraordinary letter to the secretary general of the Arab League, in which Iraq's complaints against Kuwait were formally catalogued. "The Kuwait government," wrote Tariq Aziz, "has installed an oil-producing infrastructure in the southern part of the Iraqi field at Rumaila and has begun to extract oil from it . . . On the basis of prices between 1980 and 1990, the value of the oil extracted from the Rumaila field by this method . . . is estimated at $2,400 million."[26] (How Iraq arrived at this figure is not clear; if, as reported, Kuwait's production from Ratqa averaged 10,000 barrels per day, then aggregate production for 1980–1990 comes to about 40 million barrels, resulting in a value per barrel of roughly $60—wildly in excess of the actual market value of the oil over that period.) In any case, Kuwait's alleged transgressions at or near Rumaila can hardly be considered a legitimate *casus belli*, much less an excuse for disregarding an otherwise well-established frontier.

An American oilman with inside experience of Kuwait's oil operations (too much inside, he might say; he was in Kuwait when it was invaded) suggests that the Coalition forces of Operation Desert Storm missed a great opportunity: they could easily have made a military enclave of the entire Rumaila field. Production from the oilfield, under United Nations auspices, could have been used to finance the reparations and other expenses to be charged to Iraq's account under Resolution 687, without interference from or argument with the Iraqis themselves.[27]

The OPEC "Conspiracy"

"Kuwait, with the complicity of the United Arab Emirates, has hatched a plot to inundate the oil market with a surplus far in excess of the quota allocated by OPEC . . . Every time the price of crude oil drops by $1 Iraq loses $1 billion over the whole year." So said the July 15 letter from Tariq Aziz to the Arab League.[28]

Thirty years before, both Iraq and Kuwait became founding members of the Organization of Petroleum Exporting Countries (OPEC), the imperfect cartel that attempts to regulate the international crude oil market for the mutual benefit of its members. In recent years OPEC has established production quotas, but they have not always been very closely observed (Iraq itself exceeded its quotas in 1987 and 1988). OPEC has no enforcement arm to prevent what the industry calls "quota cheating"; disputes among the members are ordinarily sorted out behind closed doors. Iraq's public complaint about the overproduction of Kuwait and the United Arab Emirates therefore came as a surprise. But two weeks before Tariq Aziz's letter, at an Arab League summit in Baghdad, Saddam Hussein himself had broached the subject in fighting terms: he called the violation of OPEC quotas in Iraq's difficult economic circumstances an "act of war." In another speech just after the July 15 letter, Saddam Hussein declared that Kuwait was stabbing Iraq in the back with a "poison dagger." He warned that if Kuwait continued to cheat on its quota, he would have no alternative but to use force.[29]

After the August invasion, when Iraq was still trying to justify it to a largely hostile world, the Iraqis released what they said was an internal Kuwaiti memorandum, found in the captured Kuwait Foreign Ministry; the document was said to contain a report of a November 1989 meeting attended by Kuwait's director of state security at the headquarters of the Central Intelligence Agency, where "we agreed with the American side that it was important to take advantage of the deteriorating economic situation in Iraq in order to put pressure on that country's government to delineate our common border." The Iraqi government, citing the memorandum as evidence that the United States was involved in a plot to bring Iraq to its knees economically, sent it along to the United Nations for perusal by Secretary General Pérez de Cuéllar. The CIA issued a statement calling the remarks attributed to American officials "total fabrications."[30]

That Kuwait was actually overproducing its quota in early 1990 has not been contested; Kuwait's alleged participation in a plot involving the United States to destroy the Iraqi economy is quite another matter. Tariq Aziz, interviewed after the Gulf War by an American correspondent about these supposed intrigues, said, "I'm not a strong believer in conspiracies, but they do exist. And they exist more in our part of the world than elsewhere, because we have oil, a strategic position, and Israel."[31] History will perhaps one day tell us just how well-founded these suspicions were.

The Matter of Access

Historical arguments based on very selective analysis of diplomatic documents; a stale and self-serving assertion that a 1963 boundary agreement is invalid because it has not yet been ratified; a dispute over offtake from an oilfield; an unproved conspiracy to visit Iraq with economic disaster—such is the stuff of Iraq's rationale for having invaded and occupied Kuwait and annexed it forcibly to Iraq in an "eternal union." These explanations simply do not add up to the sort of vindication that could find much resonance anywhere beyond Saddam Hussein's immediate entourage. There is—there must be—some rich admixture of miscalculation, of megalomania, perhaps of obsessive fanaticism, underlying Saddam Hussein's rash and disastrous excursion in the summer of 1990.

One constant and abiding theme, however, will continue to inform Iraqi nationalism, regardless of who comes to power in Baghdad. It is the point attributed to Lord Halifax, the British foreign secretary in 1939, when proposing an effort to persuade Shaikh Ahmad of Kuwait to be a little more flexible in regard to his frontier with Iraq: "It is understandable that the state which controls the Mesopotamian plain should desire to have undivided control of at least one means of access to the sea . . . If Iraq were given this access, it would make for steadier conditions in that part of the world in years to come."[32] Iraq has never come to accept the harsh reality of its geographic predicament in relation to the Gulf. On August 6, 1990, four days after the invasion, a conversation took place at United Nations headquarters in New York between Jordanian Ambassador Abdullah Salah and his American counterpart, Thomas Pickering. The Jordanian was asked to pass this message along to Baghdad: "We [the United States] acknowledge your need for an opening to the Gulf, and the issue of access to the islands (Warba and Bubiyan) is one that we could look on favorably." It was later confirmed that Ambassador Pickering was, not surprisingly, speaking on instructions of his government.[33]

Saddam Hussein's reckless aggression, together with his postwar posturing, understandably reduced international sympathy for Iraq's geographic plight very nearly to the vanishing point. In adopting Resolution 687, with its specific incorporation not only of the 1963 Agreed Minutes but also of Prime Minister Nuri Said's letter of July 21, 1932, the United Nations Security Council closed the door on the "border disagreement with Kuwait" mentioned by Ambassador Glaspie in her prewar interview with Saddam Hussein. With all that happened afterward, the Security Council could hardly have been expected to do otherwise. Nevertheless, by its reactions to the resolution, Iraq has shown that it still does not regard the boundary matter as settled. Policymakers concerned with the application of Security Council Resolution 687 cannot disregard the intensity behind Iraq's extraordinary efforts to make the 1963 Agreed Minutes disappear.

Abbreviations

Notes

Index

Abbreviations

Ashtiany   Julia Ashtiany, *The Arabic Documents in the Archives of the British Political Agency Kuwait, 1904–1949* (London: India Office Library and Records, 1982).

BDFA   Kenneth Bourne and D. Cameron Watt, general eds., *British Documents on Foreign Affairs: Reports and Papers from the Foreign Office Confidential Print* (Frederick, Md.: University Publications of America, 1984–1986). Part I, Series B, David Gillard, ed., *The Near and Middle East, 1856–1914*, vol. 17: *The Ottoman Empire, Arabia, and the Gulf: British Strategic Interests, 1885–1907* (cited as *BDFA* I, vol. 17); vol. 18: *Arabia, the Gulf, and the Bagdad Railway, 1907–1914* (cited as *BDFA* I, vol. 18). Part II, Series B, Robin Bidwell, ed., *Turkey, Iran, and the Middle East, 1918–1939*, vols. 1–13 (cited as *BDFA* II and volume no.).

BDOW   G. P. Gooch and Harold Temperly, eds., *British Documents on the Origins of the War,* vol. X (London: H. M. Stationery Office, 1938), Part 1: *The Near and Middle East on the Eve of War* (cited as *BDOW* I); Part 2: *The Last Years of Peace* (cited as *BDOW* II).

CO   Colonial Office, London.

FO   Foreign Office, London.

IOR   India Office Records, London. The originating source of a file is indicated by a prefix: L/P&S/ designates the India Office, R/15/1 the Persian Gulf Residency, R/15/5 the Kuwait Political Agency.

KCBD   E. Lauterpacht et al., eds., *The Kuwait Crisis: Basic Documents,* vol. I (Cambridge: Grotius Publications, 1991).

Lorimer   J. G. Lorimer, *Gazetteer of the Persian Gulf, Oman, and Central Arabia* (1908–1915; reprint, Farnborough, England: Gregg International, 1970). Part I B, *Historical* (cited as Lorimer I); Part II B, *Geographical and Statistical* (cited as Lorimer II).

MENA   J. C. Hurewitz, *The Middle East and North Africa in World Politics,* vols. I and II (New Haven: Yale University Press, 1975–1979).

NID *Iraq*   Great Britain, Naval Intelligence Division, *Iraq and the Persian Gulf* (London, 1944).

PGHS   *The Persian Gulf Historical Summaries, 1907–1953,* vols. I and II (Gerrards Cross, England: Archive Editions, 1987).

PRO   Great Britain, Public Record Office, London.

Schofield   Richard N. Schofield, *Kuwait and Iraq: Historical Claims and Territorial Disputes* (London: Royal Institute of International Affairs, 1991).

SCOR   *Security Council Official Records* (New York: United Nations, ca. 1961–1963).

TAOK   Robin Bidwell, ed., *The Affairs of Kuwait, 1896–1905,* 2 vols. (London: Cass, 1971). Vol. 1: Parts I, II, III (1899–1901); vol. 2: Parts IV, V, VI (1902–1905).

WSC   Martin Gilbert, *Winston S. Churchill,* vol. IV: *1916–1922, The Stricken World* (Boston: Houghton Mifflin, 1975) (cited as *WSC* IV); companion vol. IV, Part 2: *July 1919–March 1921;* and Part 3: *April 1921–November 1922* (Boston: Houghton Mifflin, 1978) (cited as *WSC* IV/2 and IV/3, respectively).

Notes

1. Kuwait: The Beginnings

1. In the weeks following Iraq's invasion in August 1990, the Baghdad press reached far in search of historic links between Kuwait and Iraq. One article pointed to a striking resemblance between ancient Assyrian monarchs and a 3,000-year-old clay statue found on Kuwait's Failaka Island. Another reported that Kuwait had been marked on eighth-century maps as a garrison post of Abbasid forces headquartered in Basra. Judith Miller and Laurie Mylroie, *Saddam Hussein and the Crisis in the Gulf* (New York: Times Books, 1990), 194.

2. H. V. F. Winstone and Zahra Freeth, *Kuwait: Prospect and Reality* (New York: Crone Russak, 1972), 61.

3. Geoffrey Bibby, *Looking for Dilmun* (New York: Knopf, 1970), 198–199.

4. The legends and traditions surrounding the origins of Kuwait are discussed with scholarly caution by the Kuwaiti historian Ahmad Mustafa abu Hakima in his seminal *History of Eastern Arabia, 1750–1800: The Rise and Development of Bahrein and Kuwait* (Beirut: Khayat, 1965), 14–15, 48–50. Abu Hakima has also written extensively in Arabic. Much of his research informs other recent scholarship, notably Jacqueline S. Ismael, *Kuwait: Social Change in Historical Perspective* (Syracuse: Syracuse University Press, 1982), chaps. 1 and 2. For the legends themselves, told by the greatest storyteller Kuwait has ever known, one can do no better than ramble through *Kuwait and Her Neighbours*, by H. R. P. Dickson (London: Allen & Unwin, 1956).

5. Abdul-Reda Assiri, *Kuwait's Foreign Policy: City-State in World Politics* (Boulder: Westview, 1990), 2; Rosemarie Said Zahlan, *The Making of the Modern Gulf States* (London: Unwin Hyman, 1989), 25.

6. Abu Hakima, *History of Eastern Arabia*, 182–183.

7. Lorimer II, 1051–58.

8. Abu Hakima, *History of Eastern Arabia*, 14; Glen Balfour-Paul, "Kuwait, Qatar and the United Arab Emirates: Political and Social Evolution," in Ian Richard Netton, ed., *Arabia and the Gulf: From Traditional Society to Modern States* (London: Croom Helm, 1986), 156–175. For a general description of the social institutions of the Arabs

181

of the Gulf, see Alvin J. Cottrell, ed., *The Persian Gulf States: A General Survey* (Baltimore: Johns Hopkins University Press, 1980), 44. There is a useful article by Abu Hakima, "The Development of the Gulf States," in Derek Hopwood, ed., *The Arabian Peninsula: Society and Politics* (London: Allen & Unwin, 1972).

9. Bernard Lewis, *The Emergence of Modern Turkey* (London: Oxford University Press, 1961), 24.

10. Edward W. Said, *Orientalism* (New York: Vintage, 1979), 216.

11. Samir al-Khalil, *Republic of Fear: The Inside Story of Saddam's Iraq* (New York: Pantheon, 1989), 267.

12. Gary Troeller, *The Birth of Saudi Arabia: Britain and the Rise of the House of Sa'ud* (London: Cass, 1976), 171; Ashtiany, 105.

13. See generally Gerald H. Blake and Richard N. Schofield, eds., *Boundaries and State Territory in the Middle East and North Africa* (The Cottons, Cambridgeshire: Middle East and North African Studies Press, 1987).

14. H. A. R. Gibb and Harold Bowen, *Islamic Society and the West*, vol. I, pt. I (London: Oxford University Press, 1950), 203.

15. Abu Hakima, *History of Eastern Arabia*, 182–183.

16. Ibid., 120–123.

17. Ismael, *Kuwait*, 45.

18. Schofield, 7.

19. Ibid., 9

20. Ibid., 11.

21. Albertine Jwaidah, "Midhat Pasha and the Land System of Lower Iraq," in Albert Hourani, ed., *Middle Eastern Affairs, Number Three*, St. Antony's Papers No. 16 (London: Chatto & Windus, 1963), 106–136. NID *Iraq*, 258.

22. Jwaidah, "Midhat Pasha," 114; Stephen Hemsley Longrigg, *Four Centuries of Modern Iraq* (Oxford: Oxford University Press, 1925), 280–281.

23. Troeller, *The Birth of Saudi Arabia*, 7.

24. Longrigg, *Four Centuries*, 298–303; Ali Haydar Midhat, *The Life of Midhat Pasha* (1903; reprint, New York: Arno, 1973), 54–55; Alan Rush, *Al-Sabah: History and Genealogy of Kuwait's Ruling Family, 1752–1987* (London: Ithaca Press, 1987), 139–140.

25. Schofield, 12–13; Troeller, *The Birth of Saudi Arabia*, 28n.

26. Schofield, 11–12.

27. Ibid., 13. Schofield points out that during this period the British in Whitehall and in India used terms such as *sovereignty, suzerainty, authority,* and *jurisdiction* more or less interchangeably. See also Ismael, *Kuwait*, 45–46. But Majid Khadduri's suggestion that the "ca-

pitulations" applicable to Europeans in the Ottoman Empire extended to foreign consulates in Kuwait is puzzling; there were no consulates in Kuwait until 1950. "Iraq's Claim to the Sovereignty of Kuwayt," *New York University Journal of International Law and Politics* 23, no. 1 (Fall 1990), 17.

28. Arnold T. Wilson, *The Persian Gulf* (Oxford: Oxford University Press, 1928), 163–164; Longrigg, *Four Centuries*, 107–108; George Dunbar, *India and the Passing of Empire* (New York: Philosophical Library, 1952), 61–62.

29. Ismael, *Kuwait*, 43.

30. J. B. Kelly, "The Legal and Historical Basis of the British Position in the Persian Gulf," in *Middle Eastern Affairs, Number One*, St. Antony's Papers No. 4 (London: Chatto & Windus, 1958), 119–140. The entities eventually involved, besides Kuwait, were Bahrain, Qatar, the Trucial Shaikhdoms (now grouped as the United Arab Emirates), and Oman. Kelly's more recent book, *Arabia, the Gulf, and the West* (New York: Basic Books, 1980), has a succinct and authoritative description of the Gulf treaty system, pp. 51–53.

31. *MENA* I, 506–507.

32. Troeller, *The Birth of Saudi Arabia*, 2–3, 26n.

33. Kelly, "Legal and Historical Basis," 124, 127; Cottrell, *The Persian Gulf States*, 80.

34. In 1841 Kuwait entered into a maritime truce agreement with the British, but it expired after one year and was never renewed. Ismael, *Kuwait*, 44; Schofield, 7. It is mentioned (but not reproduced) in a collection of treaties published by the government of India in 1933: C. U. Aitchison, comp., *A Collection of Treaties, Engagements and Sanads Relating to India and Neighbouring Countries*, vol. XI (Delhi: Manager of Publications, 1933), 202. In stating that "Kuwait had never been asked to subscribe to the trucial system," Kelly's 1958 article ("Legal and Historical Basis," p. 132) overlooks the 1841 agreement. The character and significance of the 1841 agreement were much overstated by the British Foreign Office in dealing with the independent government of Iraq in 1938. See Chapter 7.

2. Britain, Kuwait, and the Turks, 1899–1914

1. Malcolm Yapp in Alvin J. Cottrell, ed., *The Persian Gulf States: A General Survey* (Baltimore: Johns Hopkins University Press, 1980), 80. Lorimer I, 1014–16, has much detail about Kuwait during the reign of Abdullah II. The Hogarth quotation is from David George Hogarth, *The Penetration of Arabia* (New York: Stokes, 1904), 240.

2. Alan Rush, *Al-Sabah: History and Genealogy of Kuwait's Ruling Family, 1752–1987* (London: Ithaca Press, 1987), 120, citing Kuwaiti sources.
3. The complicated genealogy is explained in Lorimer I, 1017.
4. *TAOK* pt. I, 1–2. See also Rush, *Al-Sabah,* 120–122; Jacqueline S. Ismael, *Kuwait: Social Change in Historical Perspective* (Syracuse: Syracuse University Press, 1982), 47; and Briton Cooper Busch, "Britain and the Status of Kuwayt, 1896–1899," *Middle East Journal* 21 (Spring 1967), 187.
5. *TAOK* pt. I, 23.
6. *BDOW* II, 38.
7. Ismael, *Kuwait,* 49–50.
8. Busch, "Britain and Kuwayt," 192.
9. Stephen Hemsley Longrigg, *Four Centuries of Modern Iraq* (Oxford: Oxford University Press, 1925), 319; Lorimer I, 1012; Philip W. Ireland, *Iraq: A Study in Political Development* (New York: Macmillan, 1938), 38–39; Busch, "Britain and Kuwayt," 195. In 1872 a British parliamentary committee, examining possible railway routes to the Persian Gulf, considered that Kuwait would be a better terminus than Basra. In 1882 the Ottoman government approved an application by an English group for permission to build a line through Mesopotamia to Kuwait. Nothing came of the project at the time. H. L. Hoskins, *British Routes to India* (1928; reprint, New York: Octagon, 1966), 434, 447.
10. Busch, "Britain and Kuwayt," 195. Ismael, *Kuwait,* 181n, depicts the Russian "threat" as a mere pretext for the 1899 agreement, not the reason for it.
11. Busch, "Britain and Kuwayt," 197. See also Lorimer I, 1022–24; *MENA* I, 475–477. Text of the agreement in *KCBD,* 9–10.
12. *TAOK* pt. I, 39–40, 47–50; Ismael, *Kuwait,* 50; J. B. Kelly, "Salisbury, Curzon and the Kuwait Agreement of 1899," in K. Bourne and D. C. Watt, eds., *Studies in International History* (London: Longman, 1967), 281–282.
13. *TAOK* pt. I, 35; Kelly, "Salisbury," 283–284.
14. H. St. John Philby, *Arabian Jubilee* (New York: John Day, 1953), 9.
15. It was referred to by Prime Minister Balfour in a House of Commons debate on April 8, 1903, and in a statement in *The Times* (London), Jan. 11, 1904. Lovat Fraser, *India under Curzon and After* (London: William Heinemann, 1911), 94; Edward Mead Earle, *Turkey, the Great Powers, and the Baghdad Railway* (New York: Macmillan, 1923), 181. It was described by a prominent journalist in 1903: Valentine Chirol, *The Middle Eastern Question, or Some Political Problems of Indian Defence* (London: J. Murray, 1903), 232.

16. Some Mubarak partisans have denied that he accepted this appointment. See H. R. P. Dickson, *Kuwait and Her Neighbours* (London: Allen & Unwin, 1956), 136; H. V. F. Winstone and Zahra Freeth, *Kuwait: Prospect and Reality* (London: Crone Russak, 1972), 71. But see Lorimer I, 1018–19; J. B. Kelly, *Arabia, the Gulf, and the West* (New York: Basic Books, 1980), 169.
17. Busch, "Britain and Kuwayt," 191–192.
18. Abdul-Reda Assiri, *Kuwait's Foreign Policy: City-State in World Politics* (Boulder: Westview, 1990), 4, 12; Tareq Y. Ismael and Jacqueline S. Ismael, *Politics and Government in the Middle East and North Africa* (Miami: University Presses of Florida, 1991), 453.
19. *TAOK* pt. II, 20, 34, 47, 54, 64.
20. Ibid., 67.
21. Briton Cooper Busch, *Britain and the Persian Gulf, 1894–1914* (Berkeley: University of California Press, 1967), 196–201 (hereafter "Busch *BPG*").
22. *TAOK* pt. III, 122.
23. *TAOK* pt. I, 53. See also Kelly, "Salisbury," 283.
24. *TAOK* pt. III, 97–98.
25. *BDOW*, II, 49.
26. *TAOK* pt. III, 98–99; Lorimer I, 1031; Busch *BPG*, 208–209.
27. Curzon, Oct. 23, 1901, quoted in Busch *BPG*, 210.
28. Curzon to Lord Percy, Oct. 1, 1902, quoted in Lord Ronaldshay, *Lord Curzon*, vol. II (New York: Boni and Liveright, ca. 1928), 318.
29. *TAOK* pt. III, 140–161; Lorimer I, 1031–33; Busch *BPG*, 211–212.
30. *A Collection of First World War Military Handbooks of Arabia, 1913–1917*, vol. VI: *A Gazetteer of Arabia, Vol. I, Part I, 1917* (Gerrards Cross, England: Archive Editions, 1988), 449.
31. *TAOK* pt. IV, 67–69; and pt. V, 31–33.
32. *TAOK* pt. VI, 30, 33–34.
33. Ibid., 13–15.
34. *TAOK* pt. IV, 24, 26.
35. Ibid., 37–38, 42; Lorimer I, 1033–34.
36. *TAOK* pt. IV, 54; Busch *BPG*, 216, n. 105; *KCBD*, 17–18.
37. Peter Hennessy, *Whitehall* (London: Fontana, 1990), 60.
38. Foreign Office memorandum of 1908, quoted by Schofield, 35.
39. Schofield, 34–35.
40. Lorimer II, 1059–61.
41. *PGHS* I, 74.
42. *TAOK* pt. IV, 107–109, 124–126; Lorimer I, 1036; Chirol, *The Middle Eastern Question*, 235–236.
43. *TAOK* pt. IV, 162; Busch *BPG*, 219–220.

44. "Mubarak . . . was enormously wealthy in date gardens around Fao. His lavish expenditures were made possible by the income he received from these gardens, for he received very little from his citizens except a small export and import duty." Paul W. Harrison, M.D., *The Arab at Home* (New York: Crowell, 1924), 160.

45. For details of the early date garden litigation, see Lorimer I, 1034–35, 1040–42; also *TAOK* pt. IV, 18, 19; pt. V, 38–40.

46. Ronaldshay, *Lord Curzon,* II, 317.

47. Gary Troeller, *The Birth of Saudi Arabia: Britain and the Rise of the House of Sa'ud* (London: Cass, 1976), 12.

48. Ronaldshay, *Lord Curzon,* II, 316.

49. Ibid., 317.

50. Ibid., 319.

51. *TAOK* vol. 1, xxx.

52. Curzon was accompanied on his cruise by his first American wife, the former Mary Leiter of Chicago. She probably was the first American woman to come to Kuwait, although she never disembarked, remaining on the anchored ship in the harbor. She wrote her mother: "The air is divine here, a mixture of sea and desert. And I am very well indeed [she was expecting a child], and love the long peaceful days on deck." Nigel Nicolson, *Mary Curzon* (New York: Harper & Row, 1977), 168–169.

53. *TAOK* pt. VI, 2.

54. Ibid., 3–4.

55. Philip Graves, *The Life of Sir Percy Cox* (London: Hutchinson, 1941), 102–104; Busch *BPG,* 230–233; Lorimer I, 1038–40. Detailed correspondence in *TAOK* pt. VI, 44–105 passim. The idea of appointing a resident agent had been discussed in January 1902, long before Curzon's visit. *TAOK* pt. IV, 85–86; pt. V, 46–56, 68.

56. Ulrich Gehrke and Gustav Kuhn, *Die Grenzen des Irak: Historische und rechtliche Aspekte des irakischen Anspruchs auf Kuwait* [Iraq's Boundaries: Historical and Legal Aspects of Iraq's Claim to Kuwait], vol. II (Stuttgart: W. Kohlhammer, 1963), 15–21. Since that time details of the 1907 Lease Agreement negotiations have been published in *BDFA* I, vols. 17 and 18.

57. The inexhaustible Lorimer II (p. 1055) sheds light on this curious usage.

58. At the shaikh's insistence the agreement took the form of two reciprocal documents, one addressed by Knox to Mubarak, the other by Mubarak to Knox. Each was signed by one of the parties, not the other. Text in *KCBD,* 25–27. In 1942 the political agent in Kuwait, Tom Hickinbotham, wrote: "In my opinion [the 1907 lease agree-

ment] is defunct and it has no value except as an example of how not to make use of the English language." Ashtiany, 250.

59. Ronaldshay, *Lord Curzon*, II, 317.
60. Cox took up his new job on May 2, 1904. Until 1909 his status was "Acting." He was knighted in 1911. Graves, *The Life of Sir Percy Cox*, 91–92, 144, 154.
61. Cox to Curzon, Aug. 13, 1904. *TAOK* pt. VI, 97.
62. Mubarak to Cox, Aug. 7, 1904. *TAOK* pt. VI, 82–83.
63. Cox to Mubarak, Aug. 16, 1904. Ibid.
64. *TAOK* pt. VI, 97–99, 104.
65. Busch *BPG*, 311–312.
66. Rosemarie Said Zahlan, *The Making of the Modern Gulf States* (London: Unwin Hyman, 1989), 26.
67. Barclay Raunkiaer, *Through Wahhabiland on Camelback* (ca. 1914; reprint, New York: Praeger, 1969), 43–44.
68. *BDOW* II, 45–48; Busch *BPG*, 328.
69. Earlier that year Cox advocated publishing the 1899 Agreement and using it to force the Turks to withdraw their troops from Umm Qasr and Bubiyan. The Foreign Office declined to do so for tactical reasons related to the Anglo-Ottoman negotiations. *BDOW* I, 620–621.
70. Busch *BPG*, 328–329.
71. Gehrke and Kuhn, *Die Grenzen des Irak*, I, 80–82.
72. Busch *BPG*, 333.
73. Ibid., 335.
74. Graves, *The Life of Sir Percy Cox*, 168.
75. Report, May 3, 1913, by Louis Mallet and Arthur Hirtzel. *BDOW* II, 114–115.
76. The concept of two separate areas appears to have originated with Sir Percy Cox. Schofield, 43.
77. *BDOW* II, 114–115.
78. Text of the Convention in *BDOW* II, 190–194 (French original); *MENA* I, 567–570 (English translation). See also *KCBD*, 29–35.
79. This hypothesis is supported by recently published diaries of the Ottoman grand vizier; on March 11, 1913, he wrote: "[The Cabinet] discussed the English demand for Qatar as well as Kuwait . . . What benefits could we hope for from these unimportant lands? I decided it was better to leave Kuwait and Qatar to England and concentrate on the rich provinces of Iraq." Quoted in Feroz Ahmad, "A Note on the International Status of Kuwait before November 1914," *International Journal of Middle Eastern Studies* 24 (1992), 184. See also John C. Wilkinson, *Arabia's Frontiers: The Story of Britain's Boundary Drawing in the Desert* (London: Tauris, 1991), 91–92.

80. Busch *BPG,* 337–338.
81. There is a good biography: W. V. F. Winstone, *Captain Shakespear* (London: Cape, 1978).
82. Ashtiany, 106–107.
83. Graves, *The Life of Sir Percy Cox,* 169–170; Gehrke and Kuhn, *Die Grenzen des Irak,* 83.
84. Busch *BPG,* 339.

3. Britain Takes Charge in Iraq and Kuwait

1. NID *Iraq,* 270–274, 294. This source, however, makes no allusion to raids on Mesopotamia thought to have been made by the "Sea Peoples" during the Bronze Age.
2. *BDFA* II, vol. 3, 138.
3. Text of November 3, 1914, letter in *MENA* II, 6–7; also in *KCBD,* 37.
4. Office note by Shakespear, August 12, 1910. Ashtiany, 104.
5. Sir Arnold Wilson, for one, later described the tax-exemption promise as "probably superfluous." *Loyalties: Mesopotamia, 1914–1917* (London: Oxford University Press, 1931), 9n.
6. Peter Sluglett, *Britain in Iraq, 1914–1932* (London: Ithaca Press, 1976), 21. A staff exercise in India in 1912 developed plans for the permanent occupation of Fao and Basra. Philip W. Ireland, *Iraq: A Study in Political Development* (New York: Macmillan, 1938), 23. As late as April 1918 Sir Percy Cox wrote from Baghdad: "We should still hope to annex the Basra Vilayet and exercise a veiled protectorate over the Baghdad Vilayet." Aaron S. Klieman, *Foundations of British Policy in the Arab World: The Cairo Conference of 1921* (Baltimore: Johns Hopkins University Press, 1970), 20n. But see Alvin J. Cottrell, ed., *The Persian Gulf States: A General Survey* (Baltimore: Johns Hopkins University Press, 1980), 85, where Malcolm Yapp suggests that the motivation behind the Mesopotamian campaign was not control of Iraq, but rather "to avoid the possibility that Ottoman successes in the Gulf area might influence Muslim sentiment in India against British rule."
7. F. J. Moberly, *The Campaign in Mesopotamia* (London: H. M. Stationery Office, 1923–1927); H. R. P. Dickson, *Kuwait and Her Neighbours* (London: Allen & Unwin, 1956), 150. Dickson mentions that he served in this force as a cavalry officer. In his recent historical survey Richard Schofield considers it "unlikely" that Mubarak or either of

the sons who succeeded him during the war "actively participated" in it (p. 51).

8. *MENA* II, 6.
9. Alan Rush, *Al-Sabah: History and Genealogy of Kuwait's Ruling Family, 1752–1987* (London: Ithaca Press, 1987), 94.
10. *A Collection of First World War Military Handbooks of Arabia, 1913–1917,* vol. IV: *A Handbook of Arabia, Volume I, General* (Gerrards Cross, England: Archive Editions, 1988), 38.
11. Rush, *Al-Sabah,* 94.
12. *PGHS* I, 75.
13. Robert Lacey, *The Kingdom: Arabia and the House of Saud* (New York: Harcourt Brace Jovanovich, 1981), 125.
14. *PGHS* I, 75.
15. Lacey, *The Kingdom,* 125.
16. Rush, *Al-Sabah,* 96.
17. Ibid., 95.
18. *PGHS* I, 75.
19. Rush, *Al-Sabah,* 81.
20. "The Situation at Kuwait," *Arab Bulletin* (Cairo), May 7, 1918, 145–150. For the fascinating story of the *Arab Bulletin,* see David Fromkin, *A Peace to End All Peace* (New York: Avon, 1989), 221–222.
21. Rush, *Al-Sabah,* 96. British officers found that camels could manage terrain in Mesopotamia that mules and horses could not. Donald Millar, *Death of an Army* (Boston: Houghton Mifflin, 1970), 213.
22. Memorandum by John W. Field, FO, March 29, 1922. IOR, L/P&S/18/B 391. See also Dickson, *Kuwait and Her Neighbours,* 243–244; Schofield, 53; *BDFA* II, vol. 9, 103; C. U. Aitchison, comp., *A Collection of Treaties, Engagements and Sanads Relating to India and Neighbouring Countries,* vol. XI (Delhi: Manager of Publications, 1933), 205. Deposing Shaikh Salim was under consideration by the British in September 1918. Ashtiany, 150.
23. IOR, L/P&S/12/3737, folio 275. The £12,500 was for a water distillation plant to be installed for the shaikh by the Anglo-Persian Oil Company. *PGHS* I, 74.
24. Rush, *Al-Sabah,* 80.
25. Ibid.; Gary Troeller, *The Birth of Saudi Arabia: Britain and the Rise of the House of Sa'ud* (London: Cass, 1976), 171–172. Shaikh Salim was told firmly by the British that the 1913 Convention boundary provisions were no longer binding on Ibn Saud. Ashtiany, 144–146. See also Christine Moss Helms, *The Cohesion of Saudi Arabia* (Baltimore: Johns Hopkins University Press, 1981), 207–209.

26. H. V. F. Winstone and Zahra Freeth, *Kuwait: Prospect and Reality* (New York: Crone Russak, 1972), 83.
27. Dickson, *Kuwait and Her Neighbours,* 243–257; *PGHS* I, 79–80. Ashtiany, 147–148.
28. Jacqueline S. Ismael, *Kuwait: Social Change in Historical Perspective* (Syracuse: Syracuse University Press, 1982), 71–72; Tareq Y. Ismael and Jacqueline S. Ismael, *Politics and Government in the Middle East and North Africa* (Miami: University Presses of Florida, 1991), 460–461; Rosemarie Said Zahlan, *The Making of the Modern Gulf States* (London: Unwin Hyman, 1989), 25–27; *PGHS* I, 73 (where the number of members is given as six, not twelve); Rush, *Al-Sabah,* 54–55; Ashtiany, 149.
29. Sluglett, *Britain in Iraq,* 19; Fromkin, *A Peace to End All Peace,* 258.
30. NID *Iraq,* 287.
31. Ireland, *Iraq,* 338–342. The treaty was ratified by Iraq's Constituent Assembly in June 1924, but not with much enthusiasm. Only 69 of the 100 delegates were present; 37 voted for the treaty, 24 voted against, and the rest abstained. John Marlowe, *The Persian Gulf in the Twentieth Century* (New York: Praeger, 1962), 260.
32. *WSC* IV/2, 1296.
33. Jeremy Wilson, *Lawrence of Arabia* (New York: Macmillan, 1990), 954.
34. Ashtiany, 372.
35. When news of Britain's mandate reached Baghdad in late May 1920, a delegation of notables approached Wilson to protest. He dismissed them as "a handful of ungrateful politicians." Helen Chapin Metz, ed., *Iraq: A Country Study,* 4th ed. (Washington, D.C.: U.S. Government Printing Office, 1990), 34.
36. C. J. Edmonds, *Kurds, Turks and Arabs* (London: Oxford University Press, 1957), 117.
37. *WSC* IV, 496.
38. *WSC* IV/2, 1309–13.
39. IOR, L/P&S/12/3737.
40. Cox to Curzon, July 23, 1921. *WSC* IV/3, 1939–40, where this letter, found in Curzon's papers, was printed out of chronological order among documents dated July 1922.
41. *WSC* IV/2, 1389.
42. Ibid., 1392–93.
43. Ibid., 1398–99.
44. Ibid., 1407.
45. *WSC* IV/3, 1567.
46. The "authorized" biography of Lawrence mentions meetings be-

tween Lawrence and Faisal in Egypt on April 15 and April 21, 1921, but sheds no light on what passed between them about Iraq. Wilson, *Lawrence of Arabia*, chap. 30. See also Klieman, *Foundations of British Policy in the Arab World*, 152.

47. Churchill to John Shuckburgh, July 9, 1921. *WSC* IV/3, 1547.
48. Ibid., 1580.
49. Ibid., 1604–05.
50. Ibid., 1601–03.
51. Ibid., 1675.
52. Ibid., 1840–41. Cox "had no liking for Lawrence, and regarded his intrigues on behalf of Faisal as a principal cause of the [1920] Iraq rebellion." H. St. John Philby, *Arabian Jubilee* (New York: John Day, 1953), 65. Wilson's *Lawrence of Arabia* does not mention Churchill's proposal that Lawrence go to Baghdad.
53. *WSC* IV/3, 1973–74.
54. Ibid., 1987.
55. Ibid., 1988.

4. First Lines in the Sand, 1923

1. Paul W. Harrison, M.D., *The Arab at Home* (New York: Crowell, 1924), 140–141.
2. Joseph Kostiner, "Britain and the Northern Frontier of the Saudi State, 1922–1925," in Uriel Dann, ed., *The Great Powers in the Middle East, 1919–1939* (New York: Holmes & Meier, 1988), 29; Schofield, 57–58.
3. IOR, L/P&S/12/3737. It has been asserted that Cox derived his dual authority at Uqair from a wartime directive of the War Office to the effect that Kuwait and the Persian Gulf were to be administered from Basra. Edward Hoagland Brown, *The Saudi Arabia–Kuwait Neutral Zone* (Beirut: Middle East Research and Publishing Center, 1963), 52. That order may have been in the background, but the arrangement made in 1921 was personal to Cox and was very specifically limited to his tenure in Baghdad.
4. Dickson, as political agent in Kuwait, included an account of the conference in a memorandum to the political resident in 1934, which has not been published: IOR, R/15/5/184. Amin Rihani, an Arab-American writer who came to Uqair with Ibn Saud's entourage, included excerpts from his diary during the conference in *Ibn Sa'oud of Arabia* (London: Constable, 1928). Cox's own report to the Colonial Office, dated December 20, 1922, is in *KCBD*, 48–49. There is a definitive discussion of Uqair in John C. Wilkinson's *Arabia's Fron-*

tiers: The Story of Britain's Boundary Drawing in the Desert (London: Tauris, 1991), chap. 6.

5. H. St. John Philby, *Arabian Days* (London: Hale, 1948), 113–114.
6. One of the baptismal names given to the Dicksons' son, born in 1923 in Switzerland, was "Saud." The Anglican clergyman who performed the ceremony thought this inappropriate and changed it to "Sand" on the certificate. Violet Dickson, *Forty Years in Kuwait* (London: Allen & Unwin, 1971), 55. Colonel Dickson's nickname among the Arabs was "Abu Saud"—father of Saud. Zahra Freeth, *A New Look at Kuwait* (London: Allen & Unwin, 1972).
7. Dickson, *Forty Years in Kuwait*, 53–54.
8. Ibid., 54.
9. Lady Bell, ed., *Letters of Gertrude Bell*, vol. II (New York: Boni & Liveright, 1927), 659.
10. C. J. Edmonds, *Kurds, Turks and Arabs* (London: Oxford University Press, 1957), 396.
11. H. R. P. Dickson, *Kuwait and Her Neighbours* (London: Allen & Unwin, 1956), 272–274. In 1950 the U.S. government was told by the British that the original Uqair Conference map (with Cox's markings) could be seen at the Royal Geographical Society in London. U.S. Department of State, *Foreign Relations of the United States, 1950*, vol. V (Washington, D.C.: U.S. Government Printing Office, 1978), 31.
12. Dickson, *Kuwait and Her Neighbours*, 275.
13. In his 1916 report on the Anglo-Indian intelligence staff in Basra, Col. T. E. Lawrence gave More high marks: "In Basra the S.S. [Secret Service] work is being run by Captain J. C. More, the solitary member of the Intelligence Staff who speaks Arabic. He also knows Persian. He has lived and travelled in Syria, understands the Arabs, and gets on well with them." Jeremy Wilson, *Lawrence of Arabia* (New York: Macmillan, 1990), 950.
14. Dickson, *Kuwait and Her Neighbours*, 276.
15. Ibid., 279.
16. Schofield regards Dickson's analysis of the Najd-Kuwait boundary settlement as "flawed and unfair" (p. 60).
17. PRO, CO/730/26, Dispatch no. 877, Dec. 20, 1922.
18. Their ranks are legion. Examples include John Marlowe, *The Persian Gulf in the Twentieth Century* (New York: Praeger, 1962), 75; Jill Crystal, *Oil and Politics in the Gulf* (Cambridge: Cambridge University Press, 1990), 53; John Bulloch, *The Persian Gulf Unveiled* (New York: St. Martin's, 1984), 62; Glenn Frankel of the *Washington Post*, an article reproduced in Micah L. Sifry and Christopher Cerf, eds., *The*

Gulf War Reader (New York: Times Books, 1991), 16–20. The Uqair Conference is summarized correctly in *PGHS* I, 80; also by Schofield, 57–60.

19. Schofield, 55.
20. Ibid., 61. (The exact circumstances are not clear from Schofield's account.)
21. IOR, R/15/5/207, Dispatches no. 876, Dec. 19, 1922; and 877, Dec. 20, 1922.
22. IOR, R/15/5/207, Dispatch no. 874, Dec. 20, 1922.
23. IOR, R/15/5/207.
24. IOR, R/15/5/100 (original Arabic with English translation).
25. IOR, R/15/5/100. See also Ashtiany, 148–149.
26. More to Cox, April 4, 1923. IOR, R/15/5/100.
27. C. U. Aitchison, comp., *A Collection of Treaties, Engagements and Sanads Relating to India and Neighbouring Countries,* vol. XI (Delhi: Manager of Publications, 1933), 266.
28. This point is made by Husain M. al-Baharna in his useful article "The Consequences of Britain's Exclusive Treaties: A Gulf View," in B. R. Pridham, ed., *The Arab Gulf and the West* (London: Croom Helm, 1985), 36, n. 11.
29. Aitchison, *A Collection of Treaties,* 211–212.
30. In the Anglo-Iraqi treaty, the exact sense of the mandatory provision was carried over in these words (Art. VIII): "No territory in Iraq shall be ceded or leased or in any way placed under the control of any Foreign Power." *MENA* II, 311.
31. Quincy Wright, *Mandates under the League of Nations* (Chicago: University of Chicago Press, 1930), 122.
32. Iraq, High Commissioner, *Report on Iraq Administration, October 1920–March 1922* (London, ca. 1923), and reports for following periods. Great Britain, Colonial Office, *Special Report on the Progress of Iraq during the Period 1920–1931* (London, 1931). The 1920–1922 report refers (pp. 117, 121) to the need for establishing the Najd-Iraq and Najd-Kuwait frontiers, but there is no reference to Iraq-Kuwait.
33. Aitchison, *A Collection of Treaties,* 205.
34. Arnold J. Toynbee, *Survey of International Affairs, 1925,* vol. I: *The Islamic World since the Peace Settlement* (London: Oxford University Press and the Royal Institute of International Affairs, 1927), pt. III, sec. vi, 336.
35. Arnold J. Toynbee, *Survey of International Affairs, 1934* (London: Oxford University Press and the Royal Institute of International Affairs, 1935), pt. II, sec. ii, 182, with a footnote reference to the 1925 *Survey.*

36. William H. McNeill, *Arnold J. Toynbee: A Life* (New York: Oxford University Press, 1989), 133–134, and 309, n. 46.

37. The myth that Iraq itself was somehow involved in the Cox "settlement" of the Kuwait border in 1923 seems to die hard. In a 1947 "Outline of the History of Kuwait," Laurence Lockhart wrote regarding 1922–23: "The Kuwaiti-Iraqi frontier was likewise settled by friendly agreement." *Journal of the Royal Central Asian Society* 34 (July–October 1947), 273. In the article "Kuwait" in the 1968 edition of *Encyclopaedia Britannica,* XIII, 520, Lockhart stated that the northern frontier of Kuwait was "agreed with Iraq in 1923." In the 1986 edition (VII, 51) this had been amended to: "The northern frontier with Iraq was agreed upon in 1923," which is somewhat less misleading, but not much. Even Schofield's otherwise admirable 1991 study, *Kuwait and Iraq: Historical Claims and Territorial Disputes,* published by the Royal Institute of International Affairs itself, seems to adhere to the original Chatham House version, asserting that by 1957 "Britain had failed to reconcile Iraq to the boundary it had earlier agreed in official correspondence of 1923 and 1932" (p. 99), and "In exchanges of notes of 1923 and 1932 Iraq had also agreed to the present delimitation" (p. 130). In an article in *The Spectator,* March 16, 1991, J. B. Kelly says: "the boundaries of Iraq, Kuwait and Najd were drawn in consultation with the Arab rulers concerned."

38. The official *Administration Report* for Iraq covering the period April 1923–December 1924 states that Cox was in Baghdad during the month of April but "took no active part in affairs" (with the exception of a protocol to the Anglo-Iraqi treaty) (p. 7). Gertrude Bell, who wrote the report, may not have known about Cox's April 19 memorandum to More.

39. J. B. Kelly, *Arabia, the Gulf, and the West* (New York: Basic Books, 1980), 233.

40. The vocabulary of trusts, familiar enough to students of the common law, was not much employed in connection with the work of the Permanent Mandates Commission of the League of Nations, although the similar concept of "guardianship" was often used. Perhaps this reflects the fact that trusts are little understood or appreciated in civil law jurisprudence. But the United Nations seems to work comfortably with "Trust Territories"—the functional equivalents of League of Nations mandates. See, generally, League of Nations, *The Mandates System: Origins—Principles—Application* (Geneva, 1945); Quincy Wright, *Mandates under the League of Nations* (Chicago: University of Chicago Press, 1930); Campbell L. Upthegrove, *Empire by Mandate: A History of the Relations of Great Britain with*

the Permanent Mandates Commission of the League of Nations (New York: Bookman, 1954).

5. Invisible Lines at Geneva, 1932

1. John Bagot Glubb, *War in the Desert* (New York: Norton, 1961), 64.
2. Ibid., 108–109.
3. Ibid., 272–273.
4. H. R. P. Dickson, *Kuwait and Her Neighbours* (London: Allen & Unwin, 1956), 306.
5. Glubb, *War in the Desert*, 198. There is extensive material about the Ikhwan operations as they affected Kuwait in *BDFA* II, vol. 9, 103–104. There is an official British summary in *PGHS* I, 82–83. See also Alan Rush, *Al-Sabah: History and Genealogy of Kuwait's Ruling Family, 1752–1987* (London: Ithaca Press, 1987), 55–56; and H. V. F. Winstone and Zahra Freeth, *Kuwait: Prospect and Reality* (New York: Crone Russak, 1972), 97–105.
6. H. V. F. Winstone and Zahra Freeth, *Kuwait: Prospect and Reality* (New York: Crone Russak, 1972), 90.
7. From "Editor's Preface" to Kaiyan Homi Kaikobad, *The Shatt-al-Arab Boundary Question* (Oxford: Oxford University Press, 1988).
8. Violet Dickson, *Forty Years in Kuwait* (London: Allen & Unwin, 1971).
9. Ibid., 75–81. Mrs. Dickson, who became a Dame of the British Empire in 1941, died in a Berkshire nursing home on January 4, 1991. *New York Times*, Jan. 20, 1991.
10. Zahra Dickson Freeth, *Kuwait Was My Home* (London: Allen & Unwin, 1956), 11–12. Safwan is where Gen. Norman Schwarzkopf held his historic meeting with Iraqi officers following the Gulf War, March 2, 1991.
11. H. R. P. Dickson, *The Arab of the Desert* (London: Allen & Unwin, 1949), 583. The road was first paved in the mid-1950s. Kuwait Oil Company, *The Story of Kuwait* (London, 1955), 59.
12. During the Mesopotamian campaign, the British-Indian military authorities had naturally established that in Iraq the "rule of the road" was to be to the left, as it was in India. By midcentury, independent Iraq had switched from left to right. *Pocket Guide to Baghdad*, rev. 2d ed. (Baghdad: Times Press, 1953), 74. In Kuwait the few vehicles had apparently always driven on the right. Lefthand driving has been a problem elsewhere as the British Empire shrank: in Pakistan after independence in 1947, the newly independent government shucked off one remnant of the old regime by switching traffic from left to right; the move proved controversial because draft animals

continued to plod along at night on the left as they had always done, causing a number of serious accidents.

13. Ashtiany, 242–243. The boundary signboard south of Safwan was removed and replaced many times over the next twenty-five years, until no one was certain any longer where it had originally stood. Schofield, 62, 82–87.

14. See, generally, Ulrich Gehrke and Gustav Kuhn, *Die Grenzen des Irak: Historische und rechtliche Aspekte des irakischen Anspruchs auf Kuwait*, 2 vols. (Stuttgart: W. Kohlhammer, 1963).

15. Schofield, 64.

16. The Iraq constitution ("Organic Law") provided that treaties were to be made by the king but must be ratified by the Parliament. But on Sept. 7, 1927, the Council of Ministers had enacted a resolution providing that "international agreements of minor importance or of a scientific nature and not concluded between the heads of states concerned, but between high officials of the governments of such states, need not of themselves be submitted to Parliament." Majid Khadduri, *Independent Iraq* (New York: Oxford University Press, 1960), 23. It would be interesting to know if the British authorities thought of using this provision in 1932 in connection with the Iraq-Kuwait boundary. As Khadduri has recently pointed out, an agreement about frontiers is hardly a matter of "minor importance." "Iraq's Claim to the Sovereignty of Kuwayt," *New York University Journal of International Law and Politics* 23, no. 1 (Fall 1990), 47n. But what about a letter merely "re-affirming" a frontier?

17. According to George William Rendel, Hall "had an encyclopedic knowledge of every aspect and incident of Anglo-Iraqi relations over the previous ten years." *The Sword and the Olive: Recollections of Diplomacy and the Foreign Service, 1913–1954* (London: John Murray, 1957), 65.

18. Memorandum by J. Hathorn Hall, April 8, 1932. PRO, CO/730/176/3. Hall refers to the 1913 Anglo-Turkish Convention as "unpublished." The Convention itself was apparently first published in *BDOW* II, 190–194; this official collection of prewar documents had begun to appear, but the volume in question did not come out until 1938. However, the clauses of the Convention relating to the Iraq-Kuwait boundary were printed in the original French in an Indian government publication which was available for public sale ("9 rupees or 8/6d") as early as 1933: C. U. Aitchison, comp., *A Collection of Treaties, Engagements and Sanads Relating to India and Neighbouring Countries*, vol. XI (Delhi: Manager of Publications, 1933), 266–267.

19. Memorandum by A. F. Morley, May 7, 1932. IOR, L/P&S/12/3737.

20. J. E. W. Flood, FO, to under secretary of state, IO, May 11, 1932. PRO, FO 371/16006; and IOR, R/15/1/524.
21. IO to FO, June 22, 1932. PRO, FO 371/16006.
22. IOR, R/15/1/524.
23. Ibid.
24. Political agent (Kuwait) to political resident, June 10, 1932. Ibid.
25. Political resident Persian Gulf to political agent (Kuwait), June 11, 1932. Ibid.
26. Political resident Persian Gulf to Government of India and secretary of state for India, June 11, 1932. PRO, FO 371/16006.
27. PRO, FO 371/16006.
28. Schofield, 65–66; *KCBD,* 75–76.
29. On July 18 Sir Hugh Biscoe died of a heart attack in the Gulf, on his way to Sharjah to negotiate aircraft landing rights there. Dickson, who was with him, buried Biscoe at sea and proceeded to Sharjah, where he conducted the negotiations alone. Dickson, *Kuwait and Her Neighbours,* 346–349.
30. PRO, CO/730/176/3.
31. Copies of all the documents referred to here can be found in PRO, FO 371/16006.
32. PRO, FO 371/16006.
33. "Request of the Kingdom of Iraq for Admission to the League of Nations," League of Nations Document no. A17 1932/vii, Aug. 16, 1932, quoting Iraq's memorandum, July 12, 1932. PRO, CO/730/176/3. See also Henry A. Foster, *The Making of Modern Iraq* (Norman: University of Oklahoma Press, 1935), 286–287. "Limitrophe," incidentally, is an infrequently used word meaning "adjacent." Obscure terminology is a useful gambit in many a bluff.
34. The Permanent Mandates Commission spent an enormous amount of time on Iraq's application, owing mainly to concern over the treatment of minorities. Campbell L. Upthegrove, *Empire by Mandate: A History of the Relations of Great Britain with the Permanent Mandates Commission of the League of Nations* (New York: Bookman, 1954), 131–140.
35. Gehrke and Kuhn, *Die Grenzen des Irak,* I, 31–35.
36. J. B. Kelly, *Arabia, the Gulf, and the West* (New York: Basic Books, 1980), 97.
37. *The Times* (London), July 25, 1961; quoted in Gehrke and Kuhn, *Die Grenzen des Irak,* I, 33–34, n. 7.
38. Gehrke and Kuhn, *Die Grenzen des Irak,* I, 34, n. 8.
39. C. J. Edmonds, *Kurds, Turks and Arabs* (London: Oxford University Press, 1957), is a vivid account of Edmonds' experiences as a British

political officer in northern Iraq in the 1920s. Edmonds was not the only expert to have been led astray by the deliberate murkiness of the 1932 documentation. One legal analysis refers to a nonexistent "Iraq-Kuwait Convention on Boundaries" of 1932. R. V. Pillai and M. Kumar, "Political and Legal Status of Kuwait," *International and Comparative Law Quarterly* 11 (January 1962), 114. The very well-informed Majid Khadduri wrote that Nuri had addressed his letter to the political agent in Kuwait. *Socialist Iraq* (Washington, D.C.: Middle East Institute, 1978), 153–154.

40. Rendel to Beckett, July 4, 1932. PRO, FO/371/16006.
41. Later Sir Alexander Cadogan, a distinguished British diplomat of the post–World War II era.
42. PRO, CO/730/176/3.
43. PRO, FO 371/16006.
44. *TAOK* vol. 1, v.
45. PRO, FO 371/16006.
46. "The Pink Volume" was cited by Husain M. al-Baharna in his very interesting work, *The Arabian Gulf States: Their Legal and Political Status and Their International Problems,* 2d rev. ed. (Beirut: Librairie du Liban, 1975) (256, nn. 3 and 4), as his source for the "Exchange of Letters of 21 July and 10 August 1932 between the then Prime Minister of Iraq, Nuri Pasha al-Said, and the former Ruler of Kuwait, Shaikh Ahmad al-Sabah, respectively." The correspondence published by al-Baharna is the same as that authorized by Rendel for printing. Al-Baharna's sources included the archives of the Kuwaiti Foreign Ministry, a possible unofficial repository of the elusive "Pink Volume."

6. Britain and Kuwait between the Wars

1. *PGHS* I, 85.
2. Ibid., 76–77.
3. Schofield, 62–63; *PGHS* II, 90.
4. Note by Ryan, Aug. 16, 1933. *BDFA* II, vol. 9, 99–100.
5. Ibid., 94–105. See also Jacqueline S. Ismael, *Kuwait: Social Change in Historical Perspective* (Syracuse: Syracuse University Press, 1982), 71.
6. Alvin J. Cottrell, ed., *The Persian Gulf States: A General Survey* (Baltimore: Johns Hopkins University Press, 1980), 89.
7. Kuwait Oil Company, *The Story of Kuwait* (London, 1955), 18–20.
8. KOC concession agreement of Dec. 23, 1934, Art. 19, in *MENA* II, 456ff. There was an Ottoman precedent of sorts: the original oil rights in Mesopotamia were held by the Civil List, the Sultan's personal account; after the 1908 revolution they were transferred to

the state. David H. Finnie, *Desert Enterprise: The Middle East Oil Industry in Its Local Environment* (Cambridge, Mass.: Harvard University Press, 1958), 28.

9. Frank Stoakes in Derek Hopwood, ed., *The Arabian Peninsula: Society and Politics* (London: Allen & Unwin, 1972), 196.

10. George Willaim Rendel, *The Sword and the Olive: Recollections of Diplomacy and the Foreign Service, 1913–1954* (London: John Murray, 1957), 100–102.

11. J. B. Kelly, *Arabia, the Gulf, and the West* (New York: Basic Books, 1980), 98–99; Schofield, 92–93.

12. Paul W. Harrison, M.D., *The Arab at Home* (New York: Crowell, 1924), 182.

13. John Bulloch, *The Persian Gulf Unveiled* (New York: St. Martin's, 1984), 27.

14. David Fromkin, *A Peace to End All Peace* (New York: Avon, 1989), 85, citing *The Memoirs of Sir Ronald Storrs* (New York: G. P. Putnam's Sons, 1937), 206.

15. Capt. Gerald de Gaury, who got deeply involved in the 1938 political disturbances, "became what he still is in Kuwait—a scapegoat for all who would blame an outsider for what was in truth a local power struggle." Alan Rush, *Al-Sabah: History and Genealogy of Kuwait's Ruling Family, 1752–1987* (London: Ithaca Press, 1987), 57. See also Schofield, 76.

16. Rendel, *The Sword and the Olive*, 102.

17. H. R. P. Dickson, *Kuwait and Her Neighbours* (London: Allen & Unwin, 1956), 370; Ashtiany, 242.

18. H. R. P. Dickson, "Kuwait Administration Report for 1932," typescript copy, Dickson Papers, Private Papers Collection, Middle East Centre, St. Antony's College, Oxford.

19. *BDFA* II, vol. 2, 83.

20. Note by K. R. Johnstone, March 3, 1934. PRO, FO 371/17823. *PGHS* I, 74.

21. Dickson, "Kuwait Administration Report."

22. Ibid.

23. *BDFA* II, vol. 7, doc. 302.

24. *MENA* II, 478.

25. H. V. F. Winstone and Zahra Freeth, *Kuwait: Prospect and Reality* (New York: Crone Russak, 1972), 111–117. This popular book has a surprisingly detailed discussion of the enormously complicated date garden litigation. Also *PGHS* II, 94–99.

26. Violet Dickson, *Forty Years in Kuwait* (London: Allen & Unwin, 1971), 120; Ashtiany, 245.

27. Ashtiany, 168.

28. *PGHS* II, 60.
29. Ibid.
30. For the 1938–39 political crisis in Kuwait, see *PGHS* II, 60; J. E. Peterson, *The Arab Gulf States: Steps toward Political Participation* (New York: Praeger, 1988), 27–32; Rosemarie Said Zahlan, *The Making of the Modern Gulf States* (London: Unwin Hyman, 1989), chap. 3; Jill Crystal, *Oil and Politics in the Gulf* (Cambridge: Cambridge University Press, 1990), 52–55; Ismael, *Kuwait*, 74–77; Kelly, *Arabia, the Gulf, and the West*, 276–277; Winstone and Freeth, *Kuwait: Prospect and Reality*, 118–121.
31. Glen Balfour-Paul, "Kuwait, Qatar and the United Arab Emirates: Political and Social Evolution," in Ian Richard Netton, ed., *Arabia and the Gulf: From Traditional Society to Modern States* (London: Croom Helm, 1986), 157, 170n.

7. Iraq on Its Own

1. Gerald de Gaury, *Three Kings in Baghdad* (London: Hutchinson, 1961), 91.
2. Majid Khadduri, *Independent Iraq* (New York: Oxford University Press, 1960), 23. There is an acidly detailed summary of the prerogatives retained by the British in Hanna Batatu, *The Old Social Classes and the Revolutionary Movements in Iraq: A Study of Iraq's Old Landed and Commercial Classes and of Its Communists, Ba'thists, and Free Officers* (Princeton: Princeton University Press, 1978), 545. Readers daunted by Batatu's awesome title will be missing a gem of incisive Middle Eastern political history.
3. Nuri served as prime minister fourteen times between 1930 and 1958. "Perhaps no other Arab statesman in modern times has followed a foreign policy as consistently friendly towards Great Britain." Majid Khadduri, *Arab Contemporaries* (Baltimore: Johns Hopkins University Press, 1973), 27, 237.
4. See Cecil Byford, comp., *The Port of Basrah* (Basrah Port Directorate, 1937).
5. Handwritten draft letter headed "My dear Ambassador," undated but post-1941. C. J. Edmonds Papers, Private Papers Collection, Middle East Centre, St. Antony's College, Oxford. German engineers had indeed looked over the area. See Chapter 2.
6. "Extract from Adv. Ministry of Interior's note on a visit to the Shatt al-Arab and Kuwait—March 1934—Secret." Edmonds Papers.
7. Peterson to Foreign Secretary Halifax, April 19, 1938. *BDFA* II, vol. 12, 430–431.

8. Khadduri, *Republican Iraq* (London: Oxford University Press, 1969), 168; Husain M. al-Baharna, "The Consequences of Britain's Exclusive Treaties: A Gulf View," in B. R. Pridham, ed., *The Arab Gulf and the West* (London: Croom Helm, 1985), 254–256; R. V. Pillai and M. Kumar, "Political and Legal Status of Kuwait," *International and Comparative Law Quarterly* 11, no. 108 (January 1962), 126–130.

9. It might be just barely possible to construct an argument that Britain's role at the time of the 1923 Cox-More Memorandum was still only that of a victorious Allied "Power," on the basis that the 1922 Anglo-Iraqi Treaty (incorporating the terms and principles of the mandate allotted to Britain in 1920) did not formally come into effect until it was ratified in 1924. But such an interpretation would put an inordinately heavy strain on the equitable principles of trusteeship with which the mandates were imbued from the outset. Beckett's memorandum does not make use of the point.

10. IOR, R/15/1/541 contains the Baxter-Peterson letter and enclosures, folios 35–47.

11. De Gaury, *Three Kings in Baghdad,* 103.

12. Clark Kerr to Foreign Secretary Eden, June 19, 1936. *BDFA* II, vol. 12, 5.

13. Peterson to Foreign Secretary Halifax, June 28, 1938. *BDFA* II, vol. 13, 136–138.

14. Humphrys to Ghazi, Feb. 28, 1935. *BDFA* II, vol. 10, 420–421.

15. Humphrys to Foreign Secretary Simon, March 6, 1935. Ibid.

16. Ghazi to Humphrys, March 14, 1935. Ibid., 424. To raise questions about the authorship of such a gracious royal letter may seem churlish. Ghazi did, however, have discreet British staff available to him who would have been pleased to help out on an occasion such as this.

17. Elie Kedourie, *The Chatham House Version and Other Middle Eastern Studies* (London: Weidenfeld & Nicolson, 1970), 247n.

18. King Ghazi's interest in Gulf affairs predated the broadcasts. In 1936 he was instrumental in founding an "Association of Arabs of the Gulf" in Basra to spread propaganda among the Gulf states (especially Kuwait) in favor of union with Iraq. J. B. Kelly, *Arabia, the Gulf, and the West* (New York: Basic Books, 1980), 276.

19. Ahmad Abdul Razzaq Shikara, *Iraqi Politics, 1921–1941* (Surbiton: LAAM, 1987), 154.

20. Peterson to Foreign Secretary Halifax, March 8, 1939. *BDFA* II, vol. 13, 282.

21. Kelly, *Arabia, the Gulf, and the West,* 276, where the 1932 transaction is characterized as "an exchange of letters between the Iraqi prime

minister and the ruler of Kuwait." As mentioned in Chapter 5, there was no such direct correspondence.

22. *PGHS* II, 92.
23. Kedourie, *The Chatham House Version*, 249.
24. Peterson was writing after World War II, when Abdul Ilah was acting as regent for Faisal II. Maurice Peterson, *Both Sides of the Curtain* (London: Constable, 1950), 151–152.
25. De Gaury, *Three Kings in Baghdad*, 104.
26. Khadduri, *Independent Iraq*, 140, citing *Iraq Times*, April 6, 1939.
27. Batatu, *The Old Social Classes*, 340.
28. Ibid., 342.
29. Ibid. and 343.
30. Mohammad Tarbush, *The Role of the Military in Politics: A Case Study of Iraq to 1941* (London: Kegan Paul, 1982), 263, noted a similar absence of detailed information about Ghazi's death in the records of the Foreign Office.
31. But one unpublished doctoral dissertation analyzing Gulf boundary problems characterized Qasim's 1961 claim (see Chapter 9) as "heretofore unheard of." Lenore Greenschlag Martin, "A Systematic Study of Boundary Disputes in the Persian Gulf, 1900 to Present" (Ph.D. diss., University of Chicago, 1979), 127.

8. The Undemarcated Boundary, 1938–1958

1. Peterson to Foreign Secretary Halifax. *BDFA* II, vol. 12, 430–431.
2. Jill Crystal, *Oil and Politics in the Gulf* (Cambridge: Cambridge University Press, 1990), 52.
3. Schofield, 77.
4. *PGHS* II, 118.
5. Smuggling from Kuwait into Iraq was a contentious matter throughout the 1930s; the India Office and the Foreign Office were often at loggerheads about it. See Schofield, 68–71.
6. Daniel Silverfarb, *Britain's Informal Empire in the Middle East: A Case Study of Iraq, 1929–1941* (New York: Oxford University Press, 1986), 69.
7. Houstoun-Boswall to Halifax, April 20, 1939. *BDFA* II, vol. 13, 302–303.
8. Newton to Halifax, Nov. 14, 1939. IOR, R/15/1/541.
9. Schofield, 81.
10. Silverfarb, *Britain's Informal Empire*, 69–71. Schofield, 82.
11. It has been suggested that following the end of the mandate, "owing to physical difficulties, delimitation of frontiers in a desert area was

temporarily postponed." Majid Khadduri, *Socialist Iraq: A Study in Iraqi Politics since 1968* (Washington, D.C.: Middle East Institute, 1978), 154. In fact the reasons were more political than physical.

12. The KOC concession agreement is in *MENA* II, 456–466. The map is reproduced in Archibald H. T. Chisholm, *The First Kuwait Oil Concession: A Record of the Negotiations, 1911–1934* (London: Cass, 1975).

13. Stephen Hemsley Longrigg, *Oil in the Middle East: Its Discovery and Development,* 3d ed. (London: Oxford University Press, 1968), 82.

14. Although KOC was half-owned by Gulf Oil Corporation and had many American employees, there was no U.S. consulate in Kuwait until 1950. When the question was raised by the State Department, the Foreign Office resisted, arguing that a precedent would be created for opening other, less desirable consulates, and "Kuwait would be rapidly infected with all the ultra-nationalist maladies" that had swept Iraq and Egypt. U.S. Department of State, *Foreign Relations of the United States, 1949,* vol. VI (Washington, D.C.: U.S. Government Printing Office, 1977), 1566–71.

15. This distinction follows that in S. Whittemore Boggs, "Delimitation of Seaward Areas under National Jurisdiction," *American Journal of International Law* 45 (1951), 242, n. 10.

16. Foreign Office to Baghdad, March 30, 1939. *BDFA* II, vol. 13, 284.

17. Houstoun-Boswall to Halifax, April 20, 1939. Ibid., 305.

18. Ashtiany, 244.

19. Silverfarb, *Britain's Informal Empire,* 71–72. Silverfarb's "The British Government and the Question of Umm Qasr, 1938–1945," *Asian and African Studies* 16 (1982), 215–238, covers much the same ground in more detail.

20. Silverfarb, *Britain's Informal Empire,* 72; Schofield, 92.

21. Edmonds to Minister for Foreign Affairs, dated "9/3/45." Typescript copy, unsigned, on Iraqi Interior Ministry letterhead. C. J. Edmonds Papers, Private Papers Collection, St. Antony's College, Oxford.

22. Khadduri, *Socialist Iraq,* 154. For details of Britain's efforts to map the area and demarcate the boundary in the 1950s, see Schofield, chap. 4. Sir Rupert Hay, political resident in the Persian Gulf at the time (1946–1953), called attention to the problems in "The Persian Gulf States and Their Boundary Problems," *Geographical Journal* 120 (1954), 435–436, from which the epigraph at the beginning of this book is excerpted.

23. Husain M. al-Baharna, *The Arabian Gulf States: Their Legal and Political Status and Their International Problems* (Beirut: Librairie du Liban, 1975), 332, n. 2, paras. (a) and (b); Alan Rush, *Al-Sabah: History and*

Genealogy of Kuwait's Ruling Family, 1752–1987 (London: Ithaca Press, 1987), 44; Khadduri, *Socialist Iraq,* 154; Majid Khadduri, "Iraq's Claim to the Sovereignty of Kuwayt," *New York University Journal of International Law and Politics* 23, no. 1 (Fall 1990), 29.

24. *The Independent* (London), Jan. 2, 1991; an article by a reporter sent to the Public Record Office for the first opening of 1960 documents under the thirty-year rule.
25. Waldemar J. Gallman, *Iraq under General Nuri* (Baltimore: Johns Hopkins University Press, 1964), 148–149; Rush, *Al-Sabah,* 44. An account of the same events from another perspective is given by Sir Gawain Bell in his memoirs, *Shadows in the Sand* (London: Hurst, 1983), chap. 11. Bell was political agent from 1955 to 1957.
26. Lord Birdwood, *Nuri as-Said: A Study in Arab Leadership* (London: Cassell, 1959), 257.
27. Harold Macmillan, *Riding the Storm, 1956–1959* (New York: Harper & Row, 1971), 502–504; Phebe Marr, *The Modern History of Iraq* (Boulder: Westview, 1985), 122.
28. Gallman, *Iraq under General Nuri,* 148–150.

9. Dress Rehearsal for Desert Storm, 1961

1. Milton Viorst, "Report from Baghdad," *New Yorker,* June 24, 1991, 60.
2. Quoted in Micah L. Sifry and Christopher Cerf, eds., *The Gulf War Reader* (New York: Times Books, 1991), 17.
3. Malcolm Yapp, in Alvin J. Cottrell, ed., *The Persian Gulf States: A General Survey* (Baltimore: Johns Hopkins University Press, 1980), 94.
4. *PGHS* II, 59.
5. Ibid.
6. The phrase is borrowed from the late Elizabeth Monroe's splendid book *Britain's Moment in the Middle East* (Baltimore: Johns Hopkins University Press, 1963).
7. Abdul-Reda Assiri, *Kuwait's Foreign Policy: City-State in World Politics* (Boulder: Westview, 1990), 7.
8. Schofield, 102.
9. *The Independent* (London), Jan. 2, 1991.
10. Schofield, 104–105.
11. Text of the June 19, 1961, letters in *KCBD,* 50–51.
12. It did not take the British military completely by surprise. A military planning exercise in November 1960 assessed the effort that would be required "to recapture Kuwait from the Iraqis." *The Independent,* Jan. 2, 1991. Sir William Luce, the political resident in the Gulf, told

the *New York Times* (July 6, 1961) that the British had been aware since 1958 of Qasim's "general thesis."

13. Harold Macmillan, *Pointing the Way, 1959–1961* (New York: Harper & Row, 1972), 383–384.

14. Benjamin Shwadran, "The Kuwait Incident," *Middle Eastern Affairs* 13 (1962), 10.

15. Ibid., 12.

16. Humphrey Trevelyan, *The Middle East in Revolution* (Boston: Gambit, 1970), chap. 7. The evidence available to Trevelyan is analyzed in detail in an admirable recent study: Mustafa M. Alani, *Operation Vantage: British Military Intervention in Kuwait, 1961* (Surbiton: LAAM, 1990), 101–102.

17. John Daniels, *Kuwait Journey* (Luton, England: White Crescent Press, 1972), 92.

18. Robert Litwak, *Security in the Persian Gulf 2: Sources of Inter-State Conflict* (Montclair, N.J.: International Institute for Strategic Studies, 1981), 27; Shwadran, "The Kuwait Incident," 10–11; Edith Penrose and E. F. Penrose, *Iraq: International Relations and National Development* (London: Ernest Benn, 1978), 276, 293n.; Richard Gott, "The Kuwait Incident," in Royal Institute of International Affairs, *Survey of International Affairs, 1961* (London, 1962), 527.

19. John Bulloch, *The Persian Gulf Unveiled* (New York: St. Martin's, 1984), 62–65.

20. Alani, *Operation Vantage*, 58–59, 73–75, 98, 179–185, 212. Richmond, who was interviewed by Alani in 1982, has since died.

21. There may have been something in the rumors. See Schofield, 105.

22. Majid Khadduri, *Republican Iraq* (London: Oxford University Press, 1969), 169.

23. Quotations are from British Broadcasting Corporation, Monitoring Service, *Summary of World Broadcasts, Part 4: The Middle East, Africa and Latin America* (Caversham Park, 1961), ME/675/A, June 27, 1961.

24. According to the encyclopedic Lorimer, Mubarak indeed visited Turkish territory and received a decoration in 1899. Moreover, on November 17, 1900, the shaikh visited the wali of Basra, received yet another decoration, and promised to abstain from relations with "foreign powers." However, "the Shaikh's submission was feigned." Lorimer I, 1026, 1028.

25. According to Lorimer, about that time Ambassador Sir Philip Currie in Constantinople was informed that the British government "had never admitted Kuwait to be under the protection of the Turkish Government, but that the existence of Turkish influence would probably be difficult or impossible to deny." Lorimer I, 1020.

26. Gott, "The Kuwait Incident," 525. In 1960, when Kuwait was apply-

ing for admission to UNESCO, the Foreign Office stated that "Her Majesty's Government regard Kuwait as responsible for the conduct of her international affairs." U.S. Department of State, *Digest of International Law* 1 (1963), 442.

27. *SCOR,* 957th meeting, July 2, 1961.

28. Richard H. Sanger, *The Arabian Peninsula* (Ithaca: Cornell University Press, 1954), 168–169. Pachachi's quotation is essentially accurate.

29. *SCOR,* 958th meeting, July 5, 1961.

30. Ibid.

31. It is an established, though sometimes questioned, rule of international law that "duress" does not affect the validity of treaties. Charles G. Fenwick, *International Law,* 4th ed. (New York: Appleton-Century-Crofts, 1965), 528–533; J. L. Brierly, *The Law of Nations* (Oxford: Oxford University Press, 1981), 317.

32. *SCOR,* 959th meeting, July 6, 1961, 19. There are extensive excerpts from the Security Council records in *KCBD,* 51–55.

33. *SCOR,* 959th meeting, July 6, 1961, 6. Sir Patrick Dean's telling point about the International Labour Organization corroborates other evidence that Iraqi government officials, including even Foreign Minister Hashim Jawad, were given very little, if any, advance notice of what Qasim was going to say about Kuwait on June 25, 1961.

34. *SCOR,* 960th meeting, July 7, 1961.

35. Kuwait's application for UN membership was not, as stated by Schofield, 109, considered at the July meetings of the Security Council.

36. Kuwait had considered applying for membership as early as 1958. Robert W. Macdonald, *The League of Arab States: A Study in the Dynamics of Regional Organization* (Princeton: Princeton University Press, 1965), 235. It had been participating in some Arab League committee work since 1952. Assiri, *Kuwait's Foreign Policy,* 7.

37. Iraq later attacked the validity of the vote on the grounds that unanimity is required for votes on membership matters under the Charter of the Arab League, and that this vote was not unanimous because Iraq had been absent. Hussein A. Hassouna, *The League of Arab States and Regional Disputes: A Study of Middle East Conflicts* (Dobbs Ferry, N.Y.: Oceana, 1975), 102; Embassy of the Republic of Iraq, Karachi, *News from Iraq,* no. 21 (August 1961). Just what provision of the Charter Iraq was relying upon for the unanimity rule is not apparent even on a very close reading of that document. No such provision is cited by Hussein Hassouna himself in his exhaustive account of the debates, nor by other commentators who have treated the proceedings in detail, including Macdonald and Shwadran. An Arab League staff legal opinion, announced on July 18, declared

that unanimity was not required. *Middle East Record, Vol. II: 1961* (Jerusalem: Israel Program for Scientific Translations, ca. 1966), 133.

38. Hassouna, *The League of Arab States,* 101. In the preface the author states that he is the son of Abdul Khalik Hassouna, secretary general of the Arab League at the time.

39. Ibid., 102–106. The Status of Forces Agreement, set out in full in ibid., 447–459, is remarkably comprehensive for an international agreement drawn up so quickly. Perhaps the draftsman had access to a similar agreement adopted in another context; there were United Nations precedents in the Congo and elsewhere. Excerpts from these Arab League documents appear in *KCBD,* 55–56.

40. Schofield, 110.

41. Phebe Marr, *The Modern History of Iraq* (Boulder: Westview, 1985), 181.

42. For example, Stephen Hemsley Longrigg, *Oil in the Middle East: Its Discovery and Development,* 3d ed. (London: Oxford University Press, 1968), 398 ("some scanty and uncoordinated detachments").

43. Walid Moubarak, "Kuwait's Quest for Security, 1961–1973" (Ph.D. diss., Indiana University, 1979); Regaei el Mallakh, *Economic Development and Regional Cooperation: Kuwait* (Chicago: University of Chicago Press, 1968); Walid Khalidi, "Why Some Arabs Support Saddam," in Sifry and Cerf, *The Gulf War Reader,* 168.

44. It is true, however, that Kuwait's postal service was under Iraqi administration for most of the interwar period. For details, see *PGHS* II, 114–115; also Alec Neil Donaldson, *The History of the Postal Service of Kuwait, 1775–1959* (Bombay: Jal Cooper, 1968).

45. Kuwait's point was unexpectedly corroborated in an official Iraqi publication the following year, to which the Iraqi Port Administration contributed a chapter about the projected port at Umm Qasr, stating: "As to the navigation channel from the Arab Gulf, it passes through the Warba Channel and the Iraq territorial waters lying between the Iraqi land and the Kuwaiti [*sic*] island of Warba." Government of Iraq, *The Iraqi Revolution in Its Fourth Year* (Baghdad: Committee of Propaganda and Publication, 1962), 352.

46. UN Doc. S/4852, June 30, 1961. Hassouna, *The League of Arab States,* 137, n. 89.

47. Ibid., n. 88.

48. *SCOR,* 984th meeting, Nov. 30, 1961, 2–4.

49. Ibid., 4.

50. Ibid., 5–6.

51. Ibid., 6.

52. Ibid., 6–7.
53. Ibid., 7. In 1950, in an ironic twist, Great Britain had found itself arguing in another context (the Buraimi arbitration) that Ibn Saud had been a Turkish subject and was therefore bound by treaties entered into by the Ottomans in 1913 and 1914. J. B. Kelly, *Eastern Arabian Frontiers* (New York: Praeger, 1964), 148.
54. *SCOR*, 984th meeting, Nov. 30, 1961, 8.
55. Ibid., 9.
56. Ibid., 10.
57. This theme had previously been taken up by Iraqi Foreign Minister Hashim Jawad in an address to the UN General Assembly on October 6, 1961. Under British neocolonialism, he declared, "it has become possible to declare a number of oil wells a state." *Bulletin of the Republic of Iraq,* November 1961.
58. *SCOR*, 984th meeting, Nov. 30, 1961.
59. *SCOR*, 985th meeting, Nov. 30, 1961.
60. Hassouna, *The League of Arab States,* 109, 137 (citing *The Times* [London], Dec. 5 and 18, 1961, and UN Doc. S/5044); *New York Times,* Dec. 4, 7, 27, 28, and 30, 1961. The Security Council did not meet, however.
61. Foreign Minister Jawad, an able and much-respected professional diplomat, tried to resign over the ambassadorial recall. "But Qasim threatened me with his revolver," he said later. Uriel Dann, *Iraq under Qassem: A Political History, 1958–1963* (New York: Praeger, 1969), 351–353.
62. Jacqueline S. Ismael, *Kuwait: Social Change in Historical Perspective* (Syracuse: Syracuse University Press, 1982), 82; Rosemarie Said Zahlan, *The Making of the Modern Gulf States* (London: Unwin Hyman, 1989), 39–40; J. E. Peterson, *The Arab Gulf States* (New York: Praeger, 1988), 12, 36–42. Moubarak has a detailed analysis of the Kuwaiti constitution, under which the ruler and Al Sabah retain a great deal of power. For text of the constitution, see Abid A. al-Marayati, ed., *Middle Eastern Constitutions and Electoral Laws* (New York: Praeger, 1968), 200–229.

10. Reconciliation, Encroachment, and the First Gulf War, 1963–1988

1. Ulrich Gehrke and Gustav Kuhn, *Die Grenzen des Irak: Historische und rechtliche Aspekte des irakischen Anspruchs auf Kuwait,* vol. I (Stuttgart:

W. Kohlhammer, 1963), 115, citing *Neue Züriche Zeitung,* Feb. 10 and 11, 1963.

2. Hussein A. Hassouna, *The League of Arab States and Regional Disputes: A Study of Middle East Conflicts* (Dobbs Ferry, N.Y.: Oceana, 1975), 106; Gehrke and Kuhn, *Die Grenzen des Irak,* I, 115.

3. Hassouna, *The League of Arab States,* 106–107; Gehrke and Kuhn, *Die Grenzen des Irak,* I, 114–115.

4. *SCOR,* 1034th meeting, May 7, 1963. Gehrke and Kuhn, *Die Grenzen des Irak,* I, 116–117; Hassouna, *The League of Arab States,* 109–110; Husain M. al-Baharna, *The Arabian Gulf States: Their Legal and Political Status and Their International Problems* (Beirut: Librairie du Liban, 1975), 251.

5. Abdul-Reda Assiri, *Kuwait's Foreign Policy: City-State in World Politics* (Boulder: Westview, 1990), 24.

6. Tim Niblock, ed., *Iraq: The Contemporary State* (London: Croom Helm, 1982), 135, citing *The Observer* (London), June 2, 1963. See also *Middle East Journal,* 17 (1963), 121, citing *Al Ahram,* June 27, 1963.

7. Gehrke and Kuhn, *Die Grenzen des Irak,* I, 117, citing press reports.

8. *United Nations Treaty Series,* vol. 485 (New York: United Nations, 1965), 321–329. English translation at 326 and 328, provided by the government of Kuwait. The published English translation has "recognized" for "recognizes." Both the original Arabic and the French translation use the present tense.

9. One commentator says that the 1963 agreement "included a provision for the creation of a joint commission to reach a final delimitation of their common frontier." Robert Litwak, *Security in the Persian Gulf 2: Sources of Inter-State Conflict* (Montclair, N.J.: International Institute for Strategic Studies, 1981), 28. There is no such provision in the document registered with the UN. If there was some ancillary agreement to this effect, it has not come to hand.

10. Gehrke and Kuhn, *Die Grenzen des Irak,* I, 118.

11. According to one source, Kuwait also paid 2 million Kuwaiti dinars into the personal account of the president of Iraq. Walid Moubarak, "Kuwait's Quest for Security, 1961–1973" (Ph.D. diss., Indiana University, 1979), 157–158.

12. J. L. Brierly, *The Law of Nations* (Oxford: Oxford University Press, 1981), 317–318.

13. British Broadcasting Corporation, Monitoring Service, *Summary of World Broadcasts, Part 4: The Middle East, Africa and Latin America* (Caversham Park, 1963), ME/1372/A, Oct. 8, 1963.

14. The UN Charter requires such registration and provides (Art. 102): "No party to any such treaty or international agreement which has not been registered . . . may invoke that treaty or agreement before any organ of the United Nations."

15. The factual information in this paragraph was courteously provided by officials of the Treaty Section, Office of Legal Affairs of the United Nations. The legal interpretation is my own. The editors of *KCBD* were informed by the UN Treaty Section that Iraq had not revoked this instrument as of August 2, 1990. *KCBD*, 56, n. 128.

16. English translation of the agreement in *International Legal Materials*, vol. V (Washington, D.C.: American Society of International Law, 1966), 1140–43.

17. Niblock, *Iraq*, 136; Schofield, 114. That the border commission was formed and met several times in 1966 and 1967 was acknowledged in an Iraqi press release on Sept. 12, 1990. *KCBD*, 77.

18. Majid Khadduri, *Socialist Iraq: A Study in Iraqi Politics since 1968* (Washington, D.C.: Middle East Institute, 1978), 154–155.

19. Ibid., 156; Richard F. Nyrop, ed., *Iraq: A Country Study*, 3d ed. (Washington, D.C.: American University, 1979), 216–217.

20. Adeed Dawisha, "Invoking the Spirit of Arabism: Islam in the Foreign Policy of Saddam's Iraq," in Dawisha, ed., *Islam in Foreign Policy* (Cambridge: Cambridge University Press, 1983), 116.

21. J. B. Kelly, *Arabia, the Gulf, and the West* (New York: Basic Books, 1980), 283, has details of the Iraqi treaty proposal, which he ascribes in part to Soviet influence.

22. Khadduri, *Socialist Iraq*, 157; Litwak, *Security*, 30–31; Al-Baharna, *The Arabian Gulf States*, 330–331; Nyrop, *Iraq: A Country Study*, 237; Helen Chapin Metz, ed., *Iraq: A Country Study*, 4th ed. (Washington, D.C.: U.S. Government Printing Office, 1990), 60.

23. The pros and cons of Britain's final withdrawal from the Gulf in 1971 will be long debated. To one observer it was "a squalid little deal by which the doctrinaire back-benchers of the Labour Party agreed to the imposition of a half-crown charge for prescriptions in return for cuts in defence expenditure." John Bulloch, *The Persian Gulf Unveiled* (New York: St. Martin's, 1984), 27.

24. *The Times* (London), April 5 and 6, 1973.

25. Khadduri, *Socialist Iraq*, 157. As his source for the important Iraqi note of May 17, 1973, Khadduri refers (159, n. 20) to interviews with a number of officials in Kuwait in June 1976. The note itself has apparently not been published.

26. Khalid Kishtiany, trans., *Saddam Hussein on Current Events in Iraq* (London: Longman, 1977), 73–74.

27. David Holden and Richard Johns, *The House of Saud* (New York: Holt, Rinehart & Winston, 1981), 425.

28. Khadduri, *Socialist Iraq*, 158.

29. Ibid., 158–159.

30. Niblock, *Iraq*, 141–142.

31. Ibid., 154; Nyrop, *Iraq: A Country Study*, 237; Colin Legum, ed., *Middle East Contemporary Survey, 1976–77* (New York: Holmes & Meier, 1978), 345.

32. Nyrop, *Iraq: A Country Study*, 237.

33. Metz, *Iraq: A Country Study*, xxviii.

34. Litwak, *Security*, 32.

35. John Bulloch and Harvey Morris, *The Gulf War: Its Origins, History and Consequences* (London: Methuen, 1989), 32.

36. Ibid., 156.

37. Assiri, *Kuwait's Foreign Policy*, 75.

38. Metz, *Iraq: A Country Study*, 207.

39. Christine Moss Helms, *Iraq: Eastern Flank of the Arab World* (Washington, D.C.: Brookings Institution, 1984), 49.

40. Bulloch and Morris, *The Gulf War*, 40.

41. Schofield, 122; Assiri, *Kuwait's Foreign Policy*, 75.

42. Gerd Nonneman, *Iraq, the Gulf States and the War* (London: Ithaca Press, 1986), 41–42, 75.

43. Adel Darwish and Gregory Alexander, *Unholy Babylon* (New York: St. Martin's, 1991), 230.

44. Ibid.

45. Walid Khalidi, "Iraq vs. Kuwait: Claims and Counterclaims," in Micah L. Sifry and Christopher Cerf, eds., *The Gulf War Reader* (New York: Times Books, 1991), 62–63.

46. Nonneman, *Iraq, the Gulf States and the War*, 58, citing *Middle East Economic Digest*, Oct. 15, 1982. In construction industry jargon, a "turn-key" project is one assigned to a single contractor responsible for delivering the completed project.

47. Nonneman, *Iraq, the Gulf States and the War*, 76, and press reports. The continuing tension between Iraq and Kuwait between the two Gulf wars is covered in a chapter by Nonneman, "Iraq-GCC Relations," in Charles Davies, ed., *After the War: Iraq, Iran and the Arab Gulf* (Chichester: Carden, 1990), 25–77.

11. Saddam Hussein and the UN

1. *New York Times*, Sept. 23, 1990. Testifying before Congress in March 1991, Ambassador Glaspie did not deny the accuracy of this much-

publicized quotation, but stated that she had also warned Saddam Hussein against the use of threats, intimidation or aggression. *New York Times,* Mar. 21, 1991.

2. UN Doc. S/RES/687 (1991): preamble (fifth clause) and paras. 2 and 3.
3. *New York Times,* Apr. 4, 5, 14, 20, and 25; May 3, 1991.
4. UN Doc. S/22558, para. 2 (citing UN Docs. S/22456 and S/22457) and Annex II, Enclosure, second para.
5. Ibid., paras. 3 and 4. Richard Schofield has pointed out that Resolution 687 makes no allowance for the pro-Iraqi British "interpretation" of 1951, which would provide Iraq with more flexibility than literal adherence to the 1932 definition. Schofield, "The Iraq-Kuwait Boundary," *Middle East International,* April 19, 1991, 21–22.
6. UN Doc. S/22558, Annex II, Enclosure.
7. *United Nations Treaty Series,* vol. 485 (New York: United Nations, 1965), 321–329.
8. See, for example, J. L. Brierly, *The Law of Nations* (Oxford: Oxford University Press, 1981), chap. 7. For a discussion of the point as applying to the 1963 Agreed Minutes, see Husain M. al-Baharna, "The Consequences of Britain's Exclusive Treaties: A Gulf View," in B. R. Pridham, ed., *The Arab Gulf and the West* (London: Croom Helm, 1985), 334–335.
9. Iraq Constitution of March 21, 1925, as amended, art. 26, sec. 4. Text in Helen Miller Davis, *Constitutions, Electoral Laws, Treaties of States in the Near and Middle East* (Durham, N.C.: Duke University Press, 1947), 107–132.
10. Provisional constitution, July 27, 1958. Text in Muhammad Khalil, *The Arab States and the Arab League: A Documentary Record,* vol. I (Beirut: Khayat's, 1962), 30–32.
11. In a recent article Majid Khadduri suggests that the appropriate body to have ratified the 1963 Agreed Minutes was "the National Revolutionary Council, the highest executive and legislative authority under the Arif regime." "Iraq's Claim to the Sovereignty of Kuwayt," *New York University Journal of International Law and Politics* 23, no. 1 (Fall 1990), 31. See also Iraq's Sept. 12, 1990, press release, in *KCBD,* 76. But the provisional constitution of 1958 (arts. 21 and 22) vested both the legislative power and the executive power in the Council of Ministers; it made no mention of the National Revolutionary Council. Khalil, *The Arab States,* 30–32. In practice, of course, the regime was a dictatorship.
12. Interim constitution, April 19, 1964, arts. 43 and 103. Text in Amos J. Peaslee, *Constitutions of Nations,* rev. 3d ed., vol. II (The Hague: M. Nijhoff, 1966), 471–483.

13. *Wall Street Journal,* Nov. 2, 1990; and Jan. 11, 1991.
14. Baghdad's announcement spoke in the name of the Revolutionary Command Council, Saddam Hussein's "cabinet"; Kuwaiti officials pointed out that the rescission would not be complete until it was also acted upon by the Iraqi National Assembly, which had enacted the annexation in the first place. *New York Times,* March 6 and 14, 1991.
15. *New York Times,* April 26, 1991.
16. *New York Times,* Aug. 2, 1991.
17. *New York Times,* Aug. 29 and 30, 1991. *The Economist,* Sept. 7, 1991, reported that the captives turned out to be a scavenging party of mixed ages and sexes (including children), and commented that Kuwait was making a "huge fuss."
18. Peter Beaumont, Gerald H. Blake, and J. Malcolm Wagstaff, *The Middle East: A Geographical Study,* 2d ed. (New York: Beekman, 1988), 323.
19. Stephen Hemsley Longrigg, *Oil in the Middle East: Its Discovery and Development,* 3d ed. (London: Oxford University Press, 1968), 356, 407–409. For earlier British views about the extent of Kuwait's seabed, see *PGHS* II, 80. See also Ali A. el-Hakim, *The Middle Eastern States and the Law of the Sea* (Syracuse: Syracuse University Press, 1979), 111–119; and S. H. Amin, *International and Legal Problems of the Gulf* (London: Middle East and North African Studies Press, 1981), 120–125, 135–159.
20. Longrigg, *Oil,* 273, 362; Schofield, 128.
21. *PGHS* II, 72. KOC had entered into a "political agreement" with the British government that gave the political agent a voice on matters affecting oil company relations with the Kuwaiti authorities.
22. Government of Kuwait, *The Oil of Kuwait* (Kuwait, 1970), 20.
23. Schofield, 126, 128; also industry sources.
24. There is an exhaustive legal discussion in Rainer Lagoni, "Oil and Gas Deposits across National Frontiers," *American Journal of International Law* 73 (1979), 215–243.
25. The issue is not mentioned in the very thorough chronicles of recent Iraq-Kuwait relations by Gerd Nonneman, which extend into 1989. Nonneman, *Iraq, the Gulf States and the War* (London: Ithaca Press, 1986) and "Iraq-GCC Relations," in Charles Davies, ed., *After the War: Iraq, Iran and the Arab Gulf* (Chichester: Carden, 1990), 25–77.
26. Pierre Salinger and Eric Laurent, *Secret Dossier: The Hidden Agenda behind the Gulf War* (New York: Penguin, 1991), 227–228.
27. Personal interview, Sept. 13, 1991.
28. Salinger and Laurent, *Secret Dossier,* 226–227.
29. Walid Khalidi, "Iraq vs. Kuwait: Claims and Counterclaims," in Mi-

cah L. Sifry and Christopher Cerf, eds., *The Gulf War Reader* (New York: Times Books, 1991), 63; Efraim Karsh and Inari Rautsi, *Saddam Hussein: A Political Biography* (New York: Free Press, 1991), 206; "The War No One Saw Coming," *Washington Post National Weekly Edition,* March 18–24, 1991; Milton Viorst, "Report from Baghdad," *New Yorker,* June 24, 1991, 60.

30. Salinger and Laurent, *Secret Dossier,* 44, 239–241; *Wall Street Journal,* Nov. 1, 1990.

31. Viorst, "Report from Baghdad," 67.

32. Quoted in Schofield, 81.

33. Salinger and Laurent, *Secret Dossier,* 149.

Index